ARAB NATIONAL COMMUNISM
IN THE JEWISH STATE

Arab National Communism

in the

Jewish State

Ilana Kaufman

University Press of Florida

Gainesville/Tallahassee/Tampa/Boca Raton

Pensacola/Orlando/Miami/Jacksonville

02 01 00 99 98 97 6 5 4 3 2 1

Library of Congress Cataloging-in-Publication Data
Kaufman, Ilana, 1948–
    Arab national communism in the Jewish state / Ilana Kaufman
    p. cm.
    Includes bibliographical references and index.
    ISBN 0-8130-1478-6 (alk. paper)
    1. Miflagah ha-komunistit ha-Yisre'elit—History. 2. Palestinian Arabs—Israel—Politics and
government. 3. Nationalism and communism—Israel—History. 4. Israel—Politics and government. I. Title.
JQ1830.A98M545 1997 96-21380
327.5'495694—dc20

The University Press of Florida is the scholarly publishing agency for the State University System of Florida, comprised of Florida A & M University, Florida Atlantic University, Florida International University, Florida State University, University of Central Florida, University of Florida,
University of North Florida, University of South Florida, and University of West Florida.

University Press of Florida
15 Northwest 15th Street
Gainesville, FL 32611

To my family

CONTENTS

TABLES

ABBREVIATIONS

ADP	Arab Democratic Party
CAW	Congress of Arab Workers (Mu'tamar)
CHAM	Committee of Heads of Arab Municipalities
CPI	Communist Party of Israel
CPSU	Communist Party of the Soviet Union
PCP	Communist Party of Palestine
PLO	Palestine Liberation Organization
PLP	Progressive List for Peace
PMP	Progressive Movement for Peace
UAL	United Arab List

Posing the Problem

Academic and political discourse since the 1970s has grappled with basic paradigmatic questions on the origins and dynamics of nationalism and ethnonationalism. These questions have become more pressing following the collapse of the Soviet system into national-territorial units, the outbreak of ethnic conflict in former Yugoslavia, and the separative tendencies in Western countries such as Canada, Belgium, and Italy. Approaches to nationalism differ in the central explanatory variables for the formation, vitality, and revival of the phenomenon, particularly in the form of substate nationalism, or ethnonationalism. They also differ in their assessment of the socioeconomic dynamics involved and of whether the impact of modernization has been universal and hence "integrative" or particularist and hence "separative."

The general purpose of this study is to make a contribution to this discussion of the nature and dynamics of ethnonationalism and its relationship to sociopolitical change. I do so by focusing on the dynamics of a case—that of the Communist Party in Israel acting as the mobilizing force among Israel's Palestinian-Arab citizens and promoting a certain brand of integrative ethnonationalism. Through this study I intend to examine both the sociopolitical conditions under which this type of ethnonationalism takes hold among a national minority and the role played in directing this process by a political party committed to a class ideology. Analytically, therefore, the study differentiates among the political and geopolitical environment of the community, the political organizations active within it, and the members at large who support or refrain from supporting these bodies.

Ethnonationalism is defined here as a form of collective consciousness of an ethnic or cultural minority expressed in political rhetoric, behavior, and ideology. It is examined as the outcome of the sociopolitical and geopolitical environment and of the interaction between the strategies of mobilization by political organizations and the community. Integrative ethnonationalism is an oppositionist strategy of a nonassimilating, subordinate national minority, aimed at its egalitarian integration into society as an alternative to strategies of accommodation on the one hand and separatism on the other. The basic questions I seek to answer are (1) what are the environmental conditions that are conducive to this type of ethnonationalism? (2) what are the factors that lead a political party to employ one or the other ethnonationalist strategies of political mobilization? (3) what social bases support this type of ethnonationalist strategy and what determines the limits of its success?

The specific purposes of this study are three: to explain how the Communist Party in Israel, using a specific ethnonationalist strategy of mobilization, gradually built its power and established a hegemonic position among the minority Arab-Palestinian citizens during the 1970s; to analyze the limits and constraints of that success, which brought its hegemony to an end in the 1980s; and to evaluate the impact of the Communist Party's brand of ethnonationalism on the Arab-Palestinian minority in Israel in the 1990s and its future role in the state.

HISTORICAL BACKGROUND

The State of Israel was declared by the Jews living in Palestine in 1948 following the UN decision to replace British Mandate rule with two independent states, one "Jewish" and one "Arab." The decision to partition Palestine was the culmination of a protracted struggle between Arabs and Jews that began in the 1920s in Palestine. The goal of the Jewish Zionist movement, organized in Europe toward the end of the nineteenth century, was to "territorialize" and concentrate the Jews of the world in their ancient biblical homeland. The rise in anti-Semitism in Europe in the 1930s gave impetus to waves of migration of Jews into Palestine: by 1947 they constituted a well-organized community of 600,000 people. The Arabs in Palestine, who numbered in 1947 about 1.3 million, saw themselves and Palestine as part of the surrounding Arab homeland and viewed the Zionist intrusion as part of the European colonial onslaught on the Arab Middle East. The refusal of the Palestinian Arabs and the Arab states to accept the partition as the solution to the conflict resulted in the 1948 Arab-Israeli war. It ended with the Arabs' failure to prevent the establishment of the Jewish state, the turning of some 650,000 Palestinian Arabs into refugees, and the division between Israel and Jordan of the area designated for the Arab-Palestinian state (Morris 1987).

In this study I focus on the Palestinian Arabs who found themselves within cease-fire lines (the Green Line) in the area controlled by Israel in 1949. They numbered about 156,000 people, located mainly in 104 Arab villages and townships, in three geographical areas of the country. Despite the growth of this population to more than 800,000 in the 1990s,[1] their demographic spread remained basically the same: over 60 percent live in the Galilee in the north; 20 percent are concentrated in the Little Triangle in the center, handed to Israel by Jordan; about 10 percent live in the Negev desert in the south; and the rest are distributed in mixed Jewish-Arab urban localities, mainly in Haifa, Acre, and Jaffa. While all share Arab culture and identity, they are split along confessional and ecological lines. The majority—70 percent in 1949 and 78 percent in the 1990s—are Muslim, mostly rural, living in the north and the center of the country. The Christians, of various denominations—constituting some 20 percent in 1949 and 12 percent in the 1990s—are mostly urban, concentrated in the north. The Druze, a Muslim sect, constitute 10 percent and live in rural localities in the north. Those living in the Negev in the south are mostly Bedouin tribes, nomads in 1949 but becoming sedentary in the 1990s.

In the early 1950s this Arab population was granted Israeli citizenship and constituted a national minority of 14–18 percent in the Jewish state. In the Israeli Declaration of Independence, issued on the eve of the war in 1948, the Arabs who were destined to become citizens of the Jewish state were promised freedom of religion and language as well as equal citizenship rights and representation. However, in the postwar years the conflict between Israel and the Arab world erupted into further armed confrontations. The Arab minority population has been treated since then as part of the defeated enemy, a potential fifth column. Concentrated in their own localities (many of them situated along the cease-fire lines), the Arabs were put under military control, which lasted up to the 1960s. At the same time, citizenship, language, religious, and voting rights were granted. In other words, no attempt was made to assimilate them into the culture and religion of the Jewish majority.

Following independence, the goals of the Zionist movement—simultaneous state- and nation-building for the Jews—became the priorities of the Jewish state. It mobilized all possible resources, seizing much of the land held previously by Arabs for the purpose of making Israel into a state, a home for the Jewish refugees from postwar Europe and for Jewish immigrants from other parts of the Middle East. Under these circumstances it could have been expected that the Palestinian-Arab minority would quickly develop an irredentist movement: as a native population and as part of the Arab and Muslim majority in the region, it was involuntarily included in the entity that declared itself to be an ethnic Jewish state.

Yet up to the 1970s the majority of the Arab population kept a low political profile, even after it was reunited with the Palestinian population in the West Bank and Gaza, which were militarily occupied by Israel in 1967. Up to 1977, the Arab citizens of Israel voted overwhelmingly for Arab representatives aligned with the ruling Zionist party, the Labor Party. In the early 1960s, an attempt to establish a Palestinian-oriented Pan-Arab political movement (al Ard) was foiled by legal action of the state. Then, after a split in the Communist Party of Israel (CPI) in 1965, the faction of the party known as CPI-Rakah gradually increased its share of the Arab vote and, after setting up a front with non-Communists, became the single most organized and powerful political force among Arab voters (though it lost its base in the Jewish electorate). To a large extent under CPI's auspices and goading, in the mid-1970s the Arab minority began to express political discontent and civic unrest while reaffirming its nonirredentist intentions. This was in contrast to the armed struggle outside Israel led by the Palestine Liberation Organization (PLO), whose goal was to replace the State of Israel with a "secular, democratic state" in Palestine. The restive mood among the Arab citizens in Israel persisted in the 1980s and up to the September 1993 agreement between Israel and the PLO. However, during the 1980s, even before the collapse of the Soviet Union, the Communist Party–led front lost ground within the Arab electorate, though it won some of its support back in 1996 and remained the single largest party among the Arab voters.

The Communist Party of Israel has been unique on the Israeli political scene in more than one way. Its historical roots lie in the Communist Party of Palestine (the PCP), which in the 1920s and 1930s was operating under the directives of the Soviet-led Comintern. Throughout its existence, even after the collapse of the Soviet Union, it did not change its image of an orthodox Soviet-type party, even though the political consensus in the country since the early 1950s has been pro-Western and pro-American. Moreover, the CPI's declared ideological position is anti-Zionist, sympathetic to the Arab (anti-Western) positions in the region, while Israel, for which Zionist ideology is the state's raison d'être, has been locked in war with its Arab neighbors. Since the split in the party in 1965, the majority of the CPI-Rakah Party members and its electorate are Arabs, who form a marginal group in the society. From the electoral and policy angles, therefore, the CPI-Rakah could be viewed as an ethnonationalist party. But unlike the other Arab parties and political movements that sprang up in the 1980s and 1990s in the Arab sector, the CPI-Rakah maintained its commitment to being a Jewish-Arab party by allotting for Jewish members positions of leadership and by opposing any separatist or autonomous tendencies.

I have set out to analyze the political behavior and attitudes of Arabs in Israel via the changes in the level of Arab support for the Communist Party of Israel. The CPI serves here as vantage point for highlighting the broader issues of the Arab minority in Israel, caught up in social transformation and the national conflict between Palestinians and Jews. These issues touch on numerous aspects of the politics of identity, its roots, and its dynamics. Some of those theoretical issues will therefore be discussed in terms of the theoretical paradigms used to analyze the dynamics of ethnopolitics in general and of the Arab-Palestinian citizens in Israel in particular.[2]

ONE

Ethnonationalism and Palestinian-Arab Citizens in Israel

1

Ethnonationalism
Theoretical Conceptions and Dynamics

Approaches differ on the question of how to analyze nationalism and ethno-nationalism in the second half of the twentieth century as a phenomenon of industrial, postindustrial, or partially industrial societies. The key arguments, which overlap at some points and cross at others, run along two analytical axes. The first axis is the degree to which nationalism as a political movement and an ideology is predicated on existence of prior cultural givens, that is, ethnic ascriptive identities, versus the degree to which it is a product of construction and mobilization by states, elites, and movements in pursuit of change in the distribution of power. The cultural-given argument (known also as the primordialist viewpoint) tends to treat ethnic groups as undifferentiated natural collectives, whose identity becomes politicized under certain circumstances.[1]

The constructionist argument (sometimes called the instrumentalist view) is that there is no necessary link between ethnic identity and its politicization. Instead, nationalism and ethnonationalism are explained primarily by the act of *mobilization* of specific subgroups in society (classes, culturally or regionally defined groups) by a political agent, which may even invent traditions in the process. This line of argument emphasizes the transitory and flexible borders of national identity, which is rooted in some other set of factors. It also emphasizes the heterogeneity of interests within national groups, which may come to the fore in the course of political mobilization.[2]

The primordialist-instrumentalist debate is particularly relevant for ethnonationalism within partially assimilated subgroups or those that at least have open channels of assimilation into the national culture of dominant majorities. Its major relevance for cases of nonassimilated cultural subgroups is twofold: first, even when cultural or ethnic boundaries are treated as incontrovertible facts, there may still be a dispute about their political significance; second, the characteristics of the mobilizing agency may have an important impact on the outcome of such a dispute. In other words, ethnonationalist strategies may vary according to political and ideological factors guiding the mobilizers.

The second axis of approaches to analyzing nationalism and ethnonationalism concerns the way in which a change from an agrarian society to an industrial market economy affects the creation of nationalist sentiment, identity, or consciousness. The approaches based on the plural model of society argue that such a transformation may alter existing power relations between subgroups in a state. However, industrialization does not change the universal pattern of groups held together by a power balance or by domination of some groups over others, with the assistance of the state. The role of the modern state in society is such that it is inevitably involved in the construction of the economic and social opportunity structure.[3] The expression of these relationships in the form of nationalism (of the majority) or ethnonationalism (of the minority) is merely a reflection of these competitive or conflictual relations. Other approaches assign an explanatory power to the consequences of this process, albeit of a different kind.

Developmental theses, both the modernization-integrationist and diffusionist-conflictual (known as the nation-building approach and the orthodox Marxist approach, respectively), expected, for opposite reasons, that parochial, ethnic, ascriptive identities would lose their force as bases for collective identity with the advent of industrialization and capitalism and would be replaced by national or class identities. By the 1970s, the failure of this expectation to materialize in the former colonial societies was first explained by the integrationist approach as an attachment of traditional groups to primordial givens. But the revival of ethnonationalism in the industrialized countries led to the replacement of the linear developmental model with a disjointed or uneven thesis of modernization. In one of its non-Marxist versions, the sharing of high culture by the new urban classes—intelligentsia and workers—becomes the functional basis of industrial society. The role of the state is to provide the means for the standardization of culture. Social dislocation and structural obstruction hamper the processes of integration, as members of the new urban classes, who do not share in the dominant high culture, are excluded from fair competition. Exclusion is more likely to affect the intelligentsia. Hence, it is to be expected that members of this stratum will attempt to organize the co-cultural working class into a nationalist movement to achieve an autonomous or separatist solution (Gellner 1984; Hroch 1985; Smith 1986).

Neo-Marxist theories provided the rationale for working-class-based rather than intelligentsia-initiated movements of ethnonationalism. Whereas Orthodox Marxist theory and doctrine expected that with the spread of capitalism, class conflict and class solidarity would displace nationalism and that anticolonial nationalist movements would be a transitional stage in the process, Neo-

Marxist approaches incorporated ethnicity into the analysis. According to Neo-Marxist analysis, colonial-type dependency of ethnically distinct peripheral regions has emerged also within the developed capitalist states because of the uneven nature of capitalistic development the world over (Hechter 1975; Niren 1981). Dependency of the periphery on the core begins with proletarization of peripheral ethnic groups, which are then confined to distinct, inferior positions within the economic structure. The confinement is institutionalized and reproduced via various mechanisms of cultural division of labor, sometimes aided by the state (Peled 1989). Mobilization of ethnic identities and separative tendencies in the industrially developed world are therefore explained as a reaction to peripheral groups' subordinate place in the labor market, on which the capitalist economy and the nation-state are based. This reaction sometimes develops into antimodern, particularly religious, positions.

These analyses lead to different generalizations about the relationship between the role of the state in peripheral socioeconomic change and class formation, on the one hand, and the strategies of political mobilization based on the ethnic identities, on the other. I seek to determine the conditions likely to support a mixed strategy of both ethnonationalism and adherence to an existing state framework on the part of a nonassimilating ethnic minority. Since in this case the mobilizing agent is the Communist Party, we need a short discussion of the positions of Marxist ideology on nationalism and the nation-state.

Marxist doctrine was formulated in the nineteenth century in opposition to the doctrine of nationalism and the concept of loyalty to the nation-state. The nation-state and nationalism, as its legitimizing ideology, were held to be tools of the ruling classes, the bourgeoisie, intended to subordinate, directly and indirectly, the working classes. Marxist doctrine instead called for struggle on behalf of working-class interests, toward the goal of international working-class solidarity that would override any national loyalties. However, despite the bitter debate on the national question in the international socialist movement in the years 1903–14, movements based on Marxist ideology realized that national consciousness did take hold among working classes during the democratization of the nation state and thus had to be incorporated into the doctrine (Hobsbawm 1990). The compatibility of social and national liberation in the consciousness of the working class was particularly acceptable in a colonial situation. Thus, in addition to the liberal principles of national self-determination and equal civil rights, the cultural rights of national minorities were also made part of the socialist revolutionary doctrine. In the Leninist version of the doctrine, however, the condition that ensured the compatibility of those liberal principles with Marxist doctrine is the leading role granted to a centralized Communist Party in the struggle and, if victorious, in the state.

In the post–Bolshevik Revolution era up to the 1960s, the authoritative interpretation of Communist theory and practice was delegated by Communist parties around the world to the Communist Party of the Soviet Union. The basic strategy for those parties vis-à-vis their states and nonproletariat classes was formulated by the Soviet Union according to its own perspectives and global interests (for instance, the Popular Front strategy in the West in the 1930s and the decision to support the UN resolution to partition and recognize the State of Israel in 1947–48). Beyond decisions of global implications, local Communist parties had of course to make their own policy decisions, according to local conditions and the parties' assessment of popular appeal.

Yet, the reaction of Communist parties to ethnonationalist claims formed a pattern. The reason was that the structure of the democratic welfare state in the West after World War II imposed a certain logic on strategies and positions of left-wing parties, including the Communists. But it was a paradoxical position. On the one hand, left-wing parties became supporters of a strong centralized state and of the liberal constitutional structure, which protected workers' social rights and the parties' own political freedom. On the other, the goals and mobilizing strategies of the left wing still aimed at radical change of the system. Challenges to the state by peripheral ethnonationalism in Western Europe forced left-wing parties to try to reconcile ideology, class, and the national interests of their supporters on the periphery. The dilemmas produced complex political and electoral strategies, sometimes based on expediency, but rarely have they supported separatism (Keating 1992; Mair and McAlister 1982).

I will introduce into the complex picture *regional-national* conflict as a factor in the investigation of ethnonationalism. My analysis will incorporate the impact of such a conflict along with insights of the proletarization thesis and the disjointed modernization thesis in an effort to explain Communist-led integrative ethnonationalism as mobilizing strategy. My basic argument is that the success of integrative ethnonationalism as a mobilizing strategy is linked to the early stages of proletarization and to the initial stages of class differentiation of a subordinate ethnic minority caught in a regional-national conflict. Under these circumstances, integrative rather than separative ethnonationalism becomes a rational survival strategy. I will argue further that the dynamics of ethnonationalist mobilization as a political strategy are dialectical: its success both changes the political environment and produces conditions for the formation of new political forces and new struggles relating to the distribution of legitimacy and power.

2

Palestinian-Arab Citizens
From Acquiescence to Activism

INTERPRETATIONS OF ETHNONATIONALISM
AMONG THE ARABS IN ISRAEL

In March 1976, the Arab population in Israel declared a general strike and launched mass demonstrations against the government's plan to expropriate land. These Land Day protests, organized by the Communist Party, marked a breakthrough in its longstanding quest for acceptance as a legitimate partner for political action by the largely non-Communist and hitherto nonconfrontationist Arab public. The protests also marked a change in political tactics: the use of "direct action" at the risk of an open clash with the authorities. The event came on the heels of a gradual increase in votes for the Communist Party by Arabs, and it was followed by the unprecedented support of half of the Arab voters. What explains this political change and what did it signify with regard to the political tendencies of the Arab public?

The theoretical approaches of studies that have analyzed diverse aspects of the lives of Arabs in Israel suggest several interpretations. Although those studies were made from different theoretical perspectives, they delineate the overlapping lines of demarcation between the Jewish majority and the Arab minority. The data collected portray a national minority that is ecologically segregated from the Jewish majority, economically and socially disadvantaged, and politically weak.

The studies differ in their explanations, whether explicit or implicit, of the sociopolitical position of the minority and of the change in their political behavior from acquiescence to activism under the auspices of the Communist Party. Yet, interestingly enough, despite their theoretical differences, these models (again, either explicitly or by implication) converge roughly into either of two basic analytical perspectives on the tendencies and dynamics of Arab political behavior, of which the vote for the CPI is a part. Following

Smooha (1989, 1992), the two perspectives will be identified as "Arab radicalization" and "Arab politicization."

The Arab radicalization perspective views the dynamics of Arab political orientation over the years as a process of increasing extremism, alienation from the Jewish state, and, by implication, movement toward autonomism and irredentism in the future. Social geographers point to Arabs' objection to Jewish settlement in Arab areas, to government planning, and to illegal use of state land (Kipnis 1987; Soffer 1988.) Social psychologists and historians point to a "Palestinization" syndrome as evidenced by the definition of their own identity, the backing of Palestinian self-determination, and the growing support for fundamentalist Islamist movements, as well as a readiness to go to the street to protest against land expropriation by the government and to support Palestinian causes on the West Bank and Gaza (Rekhess 1976, 1977, 1989; Rouhana 1993; Schnell 1994; Yiftachel 1990). On the political electoral level, the votes for the CPI and other Arab parties are similarly taken as signs of radicalization (Reiter 1989). As will be seen, this view of the political dynamics as leading to separative-inclined ethnonationalism is arrived at from different analyses. It is seen primarily either as a reaction to discriminatory treatment by the state or as related to the predicaments of modernization and development in the geopolitical Arab region.

The politicization perspective, which is taken up in this study, views Arab political tendencies and behavior *mainly* as an ongoing response to Arabs' marginal socioeconomic and political position, a response directed primarily at achieving recognition of their legitimacy as a group, and more equal integration *within* the state. In contrast to the radicalization perspective, I argue here that the Arabs' activism reflects their growing confidence in using their status as citizens in a democratic system: insisting on their rights, on the legitimacy of their national (Palestinian) identity, and on expressing their needs and views (Rouhana and Ghanem 1993). In Smooha's formulation, politicization has three components: Israelization, factionalism, and militancy. Israelization is the process by which Arabs become bilingual and are incorporated into various aspects of Israeli political culture, "independently of and parallel to Palestinization" (Smooha 1992, 10). Factionalism is the development of a plurality of political opinions, or camps, on the question of the Arabs' status as a minority in the State of Israel. These views range from integrative accommodationist to reservationist to oppositionist to separatist rejectionist. Militancy is the growing willingness to use legal extraparliamentary methods to press demands that long have been ignored by the authorities. Thus a rather thin but still important line differentiates between the politicization and radicalization perspectives—namely, the identification of the main thrust of Arab political tendencies. The ethnonationalist-separatist tendency is considered to be the growing, potentially dominant trend by the radicalization perspective, whereas it is regarded by the politicization perspective as only a single, diminishing trend. From the politicization perspective, the dominant trend is impatience with the political status quo and a willingness to challenge it by various means.

ENVIRONMENTAL FACTORS: GEOPOLITICAL REGION, STATE, ECONOMY

What factors are responsible for either the radicalization or the politicization of the Arab minority, and what role in this process should be assigned to the CPI? The cultural-modernization approach posits culture and geopolitical conditions as the major environmental factors that produce the radicalization syndrome. According to Landau (1969, 1993), the first important determinant of the Arabs' behavior and attitudes is that they are a minority differing from the Jewish majority by culture. The second, related factor is the disparity in the level of modernity between the Jewish and the Arab communities and the Arabs' desire to catch up. The explanation for the socioeconomic gap is the historic economic and cultural gap between the traditional, peasant Palestinian society before 1948 and the modern industrial Jewish society. In Landau's view, the political behavior of the Arabs in Israel is determined only indirectly by their presence in the Jewish state. The state has a modernizing influence through the changes it brought in the traditional economy and through the provision of educational and welfare services. Its influence interacts, though, with the traditional character of the Arab community and with the community's "given" natural affinity to the Arabs outside Israel's borders. With increasing modernization, Landau sees a conflict growing between two spheres: the economic and educational, and the political. In the latter, the Arabs in Israel, being of the same culture, are similar to other Arabs in the region in their irrational nationalism and endemic factionalism. In the economic and educational sphere, they are progressing toward resembling the Jews. The frustration of this conflict makes for an even more extreme brand of nationalism and protest among the most modernized. The increase over time in the Arab citizens' vote for the CPI and later for the other Arab lists are a manifestation of this process.

An updated version of this argument, which does take into account the negative impact of state policies, is provided by Rekhess (1976, 1977, 1979, 1986). According to Rekhess, modernization, coupled with policies of neglect in the socioeconomic sphere, created a sense of relative deprivation. In the 1970s, when deprivation combined with increasing self-confidence born of rapid population growth and historic convergence with the Palestinians in the occupied territories, the Arabs in Israel were "Palestinized." This process was led from the outside by the PLO and from the inside by the CPI. Rekhess claims that from 1948 up to the 1970s the CPI provided the Arabs with a legal channel for antigovernment political activity by means of ideological cover and a partnership with Jews, as well as practical ways of organizing and taking part in the political give-and-take. After the rise to prominence of the nationalist Palestinian movement, the collapse of Communism, and the ascent of fundamentalist Islam within Israel, the CPI became obsolete (Rekhess 1993, 219).

Other approaches suggest that political acquiescence, actual or potential radicalization, and politicization should be seen mainly as a *reaction* to the nature of the state and its policies. These approaches dispute the cultural-modernization argument, which also tallies with the official Zionist ideological position, namely, that Jewish nation-building has not been at the expense of the Arab Palestinian minority. Instead, these approaches argue that since the Jewish state has been defined and operated as an *ethnic* state, in the interest of the Jewish majority, it logically and empirically constructed the identity of the Arabs as a subordinate national group. As a consequence, it could only partially, if at all, live up to its stated principles of liberal democracy and universal citizenship, thus provoking an ethnonationalist reaction.

The most critical of those analyses is the application of the "internal colonialist" model (Jiryis 1976; Nakhleh 1973, 1979; Zureik 1979). The Arab citizens in Israel are viewed as a section of the Palestinian *nation* that existed prior to 1948 and that has been colonized and controlled (like the blacks in South Africa) by a European settler state. According to Zureik, under the impact of Jewish colonial rule, the Palestinian natural peasant structure changed to an abnormal structure consisting only of a lumpenproletariat (Zureik 1979, 141). Similar to white rule in South Africa before 1994, the dominance of the Jewish settler group is a built-in part of the system, maintained by measures of economic dependency, cooptation, and political control. The right to vote held by the Arabs, nationally and locally, is dismissed as inconsequential.

In this light Zureik examines the process of politicization, or what we earlier called radicalization, of the Arabs in Israel. Only groups and actions that reject the incorporation of the Arabs into the State of Israel or that lean in the direction of irredentism are considered to be manifestations of politicization, while the rest are acts manifesting cooptation. The relative success of the anti-Zionist CPI in the 1970s is taken as one of the manifestations of this process of radicalization. Its class-oriented ideology and commitment to the legal and parliamentary framework of Israel are seen as a function of necessity under the system of control. Thus, just like the cultural-modernization approach, the CPI is seen as part of the radicalization process but not necessarily as its avant-garde.

Other analyses of the Arab citizens' subordinate role in the socioeconomic and political structure of the Jewish state see in its democratic structure a potential for change. According to these analyses, both state institutions and several of the particularist Jewish national institutions that were in charge of economic development before 1948 (the Land Fund, the Jewish Agency, Histadrut) have continued to function alongside and in contradiction to other universal liberal practices of state institutions. The result has been a hybrid political system. This hybrid has been characterized in several ways: as a majoritarian control system (Lustick 1980), having ethnic competitive market mechanisms (Lewin-Epstein and Semyonov 1993), as a statist "welfare and warfare" economy (Carmi and Rosenfeld 1990), and as an ethnic democracy (Smooha 1990) based on ethnorepublican principles (Peled 1992).

The majoritarian-control and competitive-ethnic approaches focus on the political and economic structures and processes that have produced superordinate-subordinate relationships between Jews and Arabs. Writing in the 1970s, Lustick argued that after 1948 the policies of the state toward the Arab citizens bypassed the democratic liberal structure and made up a system of control. The components of the system—segmentation (isolation from Jews, encouraging sectorial differences within the Arabs), dependence (avoiding economic development of Arab localities), and cooptation (of Arab political leaders)—reinforce each other and explain the acquiescent "politics of patronage" of the Arab population. The activities of the CPI are therefore examined as an exception: a generalized, basically ineffective, Arab challenge to the system. The increase in the CPI's electoral support in the 1970s is seen merely as a sanctioned outlet for venting protest.

The competitive ethnic model exposes the economic mechanisms that maintain the Arabs in a subordinate role in the 1980s and 1990s. According to this analysis, discriminatory practices and a segmented labor market structure prevent the disadvantaged Arab citizens from closing the historic gaps separating them from the Jewish majority. Carmi and Rosenfeld arrived at a similar conclusion by employing class analysis: over the years the Arab minority crystalized as an ethnoclass section of the "lower half" within the "welfare-warfare" political economy of Israel. Contrary to Zureik's claim, however, Carmi and Rosenfeld indicate that the Arabs experienced upward economic mobility and social stratification during the first two decades of Israel's statehood, aided by the existence of the welfare state. Yet the process was constrained by the built-in total exclusion of the Arabs on a *national* basis from the emerging military-industrial-bureaucratic complex (the industry being high-tech) (Carmi and Rosenfeld 1974, 1992).

Yet in the late 1980s, after the Arab-Palestinian citizens in Israel did not actively join the Intifada of the Palestinians in the West Bank and Gaza, and even voted for Zionist parties, Lustick revised his position and argued that the system of control had been mostly dismantled. In line with the politicization perspective, he saw the Arabs as having in mind "power and political strategy" instead of "patronage and protest." They have expressed it by voting for coalitional parties, thereby carving for themselves a new, integrated role in the political system. The reduction in the electoral support for the CPI in the late 1980s, therefore, reflected a lesser need for protest (Lustick 1990).

The suggestion of viewing Arab political activism as politicization had been made by Smooha in the mid-1970s, at the zenith of the CPI's electoral success and of militant activity. Based on opinion surveys, he depicted the CPI as expressing an Arab opinion trend of a specific kind: rejecting the Zionist character of the state, which favors Jews legally and unofficially, but not rejecting the framework of the state, based on a Jewish majority (Smooha 1984). It can therefore be deduced from his findings that it was not merely a protest vote that supported the CPI but a dissenting ideology of the coexistence of Arabs and Jews, which opposes both those willing to accommodate themselves to the Zionist structure and those who reject the Israeli political framework altogether. In subsequent research projects, Smooha contended that politicization of the Arab minority and a trend of accommodation among the Jewish majority have shaped a mutual understanding of the basic guidelines governing their relationship, though not of the specifics. These guidelines, described as those of an "ethnic democracy," are likely to be fortified in the era of peace and to reduce the intensity of the inherent conflict between Jews and Arabs in the state (Smooha 1989, 1990, 1992, 1994).

But what was behind the shift in Arab political behavior from controlled acquiescence to politicization, and what nourished both militancy and accommodation to the framework of the state on the part of the Arab citizens in Israel? Smooha suggests a list of forces that fed on each other and created a cumulative impact: the democratization of the Israeli political system in the 1960s, the firm policies of the state on separating the two Palestinian communities divided by the Green Line in the 1970s, and the historical shift of opinion in the PLO and the entire Arab world away from rejection of Israel in the 1980s.

While these are important environmental factors, they project a linear progression and are not clearly grounded in the social process. Moreover, they underplay the active formative role played in the politicization process by the CPI in the late 1960s and the 1970s. My contention is that, in order to understand the historical process during which the Arab minority moved from acquiescence to politicization, it is also necessary to examine closely the oppositionist mobilizing role that the CPI played among the Arab citizens in Israel during that period.

Charting the Research Issues

I argue here that the increase in support for the CPI and the party's ability to set the political agenda of the Arab minority up to the late 1980s are rooted, first, in the socioeconomic reality that evolved for the Arab population in the first two decades of Israel's existence and, second, in the CPI's political and electoral strategy in the Arab community. This political strategy appealed to the national and class concerns of the Arab minority and suggested a non-irredentist solution to the Jewish-Arab national conflict. The explanation for the apparent paradox of a Communist party mobilizing support on the basis of integrative ethnonationalist solidarity is sought by examining three sets of factors.

The first is the manner in which the Communist Party adapted and applied its class ideology to the national question at hand. Second are the mobilizational resources—leadership and organizational capacity—at the party's disposal. The study will highlight the strengths and weaknesses of both factors—ideology and organization—in a fragmented, traditional, mostly Muslim community, which was subject to rapid change and marked by the state as a potential fifth column.

The explanation for the success of the Communist Party in becoming the hegemonic force among the Arab electorate and a political rival to the Zionist establishment in the 1970s is sought in a third set of factors: the ways in which the effects of incorporating the Arab peasant communities into the Israeli system interacted with the electoral strategies of the CPI. I will examine the contradictory impact of the uneven, disjointed incorporation of the socially fragmented Arab peasant minority in 1948 into the ethnically defined, modernizing Jewish state. I will then focus on how the Communist Party reacted to these changes in terms of electoral strategy and how, aided by the emergence of the Palestinian national movement, it mobilized the newly available social bases of support and attempted to institutionalize them. The same set of factors will be used for explaining the drop in the level of support for the CPI. The party's weaknesses and inherent contradictions, particularly in organizational style but also in its electoral strategy and integrative ethnonationalist line, all came to the fore in the mid-1980s. The continued discrimination against and subordination of the Arab educated class and Arab laborers, the persistence of unequal official treatment of Arab localities, and general exclusion from the public sphere, none of which the CPI could alter, prepared the ground for new challengers. These new challengers—both within Israel's Arab population and outside it, such as the PLO—all sought to establish a hold within this politicized Arab-Palestinian population.

I will chart the role of the CPI through two foci of analysis. (1) Focusing on the party (not on its voters), in an organizational-political perspective I will examine the strategic decisions made by the CPI leadership, its internal power structure and internal conflicts over ways to accommodate its class and national appeals, and its modes of operating as a Communist party in a competitive electoral environment. (2) Focusing on the Arab constituency that voted or did not vote for the CPI, from a sociological-historical perspective I will analyze the trajectory of the CPI's rise and fall as caused by the political, social, and economic transformations among the Arabs in Israel; the analysis will test competing interpretations of their ethnonationalist tendencies.

In parts 2 and 3 of this book I describe and analyze the historical transformations of the CPI from these two perspectives. The entire analysis is organized according to a model that relates the kind of public image a party projects to the kind of appeal it uses to attach voters to itself. The result of such a process is varying social bases of support.

Part 2 of this book deals with party image as made up of three components: "programmatic," " style," and "slogan" (chaps. 3–5). The political program of the CPI is discussed mainly in terms of the national question and its Communist interpretation. "Style" is the means by which this platform is realized: the form of activity designated for members, leaders, and the Arab public in the party's praxis; the "slogan" component is the rhetorical means employed to put the style into verbal practice and to represent the ideology of the party (see Yatziv 1972).

It is assumed that each of the three components of the party image appeal to a different level of identification by the voter:

(1) Appeal on the basis of the programmatic component—the policies advocated by the party and presented to the voter as a coherently organized system of attitudes—is directed to the rational level of the voter's consciousness. In the case of the CPI, this component had two major elements: the Marxist-Leninist ideology, which was interpreted in an orthodox way, according to the Soviet Union's line; and the party's stand on the Jewish-Arab regional-national question.

(2) Appeal on the basis of the style component—the subculture that the party developed or with which it is associated—is directed to the cultural level of the voter's consciousness. The style component of the party image is made up of its unique organizational heritage, the characteristics of its leaders and prominent members, the political vocabulary and manner of speech used, the nature of the relationship between the leadership and the rank and file, the kind of activities it undertakes, and the customs and ceremonies evident in its public conferences and meetings. In the case of the CPI, the style component refers to its historical heritage as an illegal underground party of the Comintern; the Jewish-Arab splits within it; its Soviet-style centralized organization; and the dominance of the secularized Christians within it.

(3) Appeal on the basis of the slogan component—the unique kind of expressions used in proclamations, leaflets, and speeches as a means of mobilizing the vote on the eve of an election—is directed to the emotional level of the

voter's consciousness. Such expressions present a concise answer to the simple questions "On whose side is the party?" and "Who is the enemy?" In the case of the CPI, the slogans were directed at exalting the Arab identity and glorifying the party as the only true expression of this identity.

In part 3, I examine the effect of these appeals on the Arab electorate in conjunction with their process of incorporation into the Israeli state. I give a concise historical overview in chapter 6 of the incorporation of Israel's Arabs since 1948 into the economy and society, pointing to changes in the occupations, life-style norms, and political identity. In chapters 7 and 8, I examine how these processes affected the Arab response to the appeals of the CPI and its strategy (especially in the period 1961–77). In chapter 9, I discuss how the strategies, appeals, and responses changed in both local and national elections with the rise of the CPI's new rivals: the nationalists, ethnonationalists, and members of the Islamic movement. The impact of the collapse of the Soviet Union is also assessed.

In the concluding chapter I offer generalizations on the conditions under which integrative ethnonationalism is likely to develop. I also give an overview of the CPI's transformations vis-à-vis the social forces that it had mobilized and politicized. I conclude with an assessment of the likely impact of the elections in the 1990s and the peace process on current trends in ethnonationalist politics among the Arab-Palestinian citizens in Israel.

Two

The Communist Party of Israel
An Ideological and Sociological Profile

3

The Programmatic Component

The Communist Party's formation in the 1920s at the initiative of the Comintern took place vis-à-vis the development of an Arab and Jewish working class in Palestine during the mandate period and under the shadow of the evolving conflict between Arabs and Jews. The party's basis of support was mainly among the anti-Zionist Jewish immigrants. Among the Palestinian Arabs, the party found support from the educated urban Christians and the mobilized workers. Its binational composition collapsed in 1943 into a Jewish party (the PCP) and an Arab party (the National League for Liberation). The two were reunited in 1948 to form the CPI-Maki. The unity between Jewish and Arab Communists was based on the pro-Soviet Marxist-Leninist social order, which rejected Zionism but supported the UN's "self-determination" partition as the solution to the national question. But the geopolitical national conflict split the party again in 1965, giving rise to the CPI-Rakah, with its Arab majority and Jewish minority membership. While zealously upholding Soviet Marxism, even after its collapse in 1991, the focus of the CPI-Rakah social order, particularly after 1967, was the political settlement of the national question. It had two poles: the Palestinian nationalist, for Arab Palestinians outside the State of Israel, and the integrative ethnonationalist, for the Arabs within Israel. This two-state solution of conflict along 1967 borders was formulated in 1976 as the alternative to the PLO's goal, up to the 1980s, of Palestinian self-determination at the expense of Israel. The uprising (Intifada) in the occupied territories in the late 1980s was hailed by the CPI, but the participation of Arab citizens was ruled out. The Oslo agreement between Israel and the PLO in the 1990s was welcomed with reservations.

ENCOUNTERING THE NATIONAL QUESTION:
THE PALESTINE COMMUNIST PARTY (PCP) 1919–1948

Former members of the radical Jewish Poalei-Zion-Left Party in Eastern Europe, some of whom took part in the 1917 Russian revolution, founded the Palestine Communist Party in 1923; it was admitted into the Comintern in 1924. According to the Comintern's theses, formulated by Lenin, Zionism was a bourgeois-nationalist ideology and hence played a pro-imperialistic role in Palestine.[1] The role that the Comintern assigned to the PCP, therefore, was to obstruct Zionist efforts in Palestine and to arouse the Arab peasant masses in the entire Middle East against the British and French colonial authorities. After the PCP was outlawed by the British in 1924, it operated as a clandestine political organization (Ben Avram 1978; Berger-Barzily 1968; List 1965, 86–87).

Through the late 1920s, the party remained small, numbering some 300 members, almost all of them Jewish.[2] In 1929, the Comintern ordered the PCP to Arabize from top to bottom and nominated a new central committee for the PCP, with a 3:2 ratio of Arabs to Jews (Hen Tov 1974, 147; Porat 1968, 257). The Jewish members who remained in the party accepted the Comintern demand that their role be only to aid the Arab Communists, not to be their guides or leaders. They abided by the Arabization directive and elected a majority of Arabs to the central committee. Despite such efforts, the number of Arab members in the PCP remained small. Nonetheless, individuals recruited during this period were members of the new Arab intelligentsia, who in the 1930s and 1940s were successful in developing organizational ties with the Arab working class.

Since the Comintern did not recognize the Jews in Palestine as constituting a national group, the PCP under Arab leadership in 1935 declared the entire Jewish Yishuv (organized community) to be a colonizing entity, and it took further steps to identify with and actively support the developing Arab nationalist struggle. However, the increased national strife in Palestine in the 1930s and the stream of Jewish refugees from Nazi Germany and Austria pushed many of the Jewish members (still the majority in the party) toward greater identification with the cause of the Yishuv. In Communist terms, the situation was set for "rightist" and "opportunist" deviations on the part of both Arab and Jewish members of the party, which eventually tore it in two in the late 1930s and early 1940s.

The war in Europe, especially the attack on the Soviet Union in June 1941, reunited the two parts of the PCP in 1942 but only for a short while. The decision to unite on the basis of a single popular front strategy could not be carried out because of the divergent attitudes toward the war in the two national communities. While the Jewish cadre swung into helping the war effort by establishing the V League to collect money for the Red Army and by calling for enlistment in the British army, the Arab cadre, which now included members of the intelligentsia, occupied itself with Arab trade union matters and cultural clubs. In both sectors, however, the central political theme was the demand for self-determination of Palestine, freeing it from British imperialism (Budeiri 1979, 139–45). By mid-1943, most of the Jewish cadre demanded that the PCP recognize the collective national rights of the Jews in Palestine and that the party should take part in the Jewish proletariat's struggle (Porat 1964, 359). The de facto split came in May 1943, when Jewish leadership supported, and the Arab leadership opposed, the Histadrut-initiated strike in the British army camps, where both Jews and Arabs worked. Thereupon, the PCP leadership was taken over by the Jewish oppositionist group (Mikunis, Vilenska, Vilner), and the Arab cadre in September 1943 set up a separate, purely Arab organization, the League for National Liberation.

The Cultural Tie: The League for National Liberation

The Arab members of both the PCP and the League for National Liberation came mostly from the urban centers, the only places where the Communist Party was active in those days. The Arabs belonged to either of two circles in which leftist ideas had made some inroads in the late 1930s and 1940s: the educated, who lacked the religious or familial status that would make them politically significant, and the organized workers in the new industrial economy. The former were mostly Christians and resided in Haifa, Jaffa, Jerusalem, and Nazareth; the latter were mostly Muslims, of both urban and rural origins, who were introduced to Communist ideas through membership in one of the three Arab trade unions active in the period (Budeiri 1979, 160).

At the start, apparently for tactical reasons, the League for National Liberation did not identify itself as a Communist organization.[3] It was constructed according to the principles of a Leninist party. However, it excluded the membership of non-Arabs, and its official platform avoided specific commitment to revolutionary socialism (Budeiri 1979, 212; Porat 1964, 359). Although after 1945 the league identified itself more openly as part of the Communist movement and advocated equal civil rights for the Jews, it nevertheless conceived of itself as an organization devoted to promoting the Arab national cause. It opposed Zionism and demanded an end to the British Mandate and the establishment of an independent democratic Palestinian state.[4]

The Arab Communists built organizational roots among the working class, first by taking control of the two existing unions with reformist tendencies and then in 1945 by organizing a separate union, the Congress of Arab Workers (CAW). Heavy involvement in the activities of the trade unions formed the major popular base for the league and greatly aided in rebuilding the organizational network of the Communist Party in the post-1948 era.[5] The newspaper the league initiated in 1944, *al Ittihad*, which in 1945 became CAW's publication, turned out to be the party's most important asset in disseminating its views to the Arab population after 1948. Almost forty years later, it is the only daily newspaper in Arabic. The other successful organizational effort was among the urban intelligentsia, where the league's cultural-ideological clubs in nine main towns won increasing popularity (Budeiri 1979, 201).

However, these successes were not enough to win legitimacy and recognition for the league. In the eyes of the Arab political establishment, its positions toward the Jews were too liberal (Nevo 1977, 352). Consequently, it remained a marginal force in the Arab national movement. Up to the 1948 war, the Arab national movement continued to be dominated by the traditional power groups based on the big Muslim families of Jerusalem, Jaffa, Nablus, and Hebron (Shim'oni 1977, 282–95). Late in 1945, when this traditional leadership set up the Arab High Command, it ignored the league's demand to be included.[6]

The socioeconomic roots of leftist activity among the Arabs in the 1930s and 1940s explain the origin of the cultural tie between the modernized section of Arab society—the Christians and the urban workers—and the Communist Party after 1948. Geographically, these roots developed in Haifa and Jaffa, less traditional cities on the coast. Historically, the Christians in Palestine, as in most of the rest of the Middle East, were a minority with an inferior political position in Muslim society. Consequently, they had little influence among the traditional Palestinian elite even during the British Mandate (Shim'oni 1977, 210). But the economic and political dynamics of the mandate era, particularly the development of the two coastal towns, provided new opportunities for both Christians and Muslims who were not members of the traditional elite. From a town of 24,600 in 1922, the population of Haifa grew sixfold, to 128,000 in 1944, half Jews and half Arabs (Ben-Artzi 1986, 39). Jaffa grew from 32,524 in 1922 to 65,000 in 1944, making it the second largest Arab town (after Jerusalem).[7] During the 1930s and 1940s it was the major commercial and trading hub of the Arab community in Palestine and the center of Arab journalism. Communist activities here centered on the trade union front. Toward the end of 1942, the massive increase in public works in the British army camps in the area drew tens of thousands of workers from the rural areas. The British government, interested in organizing these workers, supported the activities of the Society of Arab Palestinian Workers in Jaffa, even though it was headed by members of the Communist Party.[8] Commu-

nist activity in the area came to an abrupt halt when most of the Arab population deserted Jaffa during the 1948 war.

The organizational roots of the league were in Haifa and the north, an industrial and binational area that had a sizable Christian community. In Haifa
itself, Christians accounted for 42 percent of the Arab population in 1944 (compared with 22 percent in the whole of Palestine). Most of them belonged to
the middle class—merchants and professionals—as was characteristic of the
Christian community throughout the country. In Haifa particularly, they stood
out as the prominent members of the middle class. The league was relatively
successful among Christians because they were the least traditional element
in Palestinian society and their links to Western culture made them more re-
ceptive to foreign ideas. Their major channel for the transmission of Western
concepts was a Christian educational system, which was more developed than
the Arab state schools serving the Muslims.

Among the Christians, the Greek Orthodox were salient in their political
activism, in both the Communist and the Arab nationalist movements (Shi-
m'oni 1977, 118). This was arguably a result of their special political situation:
on the one hand, their Arab national consciousness was particularly developed, but on the other, they belonged to a religious minority that, despite
their high economic and sociocultural status, held a minor position in the political leadership of the Palestinian Arabs and other Arabs (Tsimhoni 1986,
21). The secular basis of socialist and national ideologies and the stress on the
common cultural heritage provided a framework in which the Christian minorities could be equal in status to the Muslims (Haim 1976, 36–43). Communist ideology had another attractive feature: it assigned a role to the intelligentsia. In terms of the electoral politics in the post-1948 period, the Greek
Orthodox were a culture group with ties of traditional loyalty to the Communist party.

During the years 1944–48, there were two Communist parties in Palestine,
one Jewish and one Arab. The program component of the political image that
the Arab Communists projected during this period was not very different from
that of the other Arab parties in Palestine. Rather, what made them different
was their particular style of political activity, their emphasis on multiclass and
multireligious mobilization, and the possibilities they left open for political
cooperation with the Jews. The Jewish Communists also objected to the idea
of the partition of Palestine into an Arab and a Jewish state. However, unlike
the league, which advocated "a democratic state with equal civil rights to all
inhabitants," Jewish Communists were advocating more clearly a binational
state.[9] In the united party set up in 1948, the members of the central committee of the league were accepted into the central committee of the PCP, re-

named the Communist Party of Israel. The general secretary of the party
and the majority in the central committee were Jewish. This was in line with
the territorialization principle, as the majority of the state's population was
Jewish.

The Marxist-Leninist Social Order

The reunification of the Jewish and the Arab Communists came about in October 1948, six months after the proclamation of State of Israel, to which the
Jewish Communist Party representative put his signature. At that point, the
Israeli forces already occupied parts of the intended Arab state. The unity agreement formed the basis of the social order presented by the united Communist
Party of Israel (Maki) to the Jewish and Arab electorate for the first decade of
its existence. In a rather extraordinary statement of the central committee of
the League for National Liberation a month earlier, the league had acknowledged its "mistake" in not recognizing that the Jews in Palestine were by now
"a new nationality" and blamed the misjudgment on its failure to organize on
an internationalist basis.[10] Furthermore, it stated that the league's separate
Arab organization was responsible for the failure to create a united Jewish-
Arab front against imperialism. It had therefore "denied the Arab and Jewish
masses a living example of the unity to which they were called. Those who
gained from the political and organizational split were the Arab and Jewish
reactionaries, who deceived the masses by propagating racial hatred."[11] The
league was thus indirectly blaming itself for helping to bring about the
partition.[12]

Organizationally, the league suggested in this document that its bodies and
its membership within the State of Israel would become part of the Communist Party of Israel. It stated that the league's branches and organizations in
the Arab part of Palestine that "currently are occupied by Israel's army, such
as Nazareth, will retain their independent existence and their unity with the
League for National Liberation in the Arab part of Palestine."[13] The significance of this organizational separation was the continued adherence to partition lines. However, the league continued to exist separately only for about a
year and then was quietly merged into the CPI-Maki.[14] Correspondingly, the
League for National Liberation on the West Bank declared itself to be the Communist Party of Jordan in June 1951.

The statute of the CPI-Maki (1948–65) and that of the CPI-Rakah (1965–
95) declare adherence to Marxist-Leninist ideology. The party is therefore described in the statute as the "revolutionary party of the working class, the
vanguard of all the workers in Israel," whose aim (up to 1990) was "the establishment of a socialist regime in Israel."[15] The second basic aim of the party,
according to the statute, is "the achievement of peace in the world" and in the

region. To that end, the party "struggles for disconnecting Israel from its dependence on imperialism."[16] It also struggles "for friendship with the Soviet Union and the socialist countries."[17] While the party statute up to 1965 did not specify the conditions for peace in the region, the CPI-Rakah statute after 1965 specified that the "just and lasting peace between Israel and the Arab countries" has to be "based on the mutual recognition of the right for self-determination of the two peoples."[18] The third basic aim of the CPI was the achievement of rights for various groups in the society: "for the defence of the interests of working people, and the raising of their living standards"; for "equal civil and national rights of the Arab population in Israel"; and, in the Rakah statute, "for equality between the ethnic groups; for equal rights for women; for the defense of the rights of the youth."[19] In sum, the statute states that "joining the ranks of the Israeli Communist Party imposes the duty [on the members] and grants the right to be part of the exalted project of liberating Israel and the entire humanity from class exploitation, national oppression, discrimination against women, and the threat of wars."[20]

According to the social order as presented in the statute, the resolution of the national conflict depends on prior resolution of the class conflict. However, the detailed theses that the party published over the years reveal that the paramount concern expressed in its social order was not class contradictions but rather the world socialist/capitalist contradiction. The party platform and slogans, particularly those of the CPI-Rakah, imply that the resolution of the class conflict within Israel is postponed until the regional manifestations of the imperialist/anti-imperialist contradiction are resolved. Thus, a resolution of the 18th Congress of CPI-Rakah in 1976 stated that once "a just and lasting peace" is established, "the peoples will be interested in preventing imperialism from instigating [a conflict] between them again. The workers and the masses will be interested in concentrating all their efforts in a struggle for basic social changes in their countries, and in the final account, for socialism. . . . Within Israel there will be created better conditions for a struggle for full social and national equal rights of the Arab national minority. The struggle in Israel will be in the direction of democratization, in the direction of realizing deep political and social changes, which will bring in their turn a new system of relations between Jews and Arabs, of which our Communist party constitutes a living symbol."[21] They thus reveal the importance of the section in the statute (before 1990) that stressed the party's commitment to "brotherly relationship with the Communist parties and workers' parties in the world, especially with the CPSU, the most experienced and hardened unit in the world Communist movement, that carries the chief responsibility for world peace and freedom of the peoples."[22]

The CPI before the split in 1965, and CPI-Rakah thereafter, held to the

CPSU's traditional ideological negation of the Zionist movement, which was thought to have been born out of the "sin" of European anti-Semitism and British colonialism and to owe its continued existence to American imperialism. Rather than constituting the "national liberation movement of the Jewish people," Zionism (in the phrase used up to the late 1970s) is the "reactionary ideology of Jewish bourgeois nationalism" and "the ideological tool of the Jewish bourgeoisie" in the service of imperialism, to the detriment of the Jewish masses.[23] (Following the establishment of an electoral front with non-Communist Jews in 1977, Zionism was acting "at the service of foreign and local big capital.")[24] Nevertheless, the UN decision in 1947 on the partition of Palestine and the establishment of a Jewish state alongside an Arab one was justified on the basis of the new realities in the region: first, the creation of a "new Jewish nationality" in Palestine, to which the principle of self-determination justifiably should be applied; second, the danger that British imperialism would not be liquidated in the area if the two states were not established (Vilner 1970, 38). Hence the party did not object to the Law of Return, which granted automatic citizenship to Jewish refugees.

The second focus of the party's social order was the political settlement of the two-pronged national question in the region; first, the nationalist pole of self-determination for the Arab Palestinians outside the State of Israel, about which politically the party could do little until the 1980s; second, the ethnonationalist demands for equality for the Arab Palestinian citizens within Israel and recognition of them as a national minority. With regard to the first issue, the CPI positions, after some vacillations in the 1950s on the issue of borders, generally followed the Soviet line. The Soviet Union, for its own reasons, objected to any redrawing of the political map in the region in the 1950s (Freedman 1975, 10–11). As for the second issue, the party was relatively free to develop its own strategic goals, and it did so according to what was politically feasible and advantageous to its power. Thus the drawing of the exact line between those two poles in the party's social order was a matter of a historical process, which corresponded to the development of the integrative tendencies within the Arab minority and to Soviet reactions to geopolitical developments in the region.

Throughout the period 1949–90, the image the party projected to the Arab voter, through its program, political style, and emotional appeal was exaltation of all voters who would see themselves as anti-imperialist (pro-Soviet), antitraditional (modern), and internationalist (proud Arab but not nationalistic). The cracks that appeared in the Soviet system in the late 1980s following perestroika forced the party to reexamine its own Communist image and identity. Out of the tremendous confusion and disagreement within the party, those siding wholeheartedly with perestroika and radical rethinking lost out to a coalition of hard-line doctrinaire Communists and soft-line reformers. At the head of the former were the veteran Jewish-Christian leadership (see chapter 4), who claimed that the problems in the Soviet Union were a result of "mistakes and distortions" in the applications of the scientific Marxist-Leninist model but not in the theoretical model itself. The leadership therefore rejected the calls of the reformers within the party for reassessing the Soviet model and for turning the CPI into a social-democratic party, and it criticized the dangerous tendency of the perestroika in the Soviet Union to "deteriorate into anarchy."[25]

It therefore came as no surprise that the top echelons of the party expressed relief during the brief hours of the military coup against Gorbachev in August 1991.[26] Although in its 22nd Congress, held in 1993, the historic leadership retracted its position and criticized the coup attempt as "adventurous," it nonetheless reaffirmed its support of the old Communist Party model. The CPI, stated the (outgoing) general secretary, "will neither be Stalinist nor social democratic but Communist." The chairman of the party added, "Communism is not dead, and will never die."[27]

The collapse of the Soviet Union, however, did not affect dramatically the other programmatic focus of the CPI—its stance on the national question. In the party social order, the Arab minority is essentially envisioned as an ethnoclass minority within the Israeli capitalist structure; the peasants, the Arab masses, and the small and medium capitalists suffer equally from the policies of national discrimination.[28] Only when the party encountered opposition to its Arab authenticity (because of its pro-Sovietism) did it begin to refer to Arab "bourgeois elements," who were hostile to the Communists on a class basis. Up to the late 1970s, therefore, the contradictions within the Arab population were identified as being between the traditional and the progressive forces, the traditionalists being synonymous with "government stooges" (those who cooperated with the government and voted for Arab electoral lists, initiated and supported by the Zionist establishment) and the progressives being Communist or nationalist forces (who cooperated with or voted for the CPI).

The party social order promised the Arabs that in return for denouncing the traditional forces in Arab society across the border (the pro-Western Arab regimes) and for renouncing the traditional leaders in Israel (the "government and Zionist stooges"), they would first of all regain their honor, lost in the 1948 defeat, and though a minority in Israel, Arabs would also be recognized as a collective with equal title to the land (see chapter 7). As a result of the social changes in the Arab population, the "traditional" political enemies— Arab lists—disappeared by the 1980s. The challenge to the social order proposed by the Communist Party was then twofold: accommodators within the Zionist parties, on the one hand, and Palestinian nationalist and Islamic revivalist groups on the other (see chapter 9).

The National Question:
Tension Between Nationalism and Ethnonationalism, 1949–1961

The programmatic unity of the Jewish and Arab Communists was based on adherence to the Arab-Palestinian/Jewish self-determination principle inherent in the 1947 partition plan, on equal minority rights of the Arab population in Israel, and on identification with the Soviet Union. The three issues were intertwined and created vacillations in the party's position on the national-territorial issue. The identification with the Soviet Union was expressed in the party program as the need to ensure Israel's freedom and independence by pulling the new state toward a pro-Soviet orientation. In this, the CPI was not unique in the political arena: up to late 1952, the socialist-Zionist party, Mapam, which had a strong and dedicated following in the "pioneering" section of the Jewish population, was also a staunch supporter of the Soviet Union under Stalin. It also opposed Premier David Ben-Gurion's control policies toward the Arabs in Israel.

For the first three years after independence, the CPI-Maki and Mapam cooperated both inside and outside the Knesset in developing a strong opposition to the Labor (Mapai)-led government in the economic, foreign, and security fields, as well as opposing the policies that affected the Arab citizens. By the time of the CPI's 12th Congress in mid-1952, its leadership was optimistic of its chances of becoming, with Mapam, a political force that would have to be taken into account.[29]

The success of the plan depended on a wider appeal to the Jewish vote, especially among the new immigrants, refugees from Europe, some of whom settled in houses deserted by Arab refugees.[30] The plan could not succeed by reliance on the Arabs, who were small in number and had a low level of political consciousness.[31] Probably out of sensitivity to this reality, the resolution of the CPI's 12th Congress in support of the partition plan was vague on the issue of the partition lines, which did not correspond to the 1948 cease-fire lines (Samara 1980, 310). These were left to be determined in peace negotiations with the Palestinian Arabs. The resolution repeated, however, the demand for enabling the Arab refugees to return to Israel.

The hopes for an alliance with Mapam, however, were soon dashed. The positions of the CPI as expressed in the 12th Congress were not acceptable to Mapam, and a bitter exchange developed between the two parties.[32] The anti-Zionist and anti-Semitic political trials, first in Czechoslovakia (the Slansky trial, November 1952) and then in the Soviet Union (the "doctors' plot," January 1953), put an end to these hopes; Mapam reversed its pro-Soviet orientation and became a bitter rival of the CPI, which defended those trials.[33] However, a splinter group from Mapam, headed by the charismatic Dr. Moshe Sneh, who retained the pro-Soviet orientation, joined the CPI in 1954.

These developments and a number of major world and regional events led to the reopening of the territorial issue in the CPI in the late 1950s. First, the Soviet regime under Khrushchev had embarked on a definite pro-Arab policy in 1955, marked by the agreement to supply arms to the new Nasser regime in Egypt. Second, the deteriorating situation along the Jordanian and Egyptian borders, with infiltration of fedayeen (guerrillas) who killed civilians, and refugees who crossed the border for purposes of theft, led to the government's policy of military reprisals, culminating in the Sinai campaign in October 1956 (Morris 1993) and to a more heavy-handed policy toward the Arabs in Israel. In addition, pro-Nasserist Palestinian nationalists were becoming active among the educated Arabs, the nationalists including circles of poets, writers, educators, and clergymen (some of whom later founded the al Ard association; see chapter 5). Third, the 20th Congress of the Soviet Communist Party in February 1956, which denounced Stalin's "mistakes," sent shock waves throughout Communist parties around the world.

The impact of those developments on the CPI's political position by June 1957, the time of the 13th Congress, was to increase its identification with the Arab side in the conflict with Israel and to reopen the question of borders. While the fedayeen were denounced, the blame for the entire situation was put on the Israeli government's "policy of force against the Arab states" and "its refusal to recognize the just national rights of the Palestinian Arab people."[34] Unlike the 12th Congress, which made only vague reference to the territorial question, the 13th Congress, at the demand of the Arab members of the central committee,[35] declared explicitly that the "right of the Palestinian Arabs for self-determination included the part that is in Israel. This right for self determination . . . to which annexation of Arab territories to Israel is opposed, constitutes the basis for the solution of the territorial question which is in dispute between Israel and the Arab countries."[36]

At the same time, the party denied emphatically that recognition of this right *in principle* constituted a separatist position: it was the bourgeois elements in the Arab community who, out of despair about their oppressed condition, reacted by closing in, by escaping into nationalist separatism and political passivity, instead of struggling for Jewish and Arab proletarian unity. In a dialectical fashion, therefore, recognition of "the right to separate, the freedom to separate leads in general to the freedom of rapprochement between the peoples." In addition, Israel should recognize "the natural right of the refugees who want to return to their homeland and be rehabilitated."[37] In return for a change in the official policy, the Arab states should (and there were signs that they would) recognize Israel and sign a peace agreement with it.

According to the Jewish members of the CPI-Maki, who in 1965 went with the Mikunis-Sneh faction, this change of line in 1957 was a result of the demand by the Arab leaders in the party that the Soviet Union's recognition of Israel be categorized as a "Stalinistic mistake" (Balti 1981, 49–62). According to Isser Harel (then the head of the internal security service, the Shabac), this was an attempt by the Arab leaders to launch a new separatist strategy. The tactic was based on the hope that, given the surge of Arab nationalism under Nasser (especially after the unity with Syria in February 1958), Israel's existence would come to an end. Harel even supplied to the Jewish leaders of the party a recording of a supposedly secret meeting of some of the Arab party leaders in Nazareth, where they allegedly discussed setting up an underground movement in the Galilee (Balti 1981, 61; Harel 1987, 236). The participants in the meeting denied the allegation about the purpose of that meeting, charging that the evidence had been falsified in a plot by the security forces to discredit and harass the Arab Communists.[38] Some thirty years after the event, a CPI-Rakah official continued to deny the underground allegation and indeed no charges of conspiracy were ever pressed. However, he termed the line adopted in the 13th Congress of Maki in 1957 "a mistake," motivated by the desire to cool down the pro-Nasser elements in the Arab sector, who were thriving on the despair of the oppressed Arab population.[39]

By 1961, the "separatist" phrase was dropped from the party program. The program as presented in the 14th Congress reaffirmed the mutual rights of Arabs and Jews for self-determination and the need to employ peaceful means to achieve an agreement. Within the guiding principles of that agreement, Israel must "recognize the right of the Arab refugees to return to Israel, ensure proper compensation for the refugees who will decide not to return, and agree by way of a mutual agreement to change the temporary cease fire lines with permanent and peaceful borders. All that—on the basis of the right of self determination of the peoples."[40]

This position, it should be noted, was in line with the Soviet view on the territorial question (Golan 1976, 6). While there is no evidence of such, the position may well have been a subject of discussion between the CPI-Maki delegation and the Soviets during the Moscow talks held by Communist parties in 1960. Whether resulting from Soviet persuasion or from the break with the pro-Nasser al Ard, by the early 1960s the Arab leadership was convinced that the solution for the Palestinian national question could not be advanced by advocating the return to the borders of the partition plan. This conclusion can be drawn from the political program of the CPI-Rakah faction after the split in the party in 1965.

CPI-Rakah's Sovietism and Integrative Ethnonationalism, 1965–1977

The brewing conflict in the CPI-Maki leadership during 1964–65, which was a well-kept secret from the party cadre, came into the open on the eve of the 15th Congress in the summer of 1965. The split applied to a wide range of ideological strategic and tactical issues and emerged basically as a result of the Mikunis-Sneh (Jewish) faction's conclusion that the old theses on the regional and international orientation of the party were mistaken and unrealistic: that the conflict with the Arab states was basically a national conflict rather than the result of the world imperialist/anti-imperialist contradiction; that the Arab liberation movement by definition was not peace seeking and that in fact its intransigence toward Israel's existence in the region was no less to blame for the lack of peace than was the Israeli government; and that the "sister" Communist parties, should be publicly criticized whenever they took the side of clearly chauvinistic Arab positions (Edlestein 1973). The bottom line was that the party should recognize the more progressive elements in the Jewish public and seek to work with them for political change.

Behind these conclusions was not only the uneasiness felt among some of the Jewish leaders and cadre in face of the Soviet and Arab hostility toward Jews and Israel but also the diminishing electoral support of the CPI-Maki among Jewish voters. The entire Arab leadership and part of the Jewish leadership rejected these arguments as "opportunist" and as constituting a "Zionist deviation."[41] Nevertheless, in an unprecedented act for the Communist Party, an attempt was made to reach an accommodation by publishing the arguments of the two groups as two contending theses for the 15th congress: Opinion A (the Vilner-Toubi faction) and Opinion B (the Mikunis-Sneh faction). But efforts by the Soviet delegation and others failed to prevent a final break, and the two factions held separate congresses, each one called the 15th Congress of the CPI.

All the Arab cadre of the CPI-Maki and a small number of the Jewish leadership and cadre went over to the New Communist List, known as Rakah. The CPI-Rakah's congress accepted the theses expressed in Opinion A. They continued to regard British and American imperialism as the source of the conflict, and they saw the Arab national liberation movement (the pro-Soviet regimes) as a progressive force. At this stage, however, in line with Soviet positions, the newly formed al Fatah organization was not recognized as part of that liberation movement, and its actions were denounced as "terrorist" and "adventurous" (Golan 1976, 50).

The positions of Rakah on the solution to the conflict, including the territorial issue, repeated verbatim the decisions of the 14th Congress. In other words, the Arab leaders of the CPI-Rakah gave up their demand to return to the 1947 partition decision as the basis of their program. This decision may have been the price for keeping part of the Jewish leadership and cadre in the party, as well as leaving the door open for the return of the renegades.[42] A third possibility is that the demand was relinquished to head off accusations by the Mikunis-Sneh faction about the Arab Communists' disregard for the fate of the Jews.

In his polemic with the Mikunis-Sneh group at the other 15th Congress, Emil Habibi, one of the two top Arab leaders, defended their record on this matter:

We always told the [Arab] masses, that they need to fight for the defense of their rights, and their just cause. At the same time, our party strongly encouraged trust in Jewish democratic forces, which struggle against oppression and for equality. . . . We glorified the struggle of our party, we exalted our Jewish members, the struggle of the working class, the youth, and the Jewish democratic intelligentsia. We exalted the slogan of the common fate, the common enemy, as well as the shared glorious future. [Hence] it was not through planting illusions in the hearts of the masses, like claiming that our party *alone* could defend the interests of the people, that we gained the support of the Arab masses. This support is expressed not only in the number of votes in election time, but mainly through the *active* participation of the masses in the democratic struggle, which encourages the power of the people, and increases their self-confidence" [my emphases].[43]

To stress its integrative character, the program of the 15th Congress included a demand for "proper participation of the Arab citizens in the central and local state bureaucracy."[44]

For three years the two Communist factions—Maki and Rakah—battled for recognition by the Soviets and the world Communist movement as the legitimate Communist Party of Israel. By the time of the 16th Congress of Rakah, in January 1969, it had won the battle of recognition, but the geopolitical situation in the region had changed dramatically as a result of the 1967 war (Balti 1981, 190). The flash victory of Israel humiliated the pro-Soviet Arab regimes and left Israel in control of a major part of the Palestinian people living in the West Bank and Gaza.

Unlike the Maki faction, the CPI-Rakah appraised the war as a continuation of the 1956 imperialistic war, in which it believed that Israel was used by the West to hit the progressive Syrian and Egyptian regimes.[45] But the CPI-

Rakah also put some blame on the Arab side by noting "the lack of a positive stable program on the part of the Arab national movement for the solution of the Arab-Israeli conflict and the Palestinian question, while respecting the rights of the peoples involved." It also noted that "the chauvinistic statements made every once in a while, against the right of Israel to exist . . . made it difficult to convince the Jewish masses to support . . . the Communist party."[46] The failure of the Egyptian and Syrian regimes on the battlefield was due not to any lack of Soviet aid but to Egypt's socialist and democratic weakness, which if corrected would lead to "the acceptance of the program for the solution of the Palestinian problem, and the Israeli-Arab conflict on the basis of the right for self-determination *of the people of Israel* and of the Arab Palestinian people" [my emphasis].[47]

Thus, for the first time since 1948 the question of the political fate of the Palestinian Arab citizens in Israel became a concrete, internal Israeli political issue. The potential for irredentism was obvious, and there were a number of occurrences of nationalist slogan writing, apparently by unauthorized members of the CPI-Rakah youth organization.[48] The party had to formulate a clear stand, and it did so by shifting the emphasis in its program from the Palestinian component to the Israeli component.[49] The program was also faithful to the Soviet line, which did not at this stage support the PLO (al Fatah) as the national liberation movement of the Palestinians.

The basis of the program proposed by Rakah, therefore, was the retreat of the Israeli forces from all the territories occupied in June 1967, according to UN Security Council resolution 242 of November 22, 1967, solving the Arab refugee problem, and recognition by the Arab states of Israel's right to exist in recognized and secure borders.[50] Support for UN resolution 242 meant support for handing the territories back to "reactionary" Jordan. Although actively opposing the Israeli occupation, the party also denounced the "irresponsible deeds on the part of extremists in the Arab resistance movement . . . such as planting of grenades in the central bus station in Tel Aviv, the explosive car in the market in Jerusalem, and the attack on the civilian Israeli plane in Athens. In addition, our party emphatically rejects the political program of those leaders of the resistance movement who set as its goals not only the liberation of the occupied territories, and securing the just rights of the Arab Palestinian people, but the annihilation of the state of Israel."[51]

This party line encountered some internal opposition (see the next section), but the party formally stuck to UN resolution 242 until 1976. Toward the end of 1968, the Soviet Union began gradually to change its attitude toward the PLO, but not until the end of 1974 did it support the idea of a separate Palestinian entity (Golan 1976, 4). Hence, in its 17th Congress in 1972, the CPI-Rakah reaffirmed the line accepted in the previous Congress but hinted at the option of Palestinian self-determination. The party thus rejected the "Democratic Palestinian State" solution of the PLO as "not only unjust and unrealistic, but also . . . a solution by way of force."[52] It described the execution of the Security Council resolution as the first step in the direction of Palestinian self-determination: "From the point of view of the Arab Palestinian people, the execution of the Security Council resolution will give back its lands that were conquered by Israel in the June 1967 war, and will make it possible to arrive at a just solution for the problem of the Arab Palestinian refugees, namely, giving them the choice of returning to their homeland or receiving compensation according to the UN decisions."[53]

In other words, the traditional section of the party program concerning the refugees called for their settlement in the territories occupied in 1967, not in Israel along the pre-1967 lines. The party theses added that in the long term, out of free will, a federative state in the region should not be ruled out.

The 1973 war, as well as the decision of the Arab countries to recognize the PLO as "sole legitimate representative of the Palestinian people" during the Rabat conference of October 1974, found an echo in the now progressively politicizing Arab minority (see chapter 7). The change in the Soviet position during 1974–75 in favor of Palestinian statehood and the cautious support given to the PLO as an authorized representative of the Palestinian movement made possible a similar change in the Palestinian pole of the party program.[54] However, a clearer distinction had to be made between it and the Israeli pole of the party program. In the 1970s, the strategy was both to intensify the demands on the Israeli pole of the program and to build a political consensus among the Arab citizens on its proposed solution to the Palestinian problem. In the 1980s and 1990s, most of the party's attention was devoted to the latter.

In March 1976 the CPI pushed for the Land Day strike against government plans to requisition Arab lands in the Galilee. The strike action turned violent and resulted in casualties (see chapter 7). In the 18th party congress in December 1976, the party charged that "the government denies the Arab population in Israel equal civil and national rights, and does not recognize it at all as a national minority that deserves equal civil and national rights." It warned that the Arabs, making up 14 percent of the population, were "a quantitative and qualitative factor in the state of Israel" and that they were "no longer the same old Arab society" since in the new social structure "there is an overwhelming weight to the salaried workers and intelligentsia." The Arab population in Israel, "under the guidance of the Israeli Communist Party, and on the basis of the right program and methods of struggle," was in a position "to succeed in its struggle for its rights, and make an important contribution to the general democratic struggle for the change of the prevalent Israeli policy and for peace."[55] The fight to prevent land appropriation was seen in this context rather than as a general nationalist Palestinian measure: "Our Israeli Communist Party and the Arab population in Israel do not question the fact that the Galilee and the Triangle are part of the state of Israel. The government of Israel and the extreme right wing Likud treat the Arab residents as colonial subjects; they behave as if . . . [the regions] are not part of the state of Israel."[56]

Yet, apparently shocked by the results of Land Day, the party reversed priorities. Although the realization of the two poles of the party program—the nationalist and the integrative ethnonationalist—were to be pursued simultaneously, the nationalist Palestinian goal became the first priority. The Palestinian-Arab minority and Jewish "democratic forces" led by the party were to form a pressure group inside Israel for the Palestinian cause. Conditions in Israel would thus improve for the implementation of the ethnonationalist Israeli pole of the program—recognition for Arabs as a national minority. In the third stage, the Arab minority was envisioned as being in the vanguard in Israel; after achieving equal rights and eliminating the policy of discrimination, the Arab population within Israel would "be even a greater factor in the struggle for a progressive change of the regime in Israel."[57]

In preparation for the second stage—equal rights for Jews and Arabs—the party presented a thirteen-point program. The program called for the de-Zionization of the state by legal recognition of the national minority status of the Arab population in Israel and by abolishing all legal and semi-official clauses that either gave preference to Jews or excluded Arabs from benefits. Thus it called for a change in the citizenship law, which gave preference to Jews, and demanded that the state return land taken in 1948 from Arab refugees who eventually remained in Israel. In sum, the party program called for elements of a binational state but refrained from endorsing fully even its autonomist implications, preferring the general concept of integration.

The CPI-Front Program and the National Question, 1977–1993

Before the 1977 elections the CPI-Rakah organized to implement this two-stage strategy by forming an electoral front—the Democratic Front for Peace and Equality (Hadash)—with Arab and Jewish non-Communists (see chapter 8). The Hadash's six-point program, with the party's solution to the Palestinian national question as its first point, was almost synonymous with the party program. What it excluded was identification with the Soviet Union and the ideological revolutionary goals of changing the regime.[58] Throughout the period, the CPI-Hadash program on the national question was unchanged: support for the pro-Soviet Arab regimes and for Palestinian self-determination led by the PLO, with the provision that Arab leadership accept the "realistic" solution advocated by the Soviet Union.[59] The "phased stages" strategy the PLO adopted in the 1970s was seen by the party as proof of the PLO's increasing realism, and the leaders of both party and PLO held a series of meetings (Yodffat and Arnon-Ohana 1981, 60–65). But the CPI stance became more ambiguous when two criteria—"realism" and "pro-Sovietism"—clashed, or when the Arab regimes and the PLO were in conflict, or when the PLO itself was torn by internal feud.

Thus, the Camp David accords and the autonomy plan for the West Bank and Gaza, signed in Washington in 1978 by Israel and Egypt, were denounced by the CPI as "imperialist plots" designed to obstruct the only route to true and lasting peace—an international conference with the participation of the PLO and the Soviet Union. The CPI fully identified with the Arab countries' condemnation of the Egyptian regime and its political ostracism.[60] Needless to say, the war in Lebanon in 1982 between Israel and the PLO was denounced as an "Israeli-American aggression" in the service of the American imperialistic interests.[61] But the internal feud that developed within the PLO in 1983 because of the war, in which the pro-Soviet Syrian regime supported the anti-Arafat rebels, created a problem for the CPI. The CPI eventually came down on the side of PLO unity under Arafat, criticizing the Syrian interference with "the sovereign decision making" of the Palestinian national movement.[62]

Of the three trends that developed within the PLO in the mid-1980s—al Fatah, the pro-Syrian National Alliance, and the Marxist Alliance—the CPI naturally identified with the latter. Its warmest sympathy went to the Communist Palestinians (part of the Democratic Alliance), with whom it developed ties on the West Bank in the 1970s (Rekhess 1989, 127–32; Touma 1990, 146–47). The CPI's growing criticism of the American-oriented "Palestinian right, which represents sectors of the national bourgeoisie" came to a head with the signing of the Amman agreement between PLO leader Yassir Arafat and Jordan's King Hussein in February 1985. The party charged that Arafat's agreement to establish a future confederation with Jordan made the future Palestinian state "nothing but a Palestinian district in the Hashemite Kingdom."[63] Thus, after appearing for a long time to be an ardent supporter of the PLO, the CPI criticized its "pro-American" leanings and warned that "the agreement puts an end to the independence of the PLO and its position as the sole representative of the Arab Palestinian people."[64]

Indeed, the political cards of the geopolitical actors directly involved with the occupied territories—Israel, the PLO leadership, and Jordan—had to be reshuffled when the Intifada uprising by the Palestinians broke out on the West Bank and Gaza in December 1987. The CPI, which by then had encountered competitors for the role of the champion of the Palestinians in areas occupied by Israel (see below), saw an opportunity to demonstrate its Palestinian credentials. It immediately hailed the Intifada as a justified popular act of liberation, with which it declared its political solidarity, and it denounced the Israeli attempts to suppress it. Needless to say, the CPI welcomed the declaration of Palestinian independence in Algiers and the acceptance of the UN partition decision of 1947 by the PLO in November 1988. In the PLO's official coming to terms with Israel's existence the CPI saw a vindication of its long-standing position on the two-state solution to the Palestinian national question, and it credited itself for the change.[65] The party was eager to prove its identification with the PLO even during the 1991 Gulf war, despite the missile attacks on Israel. Although it objected to the invasion of Kuwait by Iraq, it virulently attacked the United States for organizing the war coalition against the Arabs of the Third World.[66] This attack reflected the anti-American mood of the Arabs in Israel.[67] It also tallied with the PLO's position.[68]

The Palestinian positions presented at the Madrid conference, convened in October 1991 under the auspices of the United States and Russia, were also greeted with enthusiasm by the CPI, which totally rejected those of the Israeli government (Ozacky and Kabha 1991). To stress its solidarity with the PLO leadership further, the Hadash held its third convention on November 15, 1991, the third anniversary of the 1988 declaration, and invited the senior Palestinian member of the delegation as its guest of honor.

Choosing to ignore the relationship between the fall of the Soviet Union and Arafat's decision to compromise even further, the CPI came out in support of the Oslo agreement. The declaration of principles of September 1993 between the Israeli government and the PLO on the mutual recognition and a gradual negotiation process, first working on an interim agreement and then on the final settlement, was thus welcomed by the CPI as "the first step in the right path in the direction of achieving the comprehensive permanent just peace."[69] Yet, loyal to its oppositionist style and political identification with the Palestinian left, the CPI soon implied criticism of Arafat's leadership and explicitly criticized the Israeli implementation of the agreement.

The Intifada and its political consequences had direct bearings on the ethno-nationalist Israeli pole of the party program, especially as it had to compete with challengers on its own turf—the "oppositionist" section of the Arab population. The main challenge to the CPI in the mid-1980s came from the Progressive Movement for Peace (PMP)—which had no reservations about identifying with the right-wing Fatah organization within the PLO. Between 1984 and 1992 the PMP ran in the general elections with a platform almost identical to that of the Hadash (see chapter 9). The Progressive Movement for Peace presented itself as an authentic Palestinian body, which took its cues not from Moscow but from the organization that the CPI recognized as the "sole representative of the Palestinian nation"—the PLO.

The first response of the CPI to this challenge was to draw again the line between nationalism and integrative ethnonationalism by assigning to itself the leading role: "The party argued that the widespread recognition of the PLO as the Palestinian national spokesman by the Arab public did not imply that they were under the PLO's control: . . . The Arab population, as citizens of the state of Israel, lives under different conditions than the other parts of the Palestinian people. The Arab population in Israel has representation and leadership of its own, which won its trust and guided it in its difficult and complicated struggle, with wisdom and success. This leadership is the Israeli Communist Party, the Democratic Front for Peace and Equality, and the other representative bodies of the Arab population."[70]

The CPI's failure to stem the tide of competitors on the ethnonationalist turf, evidenced by the creation in 1988 of the Arab Democratic Party, was diagnosed by the CPI as "the awakening of the petite-bourgeoisie and bour-geois elements."[71] It attested to the party's failure to sustain its hegemonic position (see chapter 9).

Furthermore, in the late 1980s and early 1990s, the Palestinian national question was seemingly on the track of negotiated settlement between Israel and the PLO, but there was no dramatic change in the subordinate position of the Arab citizens in Israel. Ideas on autonomy that were floated by Arab intel-lectuals were endorsed partly by the Progressive List for Peace (PLP), which also put on the political agenda the demand to turn Israel legally into the "state of all its citizens" as opposed to its definition by law as the "state of the Jewish people" (Ozacky-Lazar and Ghanem 1990, 14).

CPI spokesmen declared that its long-time anti-Zionist stance included the legal status of Israel, and they rejected the autonomist ideas outright. Accord-ing to the party's positions, separate Arab organizations and institutions, such as the Association of Arab Students, were only a temporary device to achieve integration and equality for the Arab citizens. Institutional separatism in edu-cational and social services (as suggested by the leader of the PLP) would push the Arab population into a "ghetto" and make their inequality and marginal-ity a permanent feature.[72] However, the integrative ethnonationalist formula offered by the CPI—"Arab unity in the struggle for equality"—did not have much to show for itself in the mid-1990s. This may partly explain the CPI's most serious challenger in the late 1980s and 1990s, the Islamic movement, which won increasing number of followers under the nonspecific slogan "Is-lam is the solution" (see chapter 9).

4

The Style Component
Structure, Membership, and Activities

In stark contrast to the fragmented nature of the Arab society within Israel, the Communist Party in its various forms has always kept a Bolshevist-like, centralized organization, which changed only slightly after the collapse of the Soviet Union in the 1990s. This rigid structure was responsible for maintaining both the Jewish-Arab character of the CPI and an organizational network unmatched by any competitor among the Arabs. But it also led to lack of turnover in leadership and to oligarchy. Turnover among rank and file, in contrast, increased in the late 1960s and early 1970s, after the abolition of military rule and the rise of Palestinian consciousness, and the new members were usually young. The CPI managed during this period to develop a successful counter-culture of grassroots political activity in Arab localities, in which youth and intellectuals participated. The contradiction between the agitated, politicized element and the oligarchic Bolshevist style undermined the CPI's ability to sustain its electoral success.

STRUCTURE: THE STALINIST HERITAGE

The CPI was formed as an illegal Communist movement during the mandate period. Its Bolshevist style persisted even when it became a legal party in the Israeli political system. This style was one of the issues over which the party split in 1965. Perhaps ironically, only the faction that did *not* de-Stalinize survived. I argue that the reason was that the Stalinist organizational strategy was the only one capable of tackling the Jewish-Arab national question, as well as being successful in the early stages of politicization of the Arab population living under political, economic, and social control.

Although the Comintern was dissolved in 1943 and replaced in 1947 by the less binding Cominform,[1] the spirit of the Comintern survived (Narkiewicz 1981, 131). Like other Communist parties in the world after World War II, the CPI continued to adhere to the Leninist principles and Soviet practices of party organization. These principles stated that the party ought to have a leading role in any kind of political participation. To achieve this role, the party organization had to adhere to the principles of democratic centralism: a strict hierarchy of command, run by a body of paid professional party activists (the cadre principle), in which discussion is compartmentalized and secrecy is maintained at the leadership level, and with a total ban on factionalism. The adoption of this organizational style by Communist parties in the West led to the odd phenomenon that the nonruling parties operated as if they were in power, creating a dissonance between themselves and their surrounding culture. In the words of Kriegel with regard to the French Communist Party, "Given its nature, the party tends to reach beyond the strictly political domain of traditional majority or opposition groups. It keeps its distance from other parties whose purely political theories it challenges. It also keeps its distance from a society whose very foundations it calls into question. In short, it is of and by itself a party-society, a party that is also a social model" (Kriegel 1972, 140–41).

In the case of the Jewish-led Communist Party during the mandate period (PCP, 1919–48), the political distance from Jewish consensus was unbridgeable, but the cultural dissonance was not great because of the dominance in the Jewish community of socialist movements with an Eastern European orientation. In the postwar period after the establishment of the state, however, cultural dissonance grew steadily as the Eastern European orientation gradually dissipated. The opposite was true with regard to the Arabs in Palestine and in Israel: during the mandate period, the political distance from the Arab consensus was small, but the cultural dissonance was great in terms of the traditional society. As the Arabs in Israel were transformed into a politicized ethnic minority that had only a marginal role in the system, the cultural dissonance between the minority and the party narrowed, although it did not disappear.

The CPI lacked the means to build an economic base for a complete model of party-society (independent trade unions, cooperatives, and such). The dominance of the Histadrut in the Jewish population, along with the weakness of the remnants of the League for National Liberation's Congress of Arab Workers, left no such option. The CPI therefore concentrated on building a political-cultural model of party-society, based on an elaborate political organization. Its ideal was an Arab-Jewish party united on the basis of anti-Zionism and pro-Sovietism. Thus, like the nonruling Communist parties elsewhere, it operated on the political sidelines of society, attacking the ideological consensus and the political status quo, while mobilizing the disgruntled groups in the society to fight politically for integration and equality in the state. This strategy became more and more attractive to the Arab population in the 1960s and 1970s. But by the early 1980s, as the political system's response to demands proved minimal, the rigid Soviet style of the CPI caused its leadership to become an oligarchy, which undermined the party's effort to sustain its leading role.

The Hierarchy of Command: Central Committee, Party Congress, Cadres

The organizational structure of the Communist Party of Israel follows the well-known elaborate structure of Communist parties elsewhere: a hierarchy of elected bodies on the national and regional levels. The national central bodies include the party congress, the central committee, the politburo, and the control committee. This structure was only slightly altered after the collapse of Communism in the 1990s. The regional bodies include the regional congress, the regional committee, the district (subdistrict) committee, the branch, and the cell, each of them having its own elected executive body.[2] In addition, the party directs other bodies aligned with it, either officially or unofficially. The most important is the official youth organization (Banki), which has an organizational structure corresponding to that of the party. Other aligned organizations are the Movement of Democratic Women, the League for Fostering Friendly Relations with the USSR, and the National Committee for the Defense of Arab Lands. Since 1976, the Democratic Front for Peace and Equality functions as an electoral allied organization, and several other ad hoc organizations—such as the Committee Against the War in Lebanon—have been formed, in which the CPI-Rakah plays a major role.

Up to 1990, the central committee—more specifically, the politburo—had the authority to determine the party representatives in the Knesset and other elected bodies, as well as the bodies related to the party; it manned the publishing organs of the party and guided their work, and it still has the authority to admit, expel, or otherwise punish a member. It also has the responsibility for the financial management of the party. The central committee has also had a main role in the process of "democratic centralism": it determined the method of elections to the party congress, as well as its agenda and the theses to be discussed in it. The latter had to be published by the central committee at least two months prior to the congress and were distributed for comment in the party's lower organs. At each of the party levels in which the theses were discussed, even in the smallest cell, a member of the central committee was present and a protocol was written. These protocols were sent to the central committee for study. Some of the comments were integrated into the final version of the theses presented for approval by the party congress. However, as the split in the party in 1965 indicates, this system of input and feedback between the central committee and the membership depended on unity in the top party bodies, particularly the politburo. Thus, during the last eight years of the united Maki (1957–65), the brewing conflict in the politburo and the central committee was kept hidden from the party cadre and membership (Balti 1981, 49–126). When the leadership could not settle their internal differences, a split was unavoidable, as no party mechanism existed for settling a public dispute or for living with an open disagreement for long.

The consequences of this centralized and secretive mechanism of decision making was to block the party cadres from any kind of participation in political debates before a decision was made by the leadership and brought before the party congress. In an effort not to reveal any internal disagreements in public, speakers mostly exalted the party and congratulated it on its moral superiority. However, since the congress was a legitimate venue for expressing criticism of the leadership, such criticism was voiced by delegates in the congress using careful, nonspecific language. In this way, strict adherence to Soviet international and regional policies was insulated from any input by party activists, and the leadership had a free hand to determine and change party positions. After the 1967 war, the leadership could thus ignore the positions of the Arab party cadres who favored of a separate Palestinian entity (as did the CPI in the 1950s) rather than the return of the occupied territories to Jordan, in accordance with the Soviet-supported UN resolution 242.[3] Similarly, there was no discussion of the party's wholehearted support of the Soviet invasion of Czechoslovakia in 1968 and no criticism of the Soviet support of Nasser in the 1970s, despite his suppression of Communists.[4] The leadership also changed its political positions diametrically, to fit the Soviet line. Following that line, the CPI first approved the American-initiated cease-fire between Israel and Egypt in 1970 and the peace plan drawn up by Secretary of State William Rogers but later retracted its positions when the Soviets criticized the plan.[5] Similarly, the leadership's political evaluation of the PLO was deemed opportunistic and uncritical, for the evaluation turned from "positive" during the PLO's pro-Soviet orientation in the early 1980s to a "rightist deviation" when the PLO agreed to sign a confederation agreement with Jordan in February 1985.[6]

Lack of open debate within the party was not, of course, limited to global matters but also affected local policy and electoral strategy as well as the issue of turnover in leadership positions. The leadership's decision after the Land Day demonstrations to lower the profile of its mass protest was seen by the young and more militant members as a retreat. Specifically, the leadership's decision to refrain from mobilizing mass demonstrations against the government's ban on the convention of a "congress of Arab masses," initiated by the party in December 1980, was criticized as a mistake emanating from the lack of open debate by the party cadre.[7] The leadership also remained adamant in the face of widespread criticism, particularly among the young cadres, of the failure of its electoral strategy in the 1980s.[8] But above all, growing complaints among party ranks in the 1980s against bossism, nepotism, and oligarchic practices were stonewalled up to the 1990s. Only after the collapse of the Communist regimes in Eastern Europe in 1989 did the general secretary of the party, Meir Vilner, and his deputy, Toufiq Toubi, resign their seats in the Knesset, which they had held for over forty years, and only then did Vilner relinquish his party post for the benefit of Toubi. It then took the collapse of the Soviet Union to bring about the election of a new general secretary.

Nevertheless, the symbolic functions of the party congresses, convened every three to four years, are extremely important for the many ways in which they exemplify the party's style. Both the united Maki and Rakah congresses were held either in Jaffa or Haifa, which are mixed Jewish-Arab cities. The entire proceedings and most of the speeches in Rakah's congresses were conducted in Hebrew, and while those in Arabic were translated, those in Hebrew were not. The Israeli flag was displayed beside the red flag, and the Israeli national anthem, "Hatikva," was played along with the "Internationale"; the president of the state was invited to the opening of the party congress, as customary for parties in Israel (the first time that the president accepted such an invitation was the 20th Congress of CPI-Rakah in 1985). One of the highlights of the congresses were the greetings and expressions of solidarity by Communist parties abroad, which were either read aloud or delivered by the attending delegations from the Soviet Union and other Communist countries. Rakah, after its 16th Congress in 1969, also received greetings from the Jordanian Communist Party and the Palestinian Communists on the West Bank. After 1985, greetings from the chairman of the PLO, Yassir Arafat, were also read. These greetings were vital to cadre and membership, since they gave a sense of belonging to a wide international camp and a recognition of the party's Palestinian credentials, in contrast to its political isolation from the Jewish public at home.

The backbone of the organizational structure was always the party cadre. What marked the cadres in particular was their professionalism: although their absolute number was small, a relatively large proportion of them—depending on the party's financial situation at any given time—were functionaries paid by the party, although their salaries were low.[9] According to a former member of the party leadership, Saliba Khamis, out of 2,000 members in 1987, 250 Arabs and 100 Jews were functionaries and 100 other Jews received a party pension.[10] A career as party functionary usually began in the youth organization, Banki, where potential functionaries were socialized according to party norms and proved their organizational ability. There followed years of dull bureaucratic work, which did not attract the more educated.[11] However, the work provided a channel of social mobility and status for the less educated, whose political education was acquired through the party.[12] The recruits in the 1960s and early 1970s, particularly from rural areas, came from this social stratum, and under the party's bureaucratic structure they formed the backbone of the CPI Arab cadre. They rarely questioned the organizational or political line of the leadership, and their speeches in the party congress tended to deal with specific problems and successes experienced in their localities. The same bureaucratic structure allowed these functionaries over the years to climb up the hierarchy of command and reach the central bodies.

Men of letters and university students were exempted from this kind of bureaucratic mobility in the party hierarchy. The party's publications, especially its literary supplements, offered in the 1950s and early 1960s a stage for talented young poets and writers, thereby attracting them to the party.[13] Thus was created a cultural milieu in the Arab sector, in which Palestinian Arab identity was nourished. Through the party organization, the writers who were associated with the party acquired a near monopoly of the Arab literary scene. As functionaries in the party press organs, some became members of the central committee of the CPI in the 1970s and 1980s, among them Toufiq Ziad, Salim Jubran, Samih al Qasem, and Muhamad Nafaa.

Another channel of mobility for functionaries in the 1970s and 1980s was activity among Arab students on the campuses, for example, Muhamad Barake, Suheil Nasar, and Amir Mahul. But the closed nature of the organizational structure limited new recruitment into the party. Although the cadre principle had tremendous organizational power in the field, especially in the 1960s and 1970s, it exacted a heavy price internally: it prevented necessary personnel changes, and it fossilized the structure, reinforcing its oligarchic tendencies.

THE SOCIAL PROFILE OF THE ARAB LEADERSHIP, CADRE, AND MEMBERSHIP

In the period 1975–90 the party leadership consisted mainly of veteran Jewish and Christian Arab leaders. The lack of turnover created organizational tension, which resulted in an increase in the size of the central committee leadership body from 31 to 47 members. It stands to reason that the more successful the party became among the Muslim Arabs, the greater the need to grant representation to the younger cadre, particularly Muslims.[14] However, like other Communist parties, CPI-Rakah had no mechanism for changing the veteran leadership without a severe crisis. In addition, the CPI leadership was not able to make room for Muslim Arabs in the leadership at the expense of either Jewish members or Christian Arabs. Reducing the Jewish number would have compromised the party's commitment to the internationalist principle, and the party had a traditional link with the Christian Arabs. Hence, the central committee was simply enlarged by adding Arab Muslims to the Christian Arabs and Jews. In the 1980s, after the breakthrough into the Druze community, its members were elected as well; one of them, Muhamad Nafaa, was elected secretary general of the party in 1993.

The effort to maintain a certain balance between Jews and Arabs in the top party bodies in order to exemplify the internationalist and territorial character of the party was a major structural imperative of the central bodies of both Maki (1948–65) and Rakah up to the 1980s. Until 1990 the general secretary was a Jew.[15] The ethnic balance within the politburo that favored Jews was reversed in 1981 for the first time.

The social profile of the Arab members of the three top bodies—the politburo, the central committee, and the control committee—reflected the weight of the party's history. During the Maki period (1948–65), the ten Arab members of the top bodies were all former high-ranking activists of the League for National Liberation. One was Muslim and the rest were Christians; all were residents of the urban centers (Haifa, Nazareth, Acre) in the north of the country. Of the ten, only two can be described as having had a proletarian background, though early in life they left work to become functionaries in the Arab trade union movement.[16] The rest were high school or college educated; most of them were engaged in party journalism. One, Emil Habibi, in addition to his career as a political commentator, became well known as a writer of literary works (Balas 1978, 330–31). Another, Dr. Emil Touma, was a scholar.[17] Two of the group, Toubi and Habibi, both Christians, served as the CPI's members of Knesset during the entire Maki period.

After the split in 1965, the same predominantly Christian-Arab leadership remained at the helm of CPI-Rakah. The presence of Muslims in the central bodies of the party began to edge upward in 1969. One of those Muslims was Toufiq Ziad, the secretary of the Rakah Nazareth branch (and a renowned poet), who in 1969 was placed in the fifth position in CPI-Rakah's list to the Knesset. However, given the Christian proportion of the Arab population (14 percent), Christians were still overrepresented in the CPI's central bodies in the 1990s.

Part of the reason why Christians remained so prominent at the top is the curious phenomenon of family ties within the historic Jewish and Arab leadership. For example, CPI's leader Toufiq Toubi's younger bother, George, was head of the foreign department in the central committee; his brother-in-law, Zahi Karkabi, was a member of the central committee; another brother, Shafiq Toubi, was a high-ranking functionary in the party apparatus; and in 1985 his sister-in-law (George's wife) was elected as a candidate to the central committee. An analysis of the members of the central bodies according to age also demonstrates the low rate of turnover in the leadership (both Jewish and Arab) and the enlargement of the bodies as an alternative to replacement. Whereas in the 1970s only half a percent of the leadership was over sixty years, 40 percent of the leadership was sixty and over in the 1980s.

Size and Social Composition of Cadre and Membership

Despite the CPI's stated goal of becoming a mass party, the ratio of voters to members has remained high throughout the period under study. In part, the reason may be the party's own ambivalent attitude toward broadening its ranks. While desiring to increase the cadre of activists, it feared contamination of its ideological purity and penetration by informers. Admission into the party was preceded by a long process of careful screening.

In the 1950s the CPI attempted to overcome these obstacles to becoming a mass party by setting up cells in the workplace and mobilizing support from workers dissatisfied with wages. However, this strategy had little chance of success in the Jewish sector because of the strength of the Zionist parties in the trade union, the Histadrut; it proved a failure once the systematic sacking from work of known Communists began. Among the Arab workers, mobilization of support from members of the former Congress of Arab Workers (the Mu'tamar) was apparently more successful.[18]

Information on the number and social background of the CPI cadre and membership was kept secret by the party. The official reason was the need to avoid harassment by hostile authorities. This may have had some validity in the early and mid-1950s, when the party was under public siege and known Communists were fired from jobs (Miller-Rubenstein 1985, 331).[19] But for thirty years after that, the real reasons were probably a mixture of tradition and the need to conceal the failure of the party among the working class and its nature as an ethnic Arab party with a small Jewish membership.

Nevertheless, information on the size of the membership has been published by other sources, and those estimates are probably not far off the mark. The picture that emerges is that throughout the period of electoral politics, the party remained small in membership—1,000 to 3,000—with a high rate of turnover among the rank and file.[20] The party itself provided partial information on the social profile of the membership and cadre when it published the percentages of distribution according to age, sex, and occupation of delegates to each of its national congresses and to some of its regional ones.

From such information it can be gathered that in the 1960s most of the Arab members—some 400—resided in the Nazareth district; they were relatively prosperous and well educated. Recruitment in rural areas followed a different, almost opposite pattern. From the history of party cells in several major villages, we may conclude that those who were attracted to membership in the CPI at this period were men with basic education from families marginal in the power structure of the village because of wealth, size, or seniority.[21] Thus, the Communist Party in the early 1960s not only was an ideological alternative to the dominant political and social forces in the Arab sector but was also an alternative sociopolitical channel for mobility in the village. The party attracted those who were literate and educated enough to read the newspaper the party put out and who developed a measure of political consciousness but who had no economic, social, or political resources to use or to protect in the village.

Following the 1967 war, membership in the party dropped, as can be inferred from comments made by participants in the 1989 and 1972 congresses. However, many Arab youngsters were attracted to the activities of Banki, the youth organization, which became the major channel of recruitment for Arab membership.[22] The large group of young people who became party members in the early 1970s brought the total membership (Arabs and Jews) to 1,000 to 1,500.[23] A second wave of Banki recruitment followed the 1973 war, and membership in the early 1980s was estimated at 1,500 to 2,000 members, of whom 80 percent (1,200 to 1,600) were Arabs.[24] This success could be attributed to the increase in the Palestinian consciousness of the Arab youth and to the new organizational strategy of Rakah, including the scholarships it granted to study abroad.

The breakdown of the education level of the delegates (provided for the 15th to the 22nd Congresses, 1965–93) shows a trend toward a higher level of education of the delegates, which was higher than the average for the population in Israel as a whole. Whereas in 1965 only 11 percent of the delegates were academically trained, the proportion in 1993 was 44.5 percent, compared with 9 percent of Arabs and 28 percent of Jews in the general population. This increase reflected the large number of party members, especially of the cadre, who were sent under scholarships to study in the Communist bloc (see chapter 8). It also reflects indirectly the class affiliation of the membership. The breakdown by class provided by the party is inconsistent over the years and may reflect an effort to underplay a profile that contradicted the party's ideal image of itself. As a Communist party, its ideal membership would be part of the working class. Indeed, 53 percent of the delegates in the 15th Congress (1965) were classified as workers and an additional 3 percent as agricultural workers; 31 percent were classified as clerks and working intelligentsia; and 13 percent were self-employed. But in the reports to congresses after that year, the category "workers" was replaced by "salaried workers," which made up 58 to 68 percent of the delegates, and 25 percent were self-employed.[25]

Perhaps the biggest gap between ideal image and actual style in the CPI was in membership of women. Although the CPI championed the equality of sexes, the number of Arab women in the party was small. Despite efforts to recruit women through an affiliate, the Organization of Democratic Women, in 1961, during the Maki period, only in the town of Nazareth were women members of the party—according to the party publication, 24 percent of party membership in the town. In the rural areas, there were few or no women members.[26] While there were three Jewish women in the CPI-Maki leadership, no Arab women was a member of the central bodies. After the death in 1968 of Fuad Khuri, one of the leading Arab members of Rakah, his wife, Samira, was elected to the central committee and put in charge of active organizing among Arab women. These activities did not result in a marked increase in membership, as indicated by the static small share of women delegates to the party congresses—14 to 16 percent.

The chronically small size of the CPI membership did not reflect the influence of the party in the Arab community, which included circles of consistent supporters who read the party papers, participated in many of its activities, and contributed money during its financial drives. For these supporters—some of whom were relatives of party members—the party was part of their lifestyle but they did not have to show the discipline required of a member. By 1976, when the hopes of increasing membership had not materialized, organization of the fellows in the Democratic Front was undertaken as part of the new strategy (see chapter 9). While this new organizational drive brought short-run electoral successes on the municipal and national levels, it did not bring about massive recruitment into the party. Furthermore, the manner in which the party conducted the affairs of the Democratic Front exposed the CPI to charges that it was unwilling to surrender its leading role and share power with nonparty activists. The organizational drive was thus one of the catalysts leading to creation of the Progressive Movement for Peace in 1984, which heralded the decline of CPI hegemony in the Arab sector.

Party Organizational Style: Summary and An Appraisal

The puzzling phenomenon of the CPI-Rakah's style is the persistence of this essentially Bolshevist structure despite crises of disintegration, splits, and reunion—even the collapse of Eastern European communism after which it was modeled. The explanation is both historical and functional. Until the collapse of the Soviet Union, the tradition of symbiotic links with the Soviets was an essential part of the party style and political culture. For the CPI leadership and cadre, these close links served as a means for gaining international recognition and standing and as compensation for extreme political isolation at home. Besides being a source of guidance for the party, the Soviets were a source of material support and a training ground for the cadre. In the absence of a party school, the CPI had to rely on Soviet political and educational courses for its activists.

Hence, only a major political crisis would cause the CPI to venture out against the Soviet Union. The revelations of the anti-Semitic "deviations" of Stalin and the pro-Arab policies of the Soviet Union in the 1950s and 1960s created such a crisis for the Jewish membership of the CPI; for the Arabs in the party, the closer links between the Arab states and the Soviets made life simpler. The Bolshevist style, while not particularly popular among the Arab electorate, held advantages in the politically underdeveloped Arab sector. The CPI was the only coherent political organization in which the Arabs of Israel felt equal to Jews; its Jewish-Arab character also gave psychological assurance against the disaster of becoming refugees like their fellow Palestinians in 1948. (The fear was reawakened in the 1980s when Jewish radical right political parties ran on platforms ranging from withdrawal of Israeli citizenship to transferral to Arab countries.) In addition, the party's Arab leadership was educated, and its activists were trained to mobilize the Arab minority as a force in Israeli politics. The CPI's adherence to the Soviet line on the national question made for a cautious approach that helped it to survive as a legal party in Israel while exalting the Arab identity.

Glasnost and Perestroika in the CPI?

However, the dogmatic adherence took its toll. According to oppositionist voices, which in the 1970s were lonely[27] and in the 1980s became much louder, the cadre principle was abused and created favoritism and bossism within the party.[28] In the 1980s, the younger generation was unwilling to accept the old political practices, which seemed so at odds with the pluralist political atmosphere around them and, after 1985, with the glasnost policies in the Soviet Union. In the late 1980s, criticism within the party could no longer be contained. The leadership and the rank and file were split over the demand for greater openness within the party. As noted in chapter 3, the minority called for major reform along Gorbachev's new line, but the majority either called for cautious change or only grudgingly accepted the changes introduced by perestroika in the Soviet Union.[29] The minority demanded admission of basic mistakes by the CPI and an end to the political culture of closed ranks and democratic centralism. The more outspoken left the party, were expelled, or were demoted from party positions during 1988–90 (Rekhess 1993, 201–6).[30] The party acknowledged the loss of some 25 percent of its membership as a result of disappointment and demoralization.[31]

To quell the tide of criticism, the central committee initiated some moderate changes. The veteran party representatives in the Knesset (Vilner, Toubi, and Ziad) resigned in December 1989 in favor three new, younger members (Mahamid, Gozanski, and Nafaa). Few small concessions were given to those demanding abolition of democratic centralism: the 21st Congress in May 1990 approved a change in the party statute (section 57) by which new members would make up at least one-third of the candidates for the central committee that were proposed to the party congress by the outgoing central committee. In addition, a new 150-member body, the party council, was set up, for which elections were held every two years. The politburo and the central committee were to be responsible to the party council between congresses, including responsibility for the selection process for the election list. Another major change was the introduction in 1990, under a new section in the party statute (section 46), of an internal paper open to all party members for purposes of debate.

Yet in an era in which other Israeli parties introduced primaries, it was obvious that such changes were insufficient. The upheaval in the CPI during preparations for the 1992 elections (see chapter 9) made it clear that further changes had to be introduced. After the elections, in a tense meeting of the newly elected central committee, the nine-member politburo was weakened by broadening it into a thirteen-member bureau of the central committee. In the new spirit of greater openness, the new central committee started to allow publication of the details of its closed meetings, not only the official decisions.[32]

ACTIVITIES FOR MEMBERS, FELLOWS, AND THE ARAB PUBLIC

The linchpin of the Communist Party's strength among the Arab electorate has been its ability to mobilize, which up to the 1980s was uncontested by any other body. In the early 1950s it had only fourteen branches in the Arab localities, and only a few cells of Arabs in workplaces. Most of its activity took place in residential cells that belonged to a regional branch. The party branch became a village institution that had to take into account local interests and sensibilities. The main organizational breakthrough was made in the early 1970s, bringing the total number of branches in Arab and Jewish localities to seventy-nine in 1981 and ninety-five in 1985. A drastic reduction, to sixty branches in the 1990s, was a result of the collapse of the Soviet Union.[33]

Important branch activity included the party youth movement (Ashbal), intended for ages ten to fourteen, and the Communist youth organization (Banki), intended for ages fifteen to twenty-two. Party members held regular meetings every two weeks, where recent national political and local events were discussed from the party's point of view. Members of the branch also took part in street activities—demonstrations, rallies, leaflet distributions, and election campaigns. Up to 1983, when al Ittihad became a daily newspaper, the chief regular duty of each Banki member was distribution of the biweekly. After the 1970s, Banki members also engaged in cultural and sports activity. Every year a Banki delegation was sent to a summer camp in the Soviet Union.

In addition, the Communist calendar included several days dedicated to special activity. Besides the famous First of May celebration, November 7 marked the October Revolution of 1917 in Russia. Celebrations each year included a mass event and a picnic in the Red Army Forest. On March 8 the party celebrated International Women's Day. In mid-May, the Movement for Soviet-Israeli Friendship sponsored lectures and cultural events to celebrate the victory of the Red Army over the Nazis. June 1 marked International Child Day. In addition, the Communist Press Festival took place in October. The volunteer work camp for Arab youth was held in Nazareth in August every year from 1976 to 1990. Thousands of Palestinians from the West Bank participated in the camp, defying the legal prohibition on spending the night in Israel. Although Arab participation was dominant, each year about one hundred Jewish sympathizers and Communist youth from abroad were also invited.

A major CPI activity since its establishment in 1948 was the publication of its newspapers in Hebrew, Arabic, and a host of other languages spoken by new Jewish immigrants. Direct access to readers on a regular basis in their own language was seen as essential for changing consciousness and gaining influence for the party. Hence, the publication and distribution of the party newspapers, particularly in Hebrew and in Arabic, consumed a great deal of the party's energy, and a major part of its budget.[34]

In the case of Arabic, the CPI-Maki benefited from the legacy of the League for National Liberation by resuming the publication of the league's *al Ittihad* and its literary supplement *al Jadid* in 1949; a few years later, it began to put out the Banki periodical *al Ghad* and the ideological periodical *a Darb*. Although the Arabs were the major group of potential readers of *al Ittihad*, during the Maki period, the Arabic-speaking Jews, particularly the immigrants from Iraq, were also important targets. Hence the paper, which was distributed in the immigrant camps (*ma'abarot*), decried the immigrants' difficult living conditions and their unemployment.[35]

But for the Arabic-speaking Jews, a newspaper in Arabic had inevitably only a temporary appeal, given the strong pressures to acculturate into the Hebrew-Israeli culture. In the Hebrew press, the Communist paper *Kol Haam* was only one of many, and it had a marginal effect on public opinion. After the 1965 split in the CPI, *al Ittihad*, which remained the property of Rakah, concentrated on appealing to the Arab audience, leaving appeal to Jewish readers to Rakah's Hebrew weekly, *Zo Haderech*. Despite its strong party bent, *al Ittihad*, given its high-caliber writers and professional editors, became the major newspaper in Arabic—the only nonestablishment oppositionary voice of the Arab population. It was in a position to carry out, in the public opinion area, the overall political strategy of the CPI-Rakah: forging the Arab population into a "destiny group" in which the party maintained a leading role.

The party press in Arabic served that strategy in a number of ways. First, via the party's organizational network, *al Ittihad* was the only paper to cover extensively the Arab local and national scene. Members of local branches passed on news items on events taking place in their communities. Of course, they did so in a manner that suited their political and organizational interests, putting in a negative light all steps of the authorities toward the Arab sector and concentrating on the maltreatment and neglect of the Arab localities.[36] The actions of the party's local activists toward solution of those problems were highlighted and emphasized. On the national level, the paper reported extensively on the speeches and actions of CPI representatives in the Knesset and in the public arena while reporting critically on government actions in the Arab sector (Abu Gosh 1965, 201–2). The links between the Arab world and the Communist bloc were the focus of its international reports, which relied primarily on the Soviet Tass news agency but also on its own reporter stationed in Moscow. However, since the selective and inaccurate reporting of the party paper sometimes led to "political mistakes," it was a subject of criticism even within the party.[37]

The paper also served as a medium for direct expression of party views through editorials, commentaries, and analyses of the various issues concerning the Arab population, the region, and the world. Particularly popular were Emil Touma's political analyses and Emil Habibi's semisatirical commentaries and editorials on political issues. The latter, using Arab proverbs and sharp, sophisticated language, would frequently scorn the enemies of the party and defend its friends—chiefly the Soviet Union.[38] Indeed, the use of the paper to attack local political rivals sometimes took the form of inaccurate reporting of their public expressions.

A major function of the party papers was the cultivation of the Arab-Palestinian literary culture. *Al Ittihad* and the periodicals *al Jadid* and *al Ghad* became an outlet for literary expression of the rage and frustration felt by politically conscious Arabs over the plight that befell the Palestinians in 1948. In the 1950s the short stories of writers such as Emil Habibi and Hana Ibrahim and the political expressions of such poets as Toufiq Ziad lamented the exile forced on the Palestinian refugees and the political oppression by the Zionist state (Ballas 1978, 33–87). Much of the poetry was published in *al Ittihad* and *al Jadid* as a reaction to political events, and it repeated many of the themes raised by the CPI in its purely political message. Thus, a poem by Ziad expressed solidarity with striking Jewish workers, who, like the Arab brethren, were victims of the "reactionary rulers." Together, promised the poem, they would struggle for the "dawn of happy life"; the opening of diplomatic relations with West Germany was "crawling to Hitler's heirs" after creating the Arabs' holocaust in Palestine; the shooting of Arab youngsters trying to escape to Arab countries in the early 1960s was done by heartless "soldiers of ice." For their part, the Arabs in Israel steadfastly clung to their land, "guarding the grass on the forefathers' graves" (Yinon 1981, 213–40).

In the 1960s and 1970s, another generation of poets, described as possessing "revolutionary zeal and national pathos," began to publish in the party papers, among them Rashid Hussein, Salim Jubran, Samih al Qassem, and Mahamud Darwish (Ballas 1987, 83). Darwish in particular won acclaim for his poetic capability and was a source of great pride for the party. His defection to Egypt to join the PLO in 1971 evoked great dismay. The poems and other literature of this generation in the 1970s were more militantly Palestinian, though expressing sympathy with the Jewish existence. Emil Habibi's short stories concentrate on the passivity of the non-Communist Arabs, who were ready to cooperate with the authorities, as leading to insanity.

In the late 1970s and 1980s, despite being the major Arab newspaper, *al Ittihad* apparently reached the limit of its expansion in terms of subscribers. The major competition came from the Hebrew dailies, which supplied more information and included catchy sports supplements. To combat this trend, *al Ittihad* began to appear as a daily in 1983 and to publish a sports weekly that covered the lower soccer leagues, in which Arab groups participated. But in the 1980s, competition sprang up from more colorful, independent Arab newspapers (though not dailies), especially from the Nazareth-based *al Sinara*, which was critical of the CPI. *Al Sinara* came to the aid of the CPI's new rival, the Progressive Movement for Peace (PLP), which organized first in Nazareth (see part 3).

Besides its monopoly over the literary scene, the CPI was also the only political body up to the 1980s that could mobilize the Arab streets. But throughout its history, its calls for mass protest were constrained by the heavy hand of the authorities and by its fear of being outlawed should mass protest get out of hand. Nevertheless, the CPI had some successes in bringing the people into the streets, sometimes resulting in a violent clash with the authorities. As will be seen in part 3, the major reason for mobilizing the population into grassroots action was the party's attempt to become an authentic popular force in the Arab sector. Mass action was designed to create pressure for cooperation from both nationalist non-Communist circles and the pragmatic, accommodationist local leaders. The first Land Day protest of 1976 broke the taboo of cooperating with the CPI (see chapter 8). But after having led the way, the CPI in the 1980s lost its distinction for mobilizing mass protest. Neither was it alone in the parliamentary arena: the CPI in the 1980s had to compete with the Progressive List for Peace as an oppositionist spokesman of the Arab citizens.

Parliamentary Activity of the CPI

The CPI traditionally accorded great importance to its activity in the Knesset, of which it made both expressive and instrumental political use (Goldberg

1981). As a permanent opposition party before 1992,[39] the CPI used the Knesset as both a forum for making its views known to the electorate and an instrument for making the government answer specific queries concerning the Arab population. Throughout its history, the CPI adopted an uncompromising oppositionist line to the government on almost every issue. But when it was reduced to an outcast minority party with little political clout, it became a strong defender of Knesset rules and procedures.

In the early 1950s, the CPI-Maki opposed the economic austerity plan, the acceptance of financial aid from the United States, the request for reparations from Germany, and the Knesset's denunciation of the Soviet-Egyptian arms deal of 1955 (Miller-Rubenstein 1985, 313–30). The CPI-Maki was the only party to denounce the Sinai campaign in 1956, and the CPI-Rakah was the only party to blame Israel for the 1967 war.[40] The 1973 war was again blamed on the government's refusal of peaceful political solutions suggested by the Soviet Union (Miller-Rubenstein 1985, 365). The party representatives voted against the Camp David accords and the peace treaty with Egypt, and during the early days of the war in Lebanon in July 1982 the party-led Democratic Front in the Knesset was the only party that submitted a no-confidence vote.

However, from the start the CPI representatives in the Knesset revealed also a strong instrumental tendency in trying to influence government action, and they were ready to cooperate with any party that would further the CPI's political concerns, especially on the laws and issues that had a direct bearing on the Arab population. Thus the CPI struck up a working relationship with Mapam from 1950 up to the latter's first break with Stalinism at the end of 1952. Members of the two parties in the Knesset collaborated, unsuccessfully, in an effort to moderate the Abandoned Property Bill of 1950, which transferred the property of the Arab refugees into the hands of an official custodian, and on the Citizenship Bill of 1950, which allowed citizenship to be granted only to certain resident Arabs.[41]

But the focuses of activity of the CPI during the 1950s and up to the mid-1960s were the Military Rule and the living conditions of the Arab inhabitants in various locations. Through formal questions and other parliamentary motions, the members of the CPI attempted to expose and thereby reverse specific actions taken by the Military Rule, such as banishment and arbitrary punishments for petty offenses by Arab citizens (Jiyris 1976, 28–29). Other questions related to pay and working conditions, water supply, health facilities, and the like.[42] Needless to say, the party also made attempts to repeal the Military Rule altogether or at least to limit its powers. Mapam and, after 1959, other opposition parties, including the right-wing Herut, also attempted to have the Military Rule abolished because it was seen as an electoral instrument serving the ruling Mapai (Labor) Party.

Through motions for the agenda and parliamentary questions to government ministers, the CPI, despite its isolated position in the Knesset, managed to extract here and there concrete benefits for Arab localities, though not to change the overall discriminatory policy. The purpose of a motion is to raise a public debate on an issue and to pass it on to a committee for a hearing. The CPI's proposals, the most critical of the government, focused on specific concerns of the Arab population. Some led to improvements in villages: financial aid for paving roads in one; a loan, refused several times, for building a school in another; promises for regulating water supplies in three; and permission for building sports facilities in yet another.[43]

The coming to power of the right-wing Likud government in 1977 created a new situation for the Democratic Front, led by CPI-Rakah in the Knesset, for the Likud coalition was less likely to cooperate with Communists. The hostile attitude against the CPI in the Knesset intensified and came to a head during Israel's war in Lebanon against the PLO, since the CPI supported the PLO. But the new parliamentary situation led to instances of cooperation with the Labor party, now also in opposition. For example, in 1983 the Democratic Front decided to vote for the Labor Party's candidate for president, Haim Herzog, and thus ensured his election. In return, it asked for greater cooperation in the Knesset with Labor on matters of mutual concern.[44]

The appearance of the Progressive List for Peace on the Knesset scene in 1984 intensified the instrumental behavior of the Democratic Front because of the competition between the two parties.[45] (The PLP won the status of city for the township of Um al Fahm in return for a vote for the Labor's candidate for speaker of the 11th Knesset.) In the late 1980s and early 1990s, both instrumental and expressive parliamentary behavior of the CPI-Front increased significantly: representatives of the Front changed in the Knesset, and the Front mobilized on behalf of the Palestinian uprising. Toufiq Ziad engaged in parliamentary brawls with the Jewish radical right representatives in the Knesset. Hashem Mahamid became the spokesman of Palestinian detainees in Israeli prisons, and Tamar Gozanski was extremely active in social legislation.[46]

In sum, the CPI's style in the parliamentary arena conformed on the whole to parliamentary procedure and the rules of the game. Its parliamentary style thus stood in stark contrast to its style of appeal for electoral support (see chapter 5).

5

The Slogan Component
of the CPI Party Image

Two potentially conflicting attributes, "Arab" and "worker," were historically used by the CPI to promote a view of an ethnically based Arab "destiny group" with which progressive Jews could identify in a common struggle against the Zionist, capitalist establishment. Appropriating the leading role in representing this Arab destiny group, the CPI delegitimized political nationalist and ethnonationalist rivals in the 1980s. "Our people here is a people of one complete class, and an inseparable part of the Palestinian people, and a democratic force in Israel that cannot be ignored" (Emil Habibi, in the 1983 municipal campaign, Nazareth).

The Communist Party of Israel, while belonging in some senses to the category of ethnic parties, differed in its commitment to class ideology. This difference generated a problem in definition, self-presentation, and appeal to the emotional level of the voter. The slogan component of the CPI's party image, as projected to the Arab electorate, made use of both Arab identity and the working-class unity of Jewish and Arab workers in its emotive appeal. These elements may seem in conflict, since the first emphasized Arab ethnicity as the criterion for a destiny group, while the latter brought Jews into a class-based destiny group. According to the CPI's class attribute, the working class as a whole, and the progressive forces identified with it, consisted of both Arabs and Jews. According to the national attribute, Arabs of all denominations and classes living in Israel formed a destiny group and should therefore unite politically under the banner of the CPI. By holding to both attributes, the party attempted to appeal to both class and national interests of Arabs, thus producing the integrative ethnonationalist image of the Communist Party.

However, while holding throughout the years to both of these elements, the CPI accentuated class and moderated the national attribute according to the political circumstances. This ideological flexibility should be also interpreted against the larger Israeli political discourse. In a Jewish-dominated, pro-American society, being a Communist Arab party amounted to somewhat of a double bind, demanding ideological flexibility and pragmatism. The following case will serve as an example of how the duality of ethnonationalism and communism in the CPI was played out.

THE ARAB ATTRIBUTE AND THE CHALLENGE OF AL ARD

In the first two election campaigns for the Knesset (1949 and 1951), the CPI was still hoping for implementation of the United Nations resolution on partition of Palestine. Its candidates ran under the slogans "Independent Democratic Arab State in the other part of Palestine"; "Full equal rights of the Arab Population"; and "Return of the Arab Refugees" (Landau 1969, 109). The slogans referred to three groups of Arabs: those who were on both sides of the cease-fire lines and, according to the partition plan, were to live in the Arab Palestinian state; those who were to stay in the State of Israel; and Arab refugees in Arab countries who, according to the partition plan, were to live in the State of Israel.

However, in April 1950, King Abdalla officially annexed the West Bank to the kingdom of Jordan, and by the time of the election campaign to the third Knesset in 1955 the chances of setting up the Arab state in Palestine no longer seemed feasible. The CPI slogans in that election were of a different nature: "Direct peace negotiation for solving the refugee problem"; "The return of the property rights to the Arab population"; "Against the national oppression of the Arab minority" (by the Military Rule); "For the return of 'internal refugees' to their villages"; and "Development of the Arab regions."[1] The last implied acceptance of the geopolitical status quo.

The enthusiasm that Nasserism created in the Arab world, particularly after the Sinai campaign of 1956, had an impact on the Arabs in Israel as well. Direct appeals to them over Cairo radio and Nasser's firebrand speeches raised hope among many politically conscious Arabs in Israel that Arab unity under Nasser would reverse the results of the 1948 war (Mansur 1975, 42–43). The political instability of the Hashemite rule in Jordan in mid-1957, as a result of the rise of Nasserism, added to this hope. These regional events, which coincided with the changes in the world Communist movement, revived in the CPI program the demand for "recognition of the *right* for self-determination up to the point of separation for the Arab Palestinian people, including its part in Israel."

The possibility of redrawing the 1949 cease-fire lines and Nasser's pro-Soviet orientation led to talks on the establishment of the Arab Front by the

CPI and non-Communist pro-Nasserists. The circumstance that led to establishment of the Arab Front was the violent First of May demonstration in 1958 in Nazareth. The platform of the Arab Front centered on the problems of the Arab population in Israel (Jiyris 1976, 186; Mansur 1975, 51). But a CPI-Maki spokesman explained that the purpose of the Front was "to restore their [the Arabs'] just national rights, of which the rulers of Israel deprived them" (Geffner 1973, 15). During the First of May demonstration, participants chanted slogans such as "Ben Gurion out! Palestine is free and Arab"; "Long live Abdul Nasser"; "Beware of what we will do to you when Nasser will come."[2]

The Arab Front, which changed its name to the Popular Front, was set up after the demonstration, but it lasted only a few months. By July 1959 it had broken up over the CPI's attack on Nasser for his acceptance of American aid, for the treatment of the Communists in Syria, and for his attack on Qassem of Iraq (see chapter 7).

The breakup of the Popular Front changed the CPI's slogans for the Arab audience. The slogans in the First of May demonstration in 1959, six months before the 1959 national elections, did not mention Nasser.[3] They only repeated "For the rights of the Arab population" and "For the national rights of the Arab people in Palestine."[4] Aware of Nasser's popularity, however, the CPI tried to avoid the Qassem-Nasser issue during the campaign and instead extolled Egypt as the victim of Israel and imperialism in the Sinai campaign. In view of the brewing conflict within the Front, still secret, the call was for unity of the Arabs in Israel. Emil Habibi, in a speech during the First of May rally in Nazareth in 1959, said, "Our people will not desert the comrades, the prisoners of the 1st of May demonstration [of 1958]; this demonstration is calling on the masses of the people for unity! unity! unity!"[5]

The significance of the short-term Popular Front episode was the Usrat al Ard (Family of the Land), a group later known as al Ard, set up by a small number of intellectuals who broke away from the Front. The intention of the group was to lay the foundation for an independent Arab party. A legal battle of four years ensued between the group and the Israeli authorities. In 1964, during the battle, the group managed to set up an association as the first step in the formation of a party. The articles of association contained two contradictory goals: Palestinian sovereignty and Pan-Arabism.

Thus, one article of al Ard stated that the association's purpose was "to find a just solution for the Palestinian question, considering it a whole and indivisible unit in accordance with the wishes of the Palestinian Arab people . . . a solution which regards it as the first possessor of the right to decide its own fate for itself, within the framework of the supreme wishes of the Arab nation" (Jiyris 1976, 190). In an appeal to the UN (after its request for a license to establish a newspaper was denied), al Ard also demanded that Israel grant total equality to the Arab citizens, accept the 1947 partition, and recognize the Arab national movement, "which calls for unity and socialism as the most progressive and reliable force on which the future of this region depends."[6]

Al Ard's appeal to register as a movement was finally rejected by the High Court in November 1964 on the grounds that its purposes disregarded the wishes of the Jewish people and did not even mention Israel by name; hence, al Ard was subversive. In the 1965 elections, a final attempt to register and run as a party was also stopped by legal means. Thus, the challenge al Ard posited to both the state and the CPI was considerable. It challenged the limits of democratic freedom of expression and association, and it forced the state to take the position that Arabs may not challenge ideologically the existence of an independent Jewish state. The CPI's double commitment to the Palestinian people and to the existence of Israel was attacked as hypocritical and inconsistent.

Al Ard called unsuccessfully for a boycott of the elections in 1959—a clear affront to the CPI. Before it was finally banned, the CPI had to deal with the presence of the group in the Arab arena in the next two election campaigns. Although the Communist Party condemned the high court's decision to outlaw the activities of the group as an "attack on democratic freedoms" (Jiyris 1976, 193), the CPI in 1961 denounced al Ard as "reactionary national bourgeoisie" and urged the population not to continue with "illusions . . . the disease of 'wait and see' [and] the expectation for salvation from an unknown source" (a reference to Nasser).[7] Nevertheless, although the CPI before the 1961 elections dropped the separatist clause in its program, it returned to the phrase used also by al Ard: "The masses of the Arab people in Israel, as part of the Arab Palestinian people . . . are fighting for their stolen rights."[8]

The first independent campaign of CPI-Rakah at the end of 1965 used the phrase "ensuring the legitimate rights of the Jewish and Arab peoples of Palestine" (for self-determination), as well as a denouncement of the "brutal discrimination of the Arab citizens." In addition, in the 15th Congress of Rakah, held shortly before the elections, Emil Habibi made it known that the Arab Communists continued to support the Arab refugees' right to return, without adding the option of compensation.[9]

The initial effects of the 1967 war on Arab public opinion, and the CPI's line on the desired political solution, dampened the effectiveness of the "Arab Palestinian" attribute in the CPI slogans. In an effort to focus on the issue of withdrawal from the occupied territories, according to UN resolution 242, the slogans of the CPI 1969 campaign concentrated on a generalized Arab attribute: "Not with imperialism against the Arab peoples, but with the Arab peoples against imperialism."[10] The national rights of the Palestinians were hardly mentioned. At the same time, in an effort to increase the sense of shared destiny with the Arab minority, the CPI renewed its assault on Zionism as a "bourgeois reactionary" ideology and on the government for its "racist" practices against the Arabs.

The bloody clash between King Hussein of Jordan and the PLO in September 1970, the 1973 war between Israel and the Arab states, and the rise of the PLO into regional and international prominence after the Arab summit of 1974 at Rabat all had an effect on the national identity of the Arab population in Israel. Hence, they also led to a renewed emphasis in the CPI-Rakah slogans on the Arab-Palestinian attribute of the Arabs in Israel. Ten days before the elections of 1973, Toufiq Ziad, then fourth in the CPI list, published in *al Ittihad* a series of poems glorifying as "sacred acts" the crossing of the Arab armies, in the 1973 war, into the territories held by Israel. The war was exalted as part of the liberation fight of his people (Yinon 1981, 234–35).

After Ziad's election as mayor of Nazareth in December 1975, and the success of the Land Day strike in 1976 (see chapter 8), Ziad became the CPI-Rakah's chief crowd pleaser (to use the party leaders' own term), using militant slogans to mobilize support. In the First of May rally in Nazareth in 1976, for instance, he declared: "The government has to decide whether it wants the Arab citizens of Israel as full citizens or to let them, and their lands, belong to a different state."[11] However, following the CPI's 18th Congress in July 1976, and the establishment of the Democratic Front for Peace and Equality, the CPI emphasized the slogan "Two states for two peoples" and "Return to the 4th of June, 1967 borders." Along with these slogans, which spelled out clearly to Arab voters the CPI's abandonment of the 1947 partition plan, the CPI continued to refer to the Arab population as the "Arab Palestinian masses,"[12] "the people of the Land Day," and "Our Palestinian people in Israel."[13]

A speech by Toufiq Ziad, published during the campaign for the 10th Knesset in 1981, demonstrated the effort to balance the integrative political program with an adherence to the Arab Palestinian attribute: "All the necessary conditions exist for the establishment of the Palestinian state, the Palestinian flag, the flag of our people. Without the Palestinians, without Palestine, and without the Soviet Union, there will be no just peace. As for the Arab Palestinian masses in Israel, they are the most interested party in our country and in our region in a solution [of the conflict], since they are part of the Arab Palestinian people, and part of the state of Israel. Our struggle for national equality . . . is tied to the struggle to stop the rise of fascism. The PLO is the leadership of the Arab Palestinian people, who are our own flesh and blood."[14]

To defend itself from the radical nationalists' accusations of being non-Palestinian and to combat their call to abstain from voting for the "Zionist Knes-set," CPI efforts from this time on were directed at receiving the endorsement of the PLO before election time. In the 1970s it competed in this effort with dovish Jewish groups that advocated negotiations with the PLO. In early May 1977, a CPI delegation of two Jews and two Arabs met PLO officials in Prague and thus indirectly won the endorsement, in competition with the mainly Jew-ish Shelli Party.[15] The meeting, explained al Ittihad, "set up an alliance be-tween the two national movements, PLO and the Democratic Front, which more than any other movements express the national aspirations of the Arabs in Israel."[16] In a special leaflet to the voters, the newly founded Democratic Front (see chapter 8) quoted PLO official Abdalla Hurani, advising against a single vote for the Zionist parties, which implied a PLO support of the Front against Shelli.

(This recommendation was the outcome of an internal struggle between the right and the left within the PLO. The right, headed by Issam Sartawi, for some time advocated developing ties with the non-Communist Jewish doves. But since the latter demanded a change in the Palestinian Covenant in return, the left in the PLO was successful in putting through a resolution to hold contacts only with the Jewish anti-Zionist forces in the 13th Palestinian Na-tional Council in March 1977.)[17]

The need for a PLO endorsement, according to the assessment of the CPI leadership, became particularly acute when, in early 1980, the various Arab radical nationalist groups, all small in size, took steps to set up a coordinating committee. In September 1980, a meeting was arranged between Toufiq Toubi and Yassir Arafat.[18] Before the elections to the Histadrut in April 1981, the CPI kept repeating, "The PLO supports the Democratic Front."[19] In 1984 com-petition on the embodiment of the national attribute came from the newly formed Progressive List for Peace. As noted, the issues separating the two lists were minute, and the PLP ran on a platform almost identical to the CPI's.[20] The fight, therefore, was over who represented more authentically the Arab Palestinian attribute.

The PLP accused the CPI of misrepresenting Arab votes (by including in third place Charlie Biton, a "black panther" non-Communist Jew) and of serving the interests of a foreign power (USSR). The CPI accused the PLP members of being the "agents of the Shabak" (Israel's internal security service), "servants of American imperialism," and servants of the "ruling circles in Israel" (for supposedly agreeing to the Camp David accords and to all of Arafat's moves for gaining American recognition.[21] The CPI also emphasized that the PLP had no social platform and that it placed in second place on its list a "Zionist ex-general" (Mati Peled). The struggle along these lines continued after the elections; when the CPI set up in 1986 the Association of Arab Writers, writers and poets close to the PMP refused to join and established the rival Organization of Palestinian Writers and Poets in Israel.

THE ANTI-IMPERIALIST AND ANTI-ZIONIST ATTRIBUTES

While the Arab attribute changed over time, two closely related elements—anti-Zionism and anti-imperialism—remained consistent in the slogans of the CPI. In the early 1950s "imperialism" was a catchphrase that explained to the Arabs the source of their tragedy and defined their present enemies. In the 1960s, American influence in the region was the source of their troubles. Thus the war in 1948, disastrous from the Arab point of view, was due to the "reactionary" leadership headed by the Mufti (the religious-political leader of the Palestinians), who would not accept the partition, as the Communists recommended after the Soviet change of policy. Election campaigns in the early 1950s still used the slogans "Long live the bastion of peace, of democracy and of socialism in the world—the USSR" and "Long live the Commander of Peace, the Friend of Nations—Stalin."[22]

In Israel, the enemies of the Arabs were the Zionist "ruling circles," who were pro-American and were "warmongers." All those Arabs who were ready to cooperate with them were also tainted. The effects of these slogans on the Arabs were exemplified by the monologue of one of S. Abu Gosh's informants, speaking of how in 1955 he became a member of the CPI: "We the Palestinian nation must learn from the tragedies of 1948. Had there been a national consciousness in 1948, events might have ended differently. We would not have been carried away by the battle cry of leaders like Abdalla, Farouq, Nuri al Said, and al-Mufti. These leaders were serving the interests of imperialism in the region. They had been misguiding the Arab nations with slogans like 'Throw the Jews into the sea' and 'We are returning to the homeland [Palestine].' The Communists, in 1948, raised the slogan 'The right of self-determination to both the Jewish and the Arab nations'" (Abu Gosh 1965, 70).

The Arab traditional accommodationist members of the Knesset who were allied with Mapai and other Zionist parties—up to 1969 the largest vote getter among the Arabs—were the constant target of scorn and abuse from the CPI (see part 3). They were called "reactionary"[23] and "feudal" lords,[24] seekers of selfish interests, lacking any national self-respect as "tails of the treacherous government" (Landau 1969, 197). Arab voters were urged not to give their vote to those "lists which trade with your rights, and conspire against you."[25] Not only were the Arab Knesset members of the allied lists "traitors" who "speak against the Arab Palestinian people," but they were also a "dead weight," an "instrument for [maintaining] ethnic and hamula [kinship] cleavages," and the "oppression itself."[26] The CPI slogans promised, therefore, that "the defeat of the Ma'arach [Alignment of Labor and Mapam] or its hired lists would constitute a blow to the policy of oppression and of stomping Arabs' rights."[27] Similar abuse was hurled a decade later at local leaders—mostly "government men"—who opposed holding the first Land Day strike. The CPI's propaganda described them as a "rubber stamp" of the authorities (Rekhess 1977, 28).

Up to 1977, the chief enemies in the CPI slogans were the Zionist parties in general and the governing Labor party (Mapai) in particular. Before 1966, the chief target was the Military Rule, but it was not alone. Other laws and institutions that made a distinction between Jews and Arabs (such as the Keren Kayemet, the Jewish Agency) were described constantly as "pure racism" (Geffner 1973, 58–59). After the breakup of the alliance with Mapam, the latter's efforts to build a strong constituency in the Arab sector in the mid-1950s made it a target; it was nothing but another of "the parties of the national oppression, pretending to love the masses, and care for their interests."[28]

The tragic massacre of Arab citizens who unknowingly violated a curfew by Israeli soldiers in the village of Kafar Qasem on the eve of the Sinai campaign in 1956 was presented by the CPI to its Arab audience as proof of its theses concerning the destiny of the Arabs. Toufiq Toubi charged, "All signs point to the fact that the hand that prepared the attacks on Egypt [in 1956] prepared the massacre at Kafar Qasem," the aim being "to induce all of the Arab inhabitants to flee in the event that the scope of the military operations were to widen" (Geffner 1973, 90). In its first independent campaign, nine years after Kafar Qasem, the CPI (Rakah) evoked the event again in its election slogans: "Waw [the letter of the party in the elections] promises that the Kafar Qasem Massacre will not be repeated."[29] Even twenty-five years after the event, when the Likud party was trying to win the second time in 1981 and the Labor party was calling on the Arab voters to help defeat it, the CPI came out with the slogan "The difference between them [the Likud and Labor] is like the difference between the Dir Yassin Massacre and the Kafar Qasem Massacre."[30]

Through such slogans, the CPI made every effort to convince the Arab voters that they formed a destiny group and that voting for Zionist parties or their Arab associates was degrading. Taking note of pressure by the authorities against votes for the Communists, some slogans tried to encourage the voters: "Vote K [CPI-Maki's letter] and do not fear."[31] Or, in Rakah's more militant slogan: "Election day is a day of [settling] your account with your oppressors . . . your security and your struggle."[32] Another: "Waw—Prepare for them all you can on election day—the day of Judgment."[33]

In accordance with the CPI's attempt to forge a sense of destiny among the Arab voters, the abolition of the Military Rule in 1966 was greeted with the statement that nothing had changed: "The Military Rule changed its snake's skin" and will be, perhaps even worse, "an eye which sees without being seen."[34] But since fear was less strong, the slogans emphasized honor and self-respect. The final appeal in *al Ittihad* to the voters in the municipal elections in Nazareth after the announcement of the abolition was: "The strong opinion of the people, harder than steel, will teach the government of oppression a lesson, so that it will learn to respect a people that respects itself. Fasten the 'Waw' ballots, as choking ties to the racist policy, that has rejected your rights, and has stomped your honor for nineteen years."[35]

The CPI-Rakah slogans in the campaign of 1969 developed the same theme in a slightly different direction, appealing to the voters to identify the fate of the party with the destiny of the Arabs. The special election supplement published by the CPI was headed "A Call from the Big Prisons." The text stated: "[We are] prisoners in our homeland. Some of us are prisoners in a city. Some of us in a village. Some of us in a room. Let this message be the hands of the prisoners outstretched toward their brethren across the wall of the big prison. . . . Let us make the prison keeper understand that he is weaker than the free word, and that his walls are weaker than our upright bodies, and that his darkness retreats before our glittering conscience. . . . Let us say no to the policy of aggression, and shout yes in favor of holding fast to our right to live. Let us raise our voice in the battle of destiny. Let us say 'Waw' and thus consolidate a nation which is persecuted in its homeland" (Abu-Gosh 1972, 250–51).

THE WORKING-CLASS ATTRIBUTE

The appeal to the class attribute of the voters can be seen mainly in slogans appearing before elections to the Histadrut trade union. But since many of the campaigns for Histadrut were held in close proximity to the national elections, the campaign slogans were aimed at both. The basic message to the Arab members of the Histadrut was that Zionist control of the body caused Arab workers to suffer from double inequality: on a national basis (because they were Arabs) and on a class basis (because they were workers). But as a class they shared the same inequality as Jewish workers, and it was with them and other progressive Jewish circles that Arabs should form an opinion group. Hence the slogans "Long live the unity of the working class" and, perhaps the most famous trademark slogan of the Communists, "Jewish-Arab fraternity."[36] The First of May rallies in particular stressed working-class solidarity slogans, although, even during the Maki period, in Nazareth there was always a marked emphasis on "Arab rights." This was often expressed through generally phrased class slogans such as "For the rights of the toilers" and "Against belligerent adventurism and impoverishment of the masses."

The first significant participation of Arabs in elections to Histadrut took place in 1965 (Arabs began to be admitted as full members in 1959). Since

1965 was also a national election year, the campaign slogans of the CPI-Rakah combined the two attributes—class and national. For instance: "'Waw'—the list of Jewish-Arab fraternity, of peace, democracy and equality"; "The list of the Jewish and Arab vanguard—the farmer, the educated and all those exploited"; "'Waw'—the workers' unity and national unity"; "The 'waw' [Arabic for *and*] that connects the Communists with the mass of the toilers and entire people; connects our people with every atom of this homeland; that connects the Jewish and Arab Communists as a bridge for fraternity and peace between the two peoples; connects every honest and decent man in the general system against the Military Rule, the robbing of land, annihilation of houses, and for the complete equality for our people." Other slogans emphasized specifically the demand for equality in the job market: "We will not surrender, and will not go back from complete equality for all the Arab workers in work and pay."[37] Or, "For job security, unemployment benefits, equality of daily and monthly workers." By the 1980s many of these demands had been fulfilled, and CPI slogans concentrated on the patronizing attitude of the Labor-ruled Histadrut: "An Arab and a foreman? The Arab can be only a worker. The one in charge has to be of the majority. Not according to us. . . . it is the Ma'arach that follows this policy. . . . For the participation of Arabs in the running of the Histadrut!"[38]

Generally speaking, in the 1970s and 1980s the class slogans were overshadowed by the issues of the occupied territories and the Palestinian problem. In the 1973 First of May rally in Taibe in the Triangle (bordering the West Bank), the slogans dealt only with the Palestinian question; in the Galilee, on the other hand, the slogans were traditional: "the toilers' struggle" and "Jewish-Arab fraternity." In the late 1970s the latter became the cry of the CPI demonstrators attempting to drown the nationalist slogans of the radical-nationalist hecklers.[39]

Attempts of the CPI to identify its own fate with the fate of the Arab minority are evident in all of the slogans cited here. Other slogans, particularly after the split of 1965, claimed that the CPI embodied the Arab minority by its structure, program, activity, and general Arabness. On this account, it claimed a leading role and delegitimized any other claim for leadership. The chief slogan expressing this claim called for "Unity of the line" (unity of forces). Thus, before the municipal elections in Nazareth in 1965, a leaflet proclaimed "No to sectarianism, no to familism, for a national united line." A similar call, paraphrasing lines from the Koran, was made during the campaign for the general elections two months later: "Waw of our unity and the gathering of our lines—be generous and take an oath." This theme was repeated in the 1969 campaign.[40] It was emphasized even more in the 1970s and 1980s when Arab competitors appeared on the political scene.

In the 1984 campaign for the Knesset, the CPI slogans tried both to attack the Progressive List for Peace and to minimize its importance. Slogans did not refer to the PLP by name but as "the list of assault on the national unity of line" or "the breakers of the ranks and merchants of nationalism."[41] Another slogan simply ignored the PLP's existence as a significant political rival and, paraphrasing a famous dictum from Islamic military history, appealed to the voters: "In front of you is the Likud, at the back of you is the Ma'arach, you have no one but the Front."[42]

The politics of identity among the Arab electorate had a sharper edge after the outbreak of the Intifada in 1987. During the 1988 campaign, the competition between the CPI-led Front and the PLP to identify with the uprising took place against the backdrop of violent clashes between stone-throwing young Palestinians and Israeli soldiers beating and shooting protesters in an effort to suppress the uprising. Both parties adopted slogans and symbols that identified them with the heroic Palestinian struggle. The Front urged, "Hurl 'waws' at the rulers of our country." It also drew a line of demarcation: whereas "self-defence with stones is the characteristic of the Intifada of our people [in the territories], our self-defence [in Israel] is by hurling 'waws' at the rulers of our country in elections [and] characterizes our Intifada that has been going on for forty years" (Al Haj 1989, 37). The PLP, for its part, made every effort to appear to be the list endorsed by the PLO in general and Yassir Arafat in particular, and it insinuated a lack of authenticity in the "fossiled" Communist leadership of the Israeli Communist party (Al Haj 1989, 38).

To this battle of identity another voice was added in 1988—the voice of the Arab Democratic Party. But rather than emphasize the *Palestinian* Arab attribute, this party projected the generalized Arab attribute, portraying itself as the "the party of Arabness." Its slogans also underlined the Islamic identity of its candidates (unlike the Jewish and Christian candidates of the Front and the PLP), urging the Muslims to vote only for a "believer in Allah and Muhamad as his messenger." Its slogans also pointed at its accommodationist strategy—a wish to become a coalition party—in contradistinction to the Front and the PLP: "A vote for influence, not for protest" (Reiter 1989, 67–68). How did this battle of representation of identity translate into votes for the CPI? The analysis in part 3 of this book will attempt to identify which components in the party image—program, organization, or slogan—appealed to which quarters of the Arab population and to identify the impact of this differentiation on the CPI's status as a rival political establishment.

Three

Political Mobilization of the Arab Sector and Bases of Electoral Support for the CPI, 1949–1996

6

Social and Economic Change among the Arab Citizens in Israel

The impact of the uneven, disjointed incorporation of the socially fragmented Arab peasant minority in 1948 into the ethnically defined, modernizing Jewish state, at war with the Arab region, created for the Arab minority a reality fraught with structural contradictions. They were left on their land and within their communities but were also turned into migratory, ethnically defined workers, dependent on the Jewish economy. Although incorporation and education provided access to the social and political goods of a modernizing state, segregation in underdeveloped localities kept the traditional lineage *(hamula)* structure dominant in local politics. With increased politicization but without equal incorporation, Arabs in Israel moved from the general ethnic self-identification as Arabs to the more specific identity of Palestinians, having an undefined civic identity.

INCORPORATION INTO THE ISRAELI MARKET ECONOMY

During the latter period of British Mandate rule, when tensions between the two communities heightened, Jewish and Arab economies ran mostly parallel to each other. Jewish organized labor, under the direction of Histadrut, attempted with considerable success to exclude Arab workers from competing with the higher-cost Jewish workers in the Jewish economy (Shafir 1989). In the short interval between the UN decision on partition (November 1947) and the Declaration of Independence (May 1948), there were initial deliberations within the Mapai leadership in Histadrut to change this traditional Labor-Zionist policy of economic separation, in preparation for the implementation of the UN partition plan (Amitay 1988, 89–90). But the Arab invasion, the mass exodus of Palestinians, the Jewish victory, and the mass Jewish immigration in the 1950s changed the entire demographic and geopolitical picture. These events, as well as internal political calculations of the ruling Mapai party, fostered an official attitude of suspicion toward the Arab citizens. This suspicion was used to justify treating the presence of Arabs in the country as dangerous and to relegate them to total marginality in the Jewish economy and society (Benziman and Mansour 1992, 14–16).

For the first decade after 1948, the Arab minority citizens—most of them peasants and part-time workers faced a difficult situation.[1] The Arabs lost ownership over considerable land through expropriation (Benziman and Mansur 1992, 157–66), and a small minority was cut off from urban Arab centers and middle-class leadership, circumscribed by the Military Rule, which also controlled movement and employment opportunities. The village economy was backward and not productive enough to support the surplus labor force for long (Carmi and Rosenfeld 1974). Lacking the minimum infrastructure for a modern economy (piped water, electricity, telephones, roads, skilled manpower), it had no attraction for industrial investment.

The economic impact of the establishment of the state on the Arab population had two main components and took place largely in two phases. First, from a basically peasant society, the Arab labor force was proletarianized but without being separated from the land and houses, which remained in their possession and served as an economic cushion at times of recession. In the second phase, the late 1960s and 1970s, this population became stratified.[2] However, stratification became almost stagnant in the 1980s and 1990s. Proletarianization characterized the first phase, which lasted for two decades, up to the 1967 war. In the early 1950s, the Military Rule severely curtailed the Arabs' ability to seek work outside their localities. They were thus forced either to stay on the land or to seek work as agricultural laborers through influential local figures with proper contacts with the military governor.

In response to labor shortages in the Jewish economy in the late 1950s, military controls were gradually relaxed and were abolished in 1966. The mandate pattern of proletarianization without permanent migration out of the rural areas reemerged, on almost a total scale (Rosenfeld 1978). As in the mandate period, Arab workers continued to live in rural localities among other Arabs, but in contrast to that period they traveled to work among Jews and were employed almost entirely by Jews. Work opportunities were controlled by the Employment Exchange Law, Histadrut's local labor council rules, and Jewish Agency projects, which had built-in preferences for Jewish labor (Benziman and Mansur 1992, 175; Lustick 1980; Shalev 1992, 51). Nevertheless, employment began to shift away from agriculture. In 1956 over 50 percent of the labor force was employed in agriculture and only 8 percent in construction. A decade later, only 39 percent worked in agriculture and 20 percent as manual workers in construction. The rest were employed in low-paying, unskilled manual jobs in services and industry.[3]

Thus, during the first decade of being incorporated "from below" into the developing economy of the new state, the Arab population gained skills and knowledge of the labor market. After the 1967 war, they were in a position to benefit from the economic boom despite the migratory nature of their employment, the segregated organizational incorporation of the Arab workers into Histadrut, and the exclusion of the Arab farmers from the latter's institutional network. (The Arabs were accepted as full members in Histadrut in 1959, which earned them job security, but they were put under the tutelage of a separate Arab Department, headed by Jews of the ruling Mapai party [Khalidi 1988, 75; Shalev 1992, 53].) First, industry in Jewish areas became an additional important branch of employment for approximately 20 percent of the skilled and unskilled workers. But the proportion of skilled and unskilled was sharply reversed. Unskilled workers, 35 percent of the workers in 1963, constituted only 12 percent in 1976; skilled workers, 15 percent in 1963, constituted 42 percent in 1976.[4] After 1967, the Arab citizens' place in the lowest-paying jobs, with no job security, was largely taken by the Palestinian noncitizens of the occupied territories (Semyonov and Lewin-Epstein 1987).

By the mid-1970s those who remained in agriculture as a main source of livelihood (16 percent in 1975, 10 percent in 1990) transformed the traditional subsistence-type farming into modern agriculture, despite severe handicaps in terms of resource allocation: small holdings, partly as a result of expropriation; small quotas of water; and no access to credit and marketing facilities, all of which were available to the Jewish farming via the state and the Histadrut-affiliated organizations (Khalidi 1988, 64–112).

Another significant development that took place between the late 1960s and mid-1970s was the growth of a sizable stratum of self-employed subcontractors (20 percent), particularly in transport and construction (Khalidi 1988, 120–21; Rosenfeld 1978). In the 1970s and 1980s, capital accumulation gave rise to further social differentiation with the growth of small enterprises (Meyer-Brodnitz and Czamanski 1986) and a narrow stratum of medium- and large-scale entrepreneurs (Khalidi 1988, 185–87). In the same period there was also a significant increase in employment of Arab citizens in public and community services (from 8 percent in 1961 to 15 percent in 1975 to 20 percent in 1990). The last change in particular was a corollary of the dramatic increase in the level of education as a consequence of compulsory primary education and the establishment of a secondary schooling system. In 1961 almost half of the population fifteen years and older was illiterate, and the median number of years of schooling was 1.2. By 1975 the median was 6.5, and by 1990 it rose to 9.0, with only 13 percent of the older generation remaining illiterate. The change is noticeable also in the secondary level (twelve years of schooling completed): from a minute 1.2 percent in 1961 to 9.1 percent in 1975 and 23 percent in 1990 (Lewin-Epstein and Semyonov 1993, 23). Academic training of some kind, which in 1970 encompassed only 4.5 percent of the adult population, by the end of the 1980s had risen to 9 percent.

The entry of the Arab labor force into the Jewish labor market, particularly between the 1960s and mid-1970s, with the exception of 1966, came at a time of full employment and economic expansion in construction, public services, and high-tech military-related sectors. Of the three areas, Arabs found employment mainly in the first and were excluded from the third. At the same time, in the mid-1970s state welfare benefits and public health services were greatly extended, particularly transfer payments to low-income families, of which Arab families formed a large proportion (Reiss 1988).[5] But whereas the state and the Zionist organizations supplied public housing and infrastructure for the Jewish population in new localities, the Arab population mainly had to fend for themselves. Using their savings and skills, Arabs improved their standard of housing between the mid-1970s and the 1980s, for instance, by installing indoor plumbing. Full employment also enabled them to purchase durable goods and modern home appliances, which had earlier become standard in Jewish Israeli homes (refrigerators, stoves, washing machines).[6]

However, despite these improvements in absolute terms, gaps in health standards, education, and socioeconomic status between the Arab minority and the Jewish majority, which had narrowed in the 1970s, persisted and even widened again in the 1980s and 1990s (Faris 1993, 35–37; Reiss 1988, 149). There were two underlying reasons. One, the incorporation of the Arabs into the educational system and the economy was segmentary and highly exclusionary. Second was the lack of state-initiated economic development of Arab localities, in contradistinction to Jewish localities, and outright discrimination in resource allocation for local government (Al Haj and Rosenfeld 1990; Khalidi 1988, 162–64; Lewin-Epstein and Semyonov 1993, 30–31). As a "security risk," Arabs as individuals were excluded from the high-paying, technologically advanced sectors, many of which were in defense-related industries. Arab citizens were also largely excluded from the public bureaucracy (other than teaching in Arab schools) and from managerial positions in private and publicly owned industry, ostensibly for security reasons (Carmi and Rosenfeld 1992; Wolkinson 1989). Thus, despite the Arabs' considerable educational upgrading, they faced a discriminatory opportunity structure and job discrimination practices that favored the Jewish majority and prevented them from converting their educational assets into occupational status (Lewin-Epstein and Semyonov 1993, 24). In essence, they were locked into the low-paying economic branches of the economy that suffered fluctuations in level of employment. The state's lack of any efforts to encourage economic development in Arab localities deprived them of the wide-scale protection of an enclave economy where they would have been shielded from competition with the ethnic majority. The underdevelopment of the Arab localities helped indirectly to increase the economic gap between Arabs and Jews: it encouraged the persistence of the low participation in the labor market of Arab women (10–18 percent compared with 44 percent of Jewish women), who for traditional reasons do not migrate out of the localities for employment, particularly after marriage (Carmi and Rosenfeld 1992; Lewin-Epstein and Semyonov 1993).

Thus, becoming part of the Jewish national economy had a two-pronged effect on the Arab citizens in Israel. On the one hand, integration from below into the economy was followed by upward mobility and improved economic status; aspects of the Arab economy were modernized; Arab educational standards were advanced; and Arabs were incorporated into the welfare system. On the other hand, this incorporation blocked further economic development of the Arab localities and generated a discrimination lasting over four decades, as well as widening the class gap between the dominant Jewish national majority and the Arab national minority.

The political implications of this pattern of economic change, which included elements of exclusion, neglect, and inclusion, were indirect. In the political sphere, the Arab sector had one resource that the politicians of the establishment wanted: votes. In the short run, this strengthened the hand of the traditional leadership, which argued that only through cooperating with the authorities and keeping a low political profile would the vital interests of the Arab minority be secured. However, as the process of incorporation into the market economy progressed, the sons of the fellaheen (peasants) who became laborers and professionals were available for oppositionist political mobilization by the CPI in the 1960s and 1970s. The CPI argued that recognizing the national dimension of the minority was a necessary condition of equality. The sense of socioeconomic progress in the 1970s lent some credence to this argument. But in the 1980s, the widening gap dampened these hopes and provided an impetus for pluralism in political organization among the Arab electorate.

Cultural Impact of Incorporation: Change of Social Values, Norms, and Identity

The entire process of incorporating the Arab population into Israeli society took place under conditions of the geographical, social, and cultural seclusion of the two national communities. To the mutual satisfaction of both communities, the state-sponsored educational system of the Arab minority uses Arabic, Arabs are exempted from the military service, and the incorporation into the market economy was done without emigration of the Arabs to the Jewish cities and localities. These facts had far-reaching social and political implications. Despite being Israeli citizens, the Arab citizens naturally remained culturally oriented to the surrounding Arab countries and open to their influences. Their cultural existence, therefore, had two facets, one influenced by Jewish society and the other by the general Arab culture.

Yet, owing to the Arab world's boycott of Israel, for the first two decades of Israel's existence the Arab minority in Israel was almost completely cut off from its Arab cultural milieu. It therefore found itself, perhaps inevitably, adopting some of the hegemonic cultural habits of a society that it did not want to resemble. This ambivalent feeling was termed antagonistic acculturation by one researcher (Kana'naa 1976). Yet the rank order of social values of Jews and Arabs has been found to be similar. The most recent study found a 0.79 Spearman correlation between Jews and Arabs, with "family" and "education of the children" being ranked by both groups among the top four. Arabs gave somewhat higher value to "freedom of speech" than Jews and significantly higher value to "standard of living," reflecting their position as a less affluent minority (Levinson, Katz, and Al Haj 1995).

The impact of Israelization on Arabs' traditional norms is attested to in various surveys concerning educational aspirations, occupational mobility, and family norms. However, differences between Arabs and Jews, on most points, continue to exist, particularly with regard to family norms and the place of women. Least problematic are language and media acculturation (Smooha 1984, 72). Although the family norms of Arabs in Israel can be seen to reflect both change and tradition (see Ginat 1980; Nakhleh 1973; Rosenfeld 1980), there is no dispute that the extended family, which prior to 1948 was the most significant economic, social, and (sometimes) political unit in a peasant society, has dwindled in importance following the economic changes.

However, hamulas—the kinship groups that link together by common ancestry a number of paternal households—are still successful in enlisting the loyalty of their members during local elections. With the exception of the city of Nazareth, the local political scene is dominated by family-based lists that run for local government to protect the hamula's interests in the locality. The importance of the hamula in providing a political framework for recruitment of local leadership and vote getting in general can be explained as a corollary of the lack of emigration out of the localities, which had the effect of preserving the patrilocal *form* of the hamula structure and hence the local interests of hamulas. The introduction of local elections while the traditional social structure was still intact helped to establish this pattern. Other factors that helped preserve the hamula as a political form included the lack of interest by the national parties, except for the Communist Party, in direct action on the Arab local scene, a lack favored by the authorities (Al Haj 1983, 165; Nakhleh 1979, 250–53).

On the level of political identity, surveys taken between the end of the 1960s and the 1980s reveal a definite movement from the general ethnic identification as Arabs to the more specific identity as Palestinians, although an Israeli component was included by two-thirds of the sample (Peres and Davis 1968; Smooha 1984, 1989, 1992; Tessler 1977). This could be explained by the paradox of change under conditions of ethnic differentiation. In other words, partial integration and acculturation has made the Arab minority both Israeli *and* more Arab Palestinian in their social and political behavior. The political significance of the shift from Arab to Palestinian identity is open to interpretation.

The question here is, first, the attitude of Arab citizens toward their civic identity as a minority and, second, the degree of freedom they feel allowed by the Jewish majority in identifying with the "enemy." Historically and ethnically, the Arab citizens of Israel *are* Palestinians, but they are also Arabs, Muslims, Christians, Druze, Bedouins, and Israeli citizens. The decision to identify as Palestinian could reflect a separatist political position, but not necessarily so, particularly when the term "Palestinian in Israel" is also used as self-definition in surveys (Smooha 1992, 78–83). It is clear, though, that in the current transitional political conditions, the majority of the Arabs in Israel find it difficult to resolve the issue of political identity on the abstract level. Since it is linked with the issue of their attitude toward the very existence of the state in which they live, it is volatile in their own minds and can be subject to redefinition under short-term political changes. It is therefore reasonable to treat the political identity as a dependent variable rather than as an independent one.

Cultivating the turf of their Palestinian identity while refusing to move to a Palestinian state, the Arabs in Israel are caught in a double bind. As a young Arab student was quoted in one study, "Emotionally I identify with the Arab world, but in fact, every Arab in Israel lives here and is tied to life here" (Hofman and Rouhana, 1976, 82). It is upon this gap between the emotional and the pragmatic levels that the CPI built its appeal to the Arab voters. As will be shown, the party argued that through support for the CPI this gap could be closed.

7

Oppositionist and Electoral Politics

The CPI established its electoral bases of support on the national level by relying initially on its traditional organizational-cultural link with the northern urban Christian population and then attempting to extend its support to the Muslims by embodying the ethnic Arab identity. Its main rivals were the Zionist parties and the hamula-based Zionist-affiliated Arab lists, which managed to maintain their electoral hold until the abolition of the Military Rule. The CPI electoral breakthrough in the late 1960s is attributed to the socioeconomic changes that followed the end of the Military Rule and the 1967 war. The rise to prominence of the PLO after the 1973 war gave it further impetus.

The Sociopolitical Milieu: Constraints and Strategies

The demographic and socioeconomic changes delineated earlier did not blur the sectarian identity that divided the Palestinian Arabs into Muslims, Christians, and Druze. These communal identities were instead strengthened with the active encouragement of the Israeli regime. The fact that these sectarian divisions overlapped the rural-urban division was to have a great effect on local politics.

In the first decade of electoral politics in the Arab sector, the CPI-Maki was clearly a minority party, winning only 11 to 22 percent of the Arab vote (see table 7.1). The overwhelming majority of the Arab voters, 52 to 58 percent, voted for the Arab lists associated with the ruling party, Mapai, and for the ruling party itself. Another small block, 6 to 12 percent, of the Arab voters gave their vote to the Zionist-Socialist Mapam party. Although the flight of the entire Arab leadership in 1948 left the Communists free of their nationalist rivals, the Arab Communists had no roots in the traditional social structure, and their eventual support of the partition decision discredited their claim

Table 7.1. Distribution of vote in Arab localities, 1949–59 (percentages)

Year	Participation	CPI	Arab lists	Labor/Zionists	Mapam
1949	79	22	51	26	—
1951	85	16.3	55	24	5.6
1955	90	15.6	58	19	7.3
1959	88	11.2	58	18	12.5

Note: The table excludes Arab voters in the "mixed" cities, who constitute about 8 percent of eligible Arab voters.

of being Arab patriots. On the other hand, they were the only organized Arab group that, with the help of the Jewish Communists, survived from the pre-1948 nationalist struggle, and the mid-1950s efforts made by non-Communist nationalist individuals to set up an Arab party failed (Landau 1969, 72–73). As noted in chapter 5, the only serious threat to challenge the CPI-Maki on Arab nationalist grounds—the al Ard group in 1959–61—never came to an electoral test because the organization was banned by the authorities.

Another competitor of the CPI was the socialist-Zionist Mapam party, the only Zionist party to accept Arabs as full members, beginning in 1954. After a period of close cooperation between Maki and Mapam, the two parties became bitter rivals in the Arab sector in the mid-1950s. Mapam invested considerable organizational efforts among the Arabs (Amitay 1988, 130–66), and in 1959 it even won more votes among the Arabs than did the CPI. However, Mapam eventually could not overcome its drawbacks among the opposition-inclined Arabs. The Arabs found its Zionist ideology hard to accept, and it was walking a tight-rope by being both a pro-government party (as a member of the coalition during 1955–61) and a fierce opponent of the Mapai's policies toward the Arabs and the Arab countries (Beinin 1991).

The CPI's chief electoral opposition, then, was the Arab minority lists affiliated with the ruling Zionist parties, particularly in the rural sector. In 1955, 57.9 percent of the rural and Bedouin population voted for those lists compared with 37.2 percent in the two Arab towns. For the CPI, the inverse was true: 34.9 percent of the residents of Nazareth and Shefaram voted for them but only 15.6 percent in the rural settlements (Landau 1969, 121). It is argued that the underlying reason for the relative electoral weakness of the CPI in the rural sector in the 1950s was the attachment of most of the Arabs to the traditional social structure; most of the Arabs accepted the traditional leaders' assessment that the Arabs as a minority should resign themselves to a peripheral role and cooperate with the ruling parties.[1]

The Arab lists, as their name indicates, were not proper parties but ad hoc electoral arrangements for the election of Arabs to the Knesset. This arrangement, initiated by the Zionist parties shortly after the establishment of the state, was designed to tap the Arab citizens' votes under rather anomalous conditions. On the one hand, the Arabs were under the Military Rule, restricting their civil liberties; on the other hand, they had the right to vote and to be represented in the Knesset. Those chosen to head the lists represented the philosophy that the minority Arabs' only hope of improving their material and political situation was through their representatives' efforts behind the scenes. By lobbying for Arab interests in government offices and by voting for the government rather than against it in the Knesset, they would eventually integrate into the system (Geffner 1973, 76).

The Arab candidates on the allied lists based their appeal for votes on kinship solidarity, or hamula discipline, and on the ability to provide services and even pecuniary benefits. As representatives in the Knesset, they acted according to the traditional concept of rural leadership, whose chief role is to intercede on behalf of individuals before the authorities. Although they could use the Knesset as a public stage to raise issues concerning the Arabs, they generally preferred to solve personal and local problems themselves. Thus the two Arab members of the second Knesset (1951–55) who were affiliated with the ruling party did not submit any motions for the agenda on particularized Arab matters. Of the seventy-six parliamentary questions submitted in the first session on matters related to the Arab citizens, they submitted only two.[2]

The composition of the Arab lists was decided by the Jewish specialists on Arab affairs in the relevant Zionist parties. The ruling party, Mapai, which sponsored three Arab lists in 1955 and 1959 and two in later election campaigns, carefully selected traditional, usually wealthy notables. Since none had more than a local reputation and since they belonged to different and sometimes rival sections of the Arab community, the choice had to circumvent, as much as possible, sectarian and hamula rivalries. Thus, there were always notables from the Triangle region (a Muslim), a Druze local notable, the leader of the largest hamula in Nazareth and the eastern Galilee, as well as a rural Greek Catholic notable.

The vote for the Arab lists may thus be said to have reproduced the traditional social structure in an electoral framework under the tutelage of the Zionist establishment. Opposition to one meant opposition to the other. Since there was pressure from the ruling Mapai government, through the Military Rule, to vote for those lists—rather than for the Communists—voting was not an act of individual free choice. Nevertheless, the pressure of the Military

Rule cannot alone explain the vote for the Arab lists. On the one hand, their decline began in 1961, before the abolition of the Military Rule, when they received only 45 percent of the Arab vote; on the other, their eventual eclipse occurred some fifteen years *after* its abolition, in the 1981 elections, when they ran without the blessing of the Labor party and lost. The integrationist philosophy that they represented—of going along with the establishment— was modernized and transformed into attempts of direct integration, through joining and voting for Zionist parties, in the 1970s. The Communists, on the other hand, posed as a counterestablishment and argued that only they had the means to achieve true integration.

THE TRADITIONAL-ORGANIZATIONAL BASIS OF ELECTORAL SUPPORT, 1949–1961

In its early days, the CPI was mostly a Christian, urban northern party in terms of membership and leadership. After 1949 the center for Arab Commu- nist activity moved to Nazareth, then the largest Arab town, as only a fraction of the Arab community in Haifa remained (3,500 out of 68,000). The Com- munist leaders in Nazareth came almost exclusively from the urban Greek Orthodox community.[3] The main rural basis of support was in the village of Kfar Yassif in the western Galilee, which had a sizable Greek Orthodox popu- lation. In this village the pre-1948 League of National Liberation had a num- ber of registered members, and the party newspaper, *al Ittihad*, was distrib- uted there prior to 1948 (Nakhleh 1979, 94–95). A few other league members were spread among other villages in the Galilee with Greek Orthodox popula- tion (Rame, Abu Snan, Iblin, Elabun, Bi'na).

The partition of Palestine and the massive exit of Arabs from the urban centers on the shore destroyed the mass proletarian base of the Arab Commu- nists—the Trade Union Congress (the Mu'tamar). The strategy of the Arab Communists in the initial period of electoral politics was to reestablish their links with the urban Christian cultural group and to attempt to forge the same kind of organizational links with the rural, mostly Muslim population. They did so by quickly resuming the publication of *al Ittihad*, in which they at- tacked the "treason" of the traditional Palestinian and Arab leaders; by re- newing the activities of the Mu'tamar and engaging in industrial action on behalf of Arab workers; and by setting up a number of food cooperatives in Nazareth and in a number of villages.[4] The CPI also began launching cultural activities, such as a choir named a Talia ("the vanguard"). The choir in par- ticular exemplified the untraditional style of the party, for it included both men and women and the women traveled, unescorted, to rehearsals.[5]

The electoral support of the CPI-Maki among the Arabs in the early years (1949–55) was based primarily on an organizational factor: the ability to set up its old network of activists. The second reason for the electoral support of the CPI in the first decade of electoral politics was sectarian identification. Because the leading Communists were Christians, mostly Greek Orthodox, the CPI was able to translate its ties to this cultural group into a "traditional" link of political loyalty. Unlike Greek Catholics, the Greek Orthodox community had no religious leadership and only a weak sectarian organization. So the Communist Party offered a means of identification on a secular basis (Landau 1969, 202–4).

The electoral behavior of the Catholic community was less homogeneous and less consistent than that of the Orthodox. Among the urban concentration of Greek Catholic population (Nazareth, Haifa, and Shefaram), there was apparently a fair amount of support for the CPI, but less so in the rural settlements. The Greek Catholic community, being the largest and most coherent and having important ties outside the country (with the Vatican), was a political target for the ruling Mapai party. In the mid-1950s it granted the church special concessions, and it made sure that in every Knesset, a Greek Catholic would be elected on one of its allied minority lists.

The Launching of the Embodiment Strategy: The Military Rule, Land, and Ethnonationalist Identity

In the early 1950s, building electoral support among the Muslim rural population on an organizational basis had few chances of success. The decision to disband the Congress of Arab workers (Mu'tamar) and work within Histadrut was rooted in the ideological logic of the union with the Jewish Communists, but it also reflected the disintegration of the Arab Communist trade union in the field. This was not surprising, since under existing conditions of massive unemployment and economic shortages, an oppositionist Arab trade union had no bargaining power. The failure of the cooperative food stores of the party because of mismanagement underscored the weakness of that strategy. To run a separate trade union was not feasible in the 1960s, when the Arab work force was incorporated into the Jewish economy and became totally dependent on it. However, the decision to disband the union had a long-term consequence for the CPI electoral strategy.[6] It signaled the shift from the pre-state attempt to build a party link with the Arab working class on an organizational basis to a combined strategy of embodiment of Arab ethnonationalist identity and representation of the interests of the working class and the intelligentsia. In other words, in addition to the rational appeal on the basis of interest, the CPI attempted to forge a charismatic link between itself and the Arab voters, a link strong on the emotional level but inherently unstable.

The essence of the strategy was to demonstrate to Arab citizens that the Communists' fearless opposition to the Zionist establishment and an independent Arab political bloc led by the Jewish-Arab party would be the only way of ensuring that their interests would be served. The CPI did so by launching struggles (sometimes with Mapam and other sympathizers) on the legal issues most pressing to the Arab population, especially citizenship laws, land laws, and the Military Rule. The first conflict between the Arab population and the authorities broke out in 1950 over the issue of registration of Arabs as citizens. In contradistinction to Jews, who were automatically entitled to citizenship under the "law of return," under the bill drafted by the government only Arabs who proved their loyalty to the state by being present in their villages on a certain date were entitled to register as citizens. Arabs who had left the country during the 1948 war and later returned to their villages did not qualify and were ordered to leave the country.

A parliamentary struggle by the CPI and Mapam representatives ensued on behalf of Arabs who demanded to be awarded citizenship as a means of retaining their right to stay (Ozacky 1990). In at least two villages affected, the party organized demonstrations, protests, and delegations to the military governor to abort, successfully, the deportation.[7] Deportations that took place during 1949–51 were publicized and strongly denounced in *al Ittihad* and in the statements and questions of the CPI-Maki members of the Knesset (see chapter 4).

The military government, which restricted the movement of Arab citizens out of their localities, originally for security reasons alone, subsequently intervened in all matters related to the civilian life of the Arab citizens. The local military governor, through his official power to grant permission to travel outside the village (to work, to visit relatives, to seek medical treatment) and through his authority to punish "troublemakers" by banishment, was able to intervene informally in all other matters, including politics.[8] Thus, the governor had a say on permits to buy agricultural equipment, land rental, and appointment and dismissal of teachers and civil servants.[9]

The tug of war that developed between the Communist activists and the Military Rule authorities was due to the latter's unofficial assignment to prevent any "hostile" political activity. On election day, this meant ensuring the vote for the ruling Mapai party. The Communist Party, which did not hide its objection to various aspects of the status quo, was seen by the authorities as inciting the Arab population to be disloyal to the state. In particular, the fear was that the internal refugees, those who had fled their villages but remained in the country, "egged on and organized by the Communists, would go back to squat on their ruins, demanding their lands back."[10]

Another example was the campaign in 1954 by party activists in the Arab sector against the special education tax imposed on Arab households after Arab local authorities became helpless with regard to tax collection. Emil Habibi, a CPI Arab member of Knesset, along with the Arab Mapam member, denounced the special tax as "racist," and the CPI activists in the villages encouraged the population not to pay it.[11] In May 1954 two members of the CPI central committee and newly elected members to the city council in Nazareth, Toufiq Ziad and Mun'am Jarjura, were detained by the military governor after they helped to organize violent demonstrations against tax collectors in the village of Arabe.

In the late 1950s and early 1960s, the clashes with the Military Rule centered around the issue of land expropriation. As noted in chapter 6, large tracts of land that Arabs in the Galilee and the Triangle claimed belonged to them, either individually or collectively as a village, were expropriated by the government. In 1957, in an effort to settle Jewish population at the heart of the Galilee, the government expropriated land around Nazareth and built Upper Nazareth for settlement of Jews. The CPI-Maki representatives in the Knesset protested, but refrained from taking the struggle to the streets.[12] Only in 1961, after expropriations were made for the establishment of another Jewish town (Carmiel) and for the national water project, did the CPI attempt to organize protest meetings to stop the expropriations, but their efforts were halted by the Military Rule (Jiryis 1976, 109).

Despite the widespread bitterness toward the Military Rule and the land expropriations of 1953–54, the Communists were not able to cash in on their activity on those issues, with a few exceptions. The explanation may have been that the cultivated land expropriated in 1954-55 belonged mainly to a small number of big landowners (Flapan 1963, 25–28). On a more general level, the lack of support for the Communists reflected the ability of the local leadership to respond to the pressure of the local military governor; in the villages in which the traditional hamula leaders remained coherent, the local leaders tended to stay on good terms with the military government and were able to put pressure on their kinsmen to disassociate from the Communists. In the eyes of those leaders, the Communists were unnecessarily provocative troublemakers who hindered rather than helped the Arabs' interest with their style of political action.[13] This was the case in almost all the small villages and in most of the medium-size and some of the large villages. For instance, in the large villages of Sachnin, Tamra, and Baqa-al Gharbiyya, where the hamula leadership remained strong, the vote for the Communists remained low compared with that in Taibe and Um al Fahem.[14]

Beyond these specific explanations for the difficulty of the CPI in breaking through into the rural Muslim sector, there was the suspicion felt by the religious-inclined Muslims toward the Communist secular-atheist worldview; although the Communist parties in the Middle East, including the CPI, made every effort to play down their theoretical views on religion and to stress their acceptance of Islamic traditions, their atheism could always be played against them by political rivals (Abu-Gosh 1972, 242–47). In the case of the Communists in Israel, the secular *style* of their activities and conduct caused objections in the traditional quarters. They resented the party's encouragement of boys and girls mixing freely and of women engaging in activities outside the home; they frowned upon cases of intermarriage between Christians and Muslims and decried alcohol consumption by party leaders, especially by Muslims.

Embodying Arabism was the other leg of the CPI's electoral strategy. As noted in chapter 3, during the mandate period the League for National Liberation sought recognition, without much success, as the progressive wing of the Palestinian Arab national movement. Amid the regional conflict and the international tension in the 1950s, the CPI saw an opportunity for renewing this effort. However, its first attempt in the late 1950s ended with an electoral loss. Success on a wide scale had to await a massive process of socioeconomic change among the Arab population, during which the ethnic Arab identity became politicized. As detailed in chapter 6, this process began in the early 1960s and grew to a massive scale in the 1970s.

The efforts of the CPI to become the embodiment of the Arab ethnonationalist movement in the late 1950s have been described previously. It was in this context that the Arab leadership decided to challenge the authorities by holding the mass First of May demonstrations in 1958 in Nazareth and in Um al Fahem to counter the tenth anniversary celebrations for the establishment of the state.[15] This action was aimed particularly at Arab high school students who had come to study in Nazareth from all over the country. The violent clashes with the police that ensued turned the 1958 First of May rally into a crucial event in the history of relations between the Arab population and the Communist Party.[16] For the CPI, the First of May demonstration, which helped mobilize the relatively educated youth, reflected both the ideology and tactics of the party vis-à-vis the Arab sector: its attempt to link Arab ethnonationalism with Communism in the minds of the Arab youth and to identify protest against the status quo with the Communist Party.[17] As noted in chapter 5, it also led to the first attempt at cooperation—in the form of the Popular Front— between the Communists and nationalist-inclined public personalities, who hitherto had acted sporadically on their own initiative. This step can be seen as an attempt to launch a strategy of representation toward the politically mobilized non-Communist Palestinian nationalists, whose electoral support for the CPI depended on the CPI's adherence to a pro-Nasser line. When the party did not stick to that line in 1959, the Popular Front collapsed, with some electoral consequences. It appears, however, that the breakup of the Popular Front occurred not only because of the Nasser-Qassem issue but also because the pro-Nasser circles saw the Jewish Communists as a political liability and would not accept the Arab Communists' argument that Jewish opinion had to be taken into account (Landau 1969, 94).

The electoral results of 1959 and 1961 reveal that two kinds of new supporters, divided by a fine line of distinction, were added to the traditional Christian voters of the CPI. In the first group were those who decided that their unsatisfactory life was related to their being part of an Arab minority in a social order that attributed no legitimacy to their existence as Arabs, nor even safeguarded their physical safety. These voters saw the CPI as the only body expressing their desire for a new social order, in which their ethnic collective attribute as Arabs would be recognized as legitimate, equal to that of a Jew. Supporters of the CPI did not necessarily adopt the specific social order—Communism—that the Communist Party professed. Not even all those who actually joined the party adopted its ideology. Consider the words of Abu-Gosh's informant who described what attracted him to the party:

> It was 1955. I was working in Tel Aviv, at the time, in construction. A Jewish immigrant from Iraq used to come to the cafe where we sat to sell "al Ittihad." Many workers used to buy it, including myself. I was familiar with "al Ittihad" before; in fact, I remember that, when still at school, I used to be fond of the slogans in the Communist paper.
>
> We, Israeli Arabs, live through new experiences every day; expropriation of land, persecution and racial discrimination. How could Arabs help but be fond of slogans like "equality between Arab and Jew; lifting Military Government; stopping all acts of discrimination and persecution, return of Arab rights"? The proverb says, "The hungry man dreams about bread." We dream about freedom and equality. (Abu-Gosh 1965, 66)

Voters and supporters of the second kind related their problems to the geopolitical place of the Palestinians within the large Arab nation. They thus saw their solution not in the framework of a new *social* order, but in the framework of a new Pan-Arab *regional* order, which Nasserism propagated. Their support for the CPI depended on the party's image as the embodiment of Nasserism. The events that surrounded the 1958 demonstration and the 1959 elections demonstrate the temporary increase in popularity of the Nasserist political undercurrent. By the time of the 1961 elections, these had subsided.

Soon after the split in the Popular Front in 1959, the elections to the fourth Knesset were held. The number of CPI-Maki seats in the Knesset was reduced from six to three. This development is often mentioned as most revealing about the nature of Arab support for the Communists (Landau 1969, 126; Nahas 1976, 40). Supposedly, it showed that the sole reason for the support for the party was its identification with the Arab nationalist cause; when the party preferred the Communist interest (that is, following Moscow's line) over the nationalist, its popularity sank. But a close look at the data shows that this conclusion is overstated and overlooks the effect of the oppositionist *style* of the CPI, rather than its program, on the Arab vote in those elections. The decline of the CPI in the polls among the Arabs can also be explained by the rivalry with the Zionist, oppositionist Mapam, which in 1959 reached the height of its popularity with 12.5 percent of the Arab vote (see table 7.1). In any case, the results of the elections held only two years later showed that the setback was only temporary among the "opposition inclined Arabs" even though the CPI continued to follow Moscow. In the 1961 elections to the fifth Knesset, the CPI doubled its support to 22.5 percent of the vote in Arab localities.

Perhaps the greater significance of the 1959 elections for the CPI-Maki lies in what they reveal about its relationship to its Jewish voters. The loss among Jews accounts for 88 percent of the votes lost, and as a consequence the percentage of Arabs among the voters for the CPI in 1959 increased slightly (from 27.8 percent to 29.6 percent).[18] The drastic fall in the Jewish vote probably reflected a lack of identification on the part of many with the party's pro-Nasser position in 1956, as well as disillusionment with Communism after the death of Stalin. It was therefore the first sign on the electoral front of the coming split into Jewish and Arab Communist parties in 1965.

THE BREAKTHROUGH: DISJOINTED CHANGE, GEOPOLITICS, AND THE VOTE FOR THE CPI, 1961–1973

The gradual building of bases of support by the Communists and their consequent turning into a rival political establishment began with the easing of the restrictions of the Military Rule in 1959 and the formal decision to accept the Arabs as full members of Histadrut the same year. The massive proletarization process that got under way created conditions for political mobilization by the CPI. But the disjointed nature of these changes had contradictory effects on identification with the party. On the one hand, the small percentage of young Arab high school graduates who sought a career in the public sector as teachers or public servants knew that such a career entailed acquiescence to the traditional political leadership, which the Zionist establishment continued to support.[19] A person who identified openly with the Communists was put on the authorities' list of security risks and hence lost public career opportunities. On the other hand, for the majority, some of them high school graduates, this dilemma hardly existed, for they became manual laborers in the Jewish settlements and towns.[20] The CPI's embodiment strategy became effective particularly among this group. It was the only political body that exalted their ethnic attribute and hailed them as being equal to the Jews.

The effects of this process on party identification of individuals were mitigated by the strength of the local traditional sociopolitical structure. While the economic changes swept through the entire Arab sector, they weakened the traditional political structure more quickly in the larger urban localities. Social and educational services (such as high schools, government agencies, Histadrut services, and small shops and coffeehouses) were located only in the two towns, Nazareth and Shefar'am, and in a number of the larger localities, creating there a more urban atmosphere. The sheer growth in the size of the larger villages increased social differentiation and weakened the former intimate social links. In those places where the cracks in the traditional social structure were larger, the Communists could establish a foothold.

By 1961 the pattern that characterized the vote for the CPI was established: the larger the locality, the higher the vote (table 7.2). However, the voting behavior of the Arabs in the mixed cities in 1961 seemed to suggest that it was not urbanization per se that was related to Communist vote but urbanization that maintained the sense of security and community. Only where urbanization was the experience of a fairly coherent social network did this sense arise. In general, in the three small cities (Ramle, Acre, Lydda) where the relative size of the Arab population was high, the support for the CPI was also high (table 7.3) compared with the three large cities (Tel Aviv, Haifa, and Jerusalem). In other words, the higher the concentration of Arab population, the higher the CPI vote. In 1992 this relationship no longer held in Tel Aviv–Jaffa and Jerusalem because of the polarization of the Arab-Christian population in Jaffa since the 1980s and the migration of Arab intelligentsia to Jerusalem.

Hence the year 1961 is a turning point in the history of support for the Communist Party among the Arabs. It marks the party's first successes in mobilizing certain sections of the rural Arab voters, particularly young men who after 1959 became migrant workers in the cities. Czudnowski and Landau (1965, 51) found that the relative increase in CPI-Maki vote between 1959 and 1961 was much greater in the smaller localities than in Nazareth. In other words, after the work and travel restrictions were relaxed, politicization of the rural population took place *outside* their places of residence, where they nevertheless continued to vote. The CPI was not the only party to benefit from politicization, for the direct vote for Zionist Jewish parties at the expense of the traditional Arab lists also increased (see table 7.4).

The challenge to the ethnonationalist integrative formula of the CPI in the early 1960s by the al Ard group was once again prevented from being tested in the polls in the mid-1960s by the High Court decision, on the eve of the

Table 7.2. Percentage of vote for CPI according to size of Arab locality

Size of locality	1959	1961	1965	1969	1973	1977	1981	1984	1988	1992	1996
Urban and semiurban[a]	26.5	45.0	42.0	48.1	49.8	65.0	48.3	45.5	39.5	32.7	47.1
Rural, large[b]	12.5	25.5	23.1	31.6	31.4	44.2	34.2	—	30.1	22.2	37.3
Rural, small[c]	5.1	13.0	13.1	13.1	15.8	27.5	20.3	23.6	13.1	11.5	21.8
National total[d]	11.3	22.5	23.1	28.5	36.9	50.6	37.9	33.0	33.8	23.2	36.8

a. Population over 5,000.
b. Population over 2,000.
c. Population up to 2,000 (excluding Bedouin tribes).
d. During the entire period, 9–15 percent of the Arab vote was given to independent Arab lists. The rest of the vote went either to Arab lists allied with Zionist parties, or directly to Zionist parties.

Sources: J. Landau, The Arabs in Israel, pp. 110–14; Y. Harari, The Elections to the 10th Knesset in the Arab Localities (Givaat Haviva, November 1982); CBS, Results of Elections to the 10th Knesset, June 30, 1981 (Special Series no. 680); Ozacky-Lazar and Ghanem, The Arab Vote for the 14th Knesset, May 29, 1996.

Table 7.3. Vote for CPI in mixed cities in relation to size of Arab community, 1961–
92 (results in mainly Arab neighborhood polling stations)

| | Eligible Arab voters | | | |
| | % of total in town | | % of vote for CP | |
City	1961	1992	1961	1992
Acre	22.5	21.7	22.9	37.1
Ramle	8.8	13.7	22.7	20.8
Lod	6.2	14.9	11.9	26.1
Haifa	3.9	8	16.6	15.8
Tel Aviv	1.1	2.9	13.7	21.5
Jerusalem	0.9	2	5.1	22.7

Source: M. Czudnowski and J. Landau, *The Israeli Communist Party* (Hoover Institute, Stanford, 1965), pp. 57, 62. For 1992: results published by the Labor party, July 28, 1992.

1965 elections, to ban its participation (see chapter 5). But, while the CPI-Maki was making headway among the Arab electorate, dissent within the party's leadership was growing, culminating in the split of 1965, which was widely perceived by the public as a split between Jews and Arabs. Yet in the 1965 elections to the Knesset, which took place only three months after the split, the Arab vote for the CPI-Rakah list did *not* shoot up, indicating the small effect of the ethnonationalist factor. This is hardly surprising. The CPI-Rakah presented to the Arab voter a list of candidates that looked similar to that of the former CPI-Maki: a Jew at the head of the list (Vilner), followed by the same Arab political figures (Toubi and Habibi). It is therefore no wonder that the CPI-Rakah held onto the Communist Party's Arab supporters but did not increase significantly its support. That came only four years later, in the 1969 elections.

The timing of actual breakthrough in the party's position among the Arab electorate came about only after the formal abolition of the Military Rule (December 1966) and after the 1967 war, and prior to the political ascent of the PLO, which came after the 1973 war. The abolition of the Military Rule removed the humiliating bureaucracy that controlled the Arabs' lives, and it seemed to imply that in the future Arabs would be judged individually on their actions. This gave a greater sense of political freedom, for it sharpened the distinction between political opposition and subversive deeds.

The direct and indirect results of the 1967 war strengthened this trend in the long run, despite the short-term difficulties that this new phase of the Israeli-Arab/Palestinian conflict—the occupation of the West Bank and Gaza by Israel—imposed on the Arab Palestinian citizens of Israel. The direct result of the war for the Arabs was that they were no longer physically isolated from the Arab world, particularly from the Palestinians on the West Bank and Gaza. But more significantly, the economic boom following the war enabled Arab citizens, now free from the Military Rule, to move more freely in the Israeli job market. As noted, during the following 10 years the Arab population was able to improve its poor standard of living and to increase its sense of economic security. For the following two decades, these developments worked to the CPI-Rakah's advantage, for openly identifying with the Communists no longer required a special measure of courage. In the longer run, however, the same factors also worked to undermine and halt the CPI's ascent: the increasing occupational differentiation in the Arab population and Arabs' greater familiarity with the political rules of the game weakened the emotional charismatic appeal of the party and created a reservoir of noncommitted Arab voters, who were ready to shift their vote from one election to another. The party's attempt to counteract those tendencies by institutionalizing its bases of support (see chapter 8) were only partially successful. The renewed cultural and religious ties with the Palestinians on the West Bank and Gaza also opened the way for challenges within the Arab population in Israel to the Communists' claim of political embodiment of the Arab population, on national Palestinian and Islamic religious grounds.

Immediately after the 1967 war, the Arabs in Israel were forced to reassess their situation vis-à-vis the Arab world. Pan-Arab nationalism, a source of hope for some that did not require any action on their part, suffered a severe blow in the humiliating victory of Israel over the Arab states. But the emerging alternative that spoke in their name—the PLO—was conducting a campaign of sabotage and terror within Israel, in the name of regaining the whole of Palestine for the entire Palestinian people. Few of those actions had the help of Arab citizens.[21] However, on the whole, Arab citizens felt caught in the middle: on the one hand, the authorities reacted with sanctions and administrative controls on all those having connections or expressing sympathy with the goals of the Palestinian movement, among them the leaders of the CPI-Rakah; on the other, the PLO, as the Arab countries had done, snubbed the Arabs in Israel, who were tainted with passivity and cooperation with the Zionist state. It was only after the 1973 war, especially after the Front's victory in Nazareth in 1975, that the PLO began to relate to the Arabs in Israel as having a role in the liberation struggle, being the "Palestinians Inside" (the homeland)(Shilo 1982, 79).

It stands to reason that the developments and events mentioned here influenced in particular the 20,000 young Arabs, mostly Muslim, who in 1969 were eligible to vote for the first time. The CPI's drawing power for the youngsters was both in its slogans (which promised that a vote for Rakah would make them feel "honorable and free people") and in its mode of operation, or its mobilizing style of activity (see chapter 4). Arab youth, still part of a socially conservative society, had almost no extracurricular activities; unlike their Jewish counterparts, who were members of youth movements and partisan sports organizations and who at the age of eighteen were drafted into the army, Arab youth had no such mobilizing collective activities. The party's youth movement and cultural activities appealed to this new generation and fulfilled needs of many among them.

The CPI's special appeal to the young included its antitraditional message. In the villages and among the working youth, the CPI argued that the party was their ally against "familism" and its exploitation by the authorities. At the same time, to soften its image as a party of Christians, the CPI stressed that the institutional religious interests of the Muslim community were also the concerns of the party (Landau 1969, 83). The positioning of a Muslim in the fifth place on the CPI-Rakah list for the Knesset in 1969 was similarly a demonstration to the young Muslim voters that the Communists were non-sectarian. The Muslim youth, who belonged to a generation that was far removed from religious practice, were probably less affected by the fierce verbal attacks on communism and its alleged contradiction to Islam, carried out by the Arab lists (Abu-Gosh 1972, 247).[22]

A measure of success of this strategy was the CPI-Rakah's success in capturing close to 30 percent of the vote in 1969 and 37 percent in 1973, making it for the first time the single largest party in the Arab sector (although the two Arab lists related to the Labor Party together won 41 percent of the Arab vote; see table 7.4). This result was attributed by observers, as well as by the party officials, to the addition of young voters who were not deterred by the warnings of the Labor Party against a vote for the Communists (Abu-Gosh 1972, 254). The party leaders' assessment after the 1969 elections was that the

Table 7.4. Distribution of vote in Arab localities, 1961–73 (percentages)

Year	Participation	CPI	Arab lists	Labor/Zionists	Mapam
1961	85	22.5	45	21	11.0
1965	88	23.1	41	24	9.0
1969	82	29.5	41	30	—[a]
1973	80	37.0	36	27	—

Note: The table excludes Arab voters in the "mixed" cities, who constitute about 8 percent of the eligible Arab voters.
a. Between 1969 and 1984 Mapam has run as part of the Labor Alignment.

CPI-Rakah's popularity among young voters went well beyond the existing organizational network and that they had to enlarge the party's organizational and cultural network in order to keep these new young voters and turn them into traditional supporters.[23] This was indeed attempted during the late 1970s.

The popularity of the CPI among the young generation in the late 1960s and early 1970s is not surprising in view of the intensification of the pattern of socioeconomic change noted in the early 1960s. The younger Arabs were better educated than the previous generation but only marginally more able to climb up the occupational ladder. Thus, although in this generation of young Arab voters there was a significantly higher percentage of youngsters with at least a partial high school education, still almost half went to work after completing only primary schooling.[24] In addition, as noted, the lack of job opportunities for those who completed high school sent many of them into manual labor.

Another indicator that this younger generation of the late 1960s and early 1970s were a new kind of hard-core supporters of the CPI-Rakah among the workers was the increase in the party's representation in the trade union organization, Histadrut. Arab membership, which began only in 1959, was growing particularly fast during the early 1960s.[25] In the 1969 Histadrut elections, held just prior to the Knesset elections, Rakah's share of the Arab vote jumped from 20 percent to 31 percent. The geographic pattern of support for Rakah in Histadrut proved similar to its support in the elections to the Knesset: high in the larger localities, low in the small villages, and high in the Galilee compared with the Triangle.

However, unlike the pattern that developed in the 1970s in the national parliamentary elections, the Labor Party remained a powerful force among both Jewish and Arab members in Histadrut before its defeat in 1994. After abolition of the Military Rule, the Labor Party's control of Histadrut became its chief instrument of patronage in the Arab sector. Only after its defeat in the Knesset elections of 1977 did the Labor Party begin to take a few steps to mitigate somewhat the effects of the asymmetrical relationship it maintained with the Arab membership (Shalev 1992, 55–57): to extend its medical and sports services, to initiate economic projects in Arab localities, and to place individuals in some high-ranking positions. Thus, it was able to contain the vote for the CPI and to keep it between a quarter and a third of the vote for Histadrut throughout the 1980s and mid-1990s.[26]

8

Instituting a Rival Political Establishment in the 1970s

After the 1970s the CPI implemented a new electoral strategy on both national and local levels. On the national level the Front alliance strategy involved organizing the intelligentsia and helping to increase the number of professionals, as well as mobilizing the local leadership. Success of this strategy in Nazareth in 1975 led to the mass mobilization of the Land Day in 1976 and to the position of a political establishment on the national scene. In the local power contests, the Front strategy consisted of forming nonideological, pragmatic alliances with local hamulas, which it had denounced in the past as government's stooges. This tactics helped to legitimize the Communists in the localities, but such local involvement also generated political opposition.

THE NEW ELECTORAL STRATEGY: THE FRONT ALLIANCES

Following the success of the CPI's strategy of embodying national identity, the party sought ways to enlarge and institutionalize its support among the Arab electorate by adding other bases of support. The need to do so became particularly acute in the mid-1970s, when the PLO's prestige as a symbol of Palestinian identity was rising among the Arab Palestinian citizens in Israel. Since the difficulties in recruitment of massive membership were not overcome (chapter 4), the CPI reinitiated the strategy of "alliance from above." The first stage in this strategy consisted of encouraging the formation of issue-oriented action groups, in which the mobilized sections of the Arab population could be active in directions agreeable to the party. Its goal was to turn the potential voters into an "opinion group" that would support the party on the basis of its ad hoc positions on various issues. The next step in this strategy foresaw the formation of organizational links between the party and as many social groups as possible, which would move the CPI into the leading role in the Arab community that it had long aspired to. The difficulty in implementing such a strategy was that it called both for persisting in the CPI's known oppositionist style and for making pragmatic compromises with groups it sought to draw into its orbit. This proved easier on the national political level than on the local level, where the political splits along hamula lines proved resilient and locally based leaders were not ready to give up their independence unconditionally.

The Front strategy on the national level was aimed also at building one alliance with the Jewish intellectuals who were critical of the official position toward the Palestinian national question and a second alliance "from below" with the Jewish working class; the hope was to create a political affiliation between the party and the most alienated section of the Jewish working class. Thus, in March 1977 the Democratic Front for Peace and Equality (Hadash) was set up, with the stated purpose of being "a permanent body of activity" and "not for electoral purposes alone."[1] It consisted of the CPI, the Jewish Black Panthers (activists in slum areas), the Israeli Socialist Left (Shasi), Arab mayors, and representatives of the Arab student association. However, after it proved a colossal electoral failure among the Jewish electorate in the 1977 and 1981 elections, it came under increasing criticism within the party (on the Front's platform, see chapter 3).[2]

The timing of the new strategy—the mid-1970s—was not accidental, for at this time the contradictions in the disjointed nature of the Arabs' incorporation into the system reached a certain peak. On the one hand, there was a significant increase in the sense of economic security among the Arab population and a significant rise in the level of education and political consciousness. On the other hand, the Arabs' special collective instrumental needs and their role as a national minority in the Jewish state were left undefined. Indeed, the decade 1970–80 is characterized by the increase in the number and scope of organizations set up by Arab citizens, whose common denominator was the emphasis on independent *Arab* action for furthering their special causes. The CPI was involved in a significant number of these organizations. In the mid-1970s the Front strategy was applied by the CPI-Rakah to the purely electoral sphere when the Democratic Front lists were set up on the local level as well. On the national level the Front served the strategy of forming both a rational link with the voters—votes in exchange for an accepted platform—and an organizational link, which would institutionalize the CPI as the party of the young upwardly mobilizing Arab youth. On the local level, the CPI attempted also to develop an alternative to the patron-client relationship of the Zionist parties but ended up offering a similar alternative: opportunities for political mobility in the village structure in return for mutual political support.

The focus of this strategy became the attempt to create a new basis for hard-core support among the emerging intelligentsia. In a tactic that exemplified the party's claim of commitment to the betterment of the Arab youth, it began to distribute scholarships for academic studies in Eastern Europe and the Soviet Union to high school graduates who were members of Banki. In this way, the CPI provided an incentive for Arab youth to join the party while creating alternative opportunities for social mobility. The electoral returns on this investment did go beyond the direct beneficiaries and their families. But in the long run, it suffered from the limit of all other trickle-down strategies—its benefits were directed only to those who completed high school.

Nevertheless, these efforts brought the CPI to the height of its electoral success in 1977 and placed the party for the first time in power on the local level (see table 8.1). However, opposition to its political style, particularly to its attempt to preserve a leading role in political partnerships, was rising. Its involvement in local hamula rivalries and its inefficiency in running local authorities cost heavily in the 1980s, bringing criticism of undemocratic and monopolizing practices and feelings of revenge by disaffected hamulas. It thus opened the way for groups of the middle-class and upwardly mobile groups to challenge the CPI's leading role and to organize support on a mass level.

Organizing the Intelligentsia

One of the characteristics of this stage of politicization among the Arab citizens was the proliferation of organizational activity by the emerging Arab intelligentsia. In 1971, the National Organization of Arab Academics and Students was formed to improve standards of the Arab high school; to encourage higher education among Arab youth, including girls; and to achieve social equality and defense of cultural and social rights of Arab citizens (Rekhess 1981, 188). The initiative for the organization was the CPI's, but it included non-Communists, former al Ard activists known for their nationalist views. The organization did not last long, but other, locally based associations of students and academicians were more successful. In 1973 a group of professionals in Nazareth formed the League of University Graduates in Nazareth. This prompted the formation of the Association of Merchants and Artisans as well as the Committee of University Students in Nazareth, which in turn formed the basis for the Nazareth Democratic Front in 1975.[3] Earlier, in 1974, the Committee of Arab High School Students, also based in the Nazareth area, was established, and a year later local committees of Arab students at the universities of Jerusalem and Haifa set up the National Association of Arab University Students (Rekhess 1981, 190).

The manner in which the CPI was involved in those initiatives demonstrates how CPI strategy interacted with the politicization process that was in progress. The initiator of the Committee of Arab High School Students, Azmi Bishara, then a high school student unattached to the party,[4] organized the committee for the purposes of (1) raising the low standard of teaching and equipment in Arab high schools, which resulted in a high level of failure in the matriculation exams, (2) changing the curriculum, which presented only the Zionist outlook and which emphasized Jewish and Hebrew culture, and (3) introducing Arab literature and culture into the school curriculum. According to Bishara, he was motivated by the patronizing and stereotyped references to Arabs in the school textbooks. After he began his organizing activity, the representatives of Banki, the CPI's youth organization, approached him with an offer of cooperation and help. He accepted their offer because through their organizational network he could reach many more schools than he could with his own resources. He himself joined Banki, and subsequently became a party member.[5]

Oppositionist tendencies and politicization in the 1970s affected also the socially most conservative and most accommodationist group among the Arab citizens, the Druze community. This Islamic sect retained its structure as a community led by hereditary religious sheikhs. It constituted 10 percent of the non-Jewish population, and Israeli authorities accorded it a separate religious legal status in the 1960s. At the request of the Druze religious leaders, after 1957 Druze men were conscripted into the army. In 1972, a small group of Druze formed the Druze Initiative Committee (DIC) for the purpose of abolishing mandatory conscription of Druze and expressing general opposition to the official distinction between the Druze and the rest of the Palestinian Arab citizens. The founders of the group were religious sheikhs who opposed the established Druze religious leadership. The other members were Druze activists of the CPI. The group began a campaign within the Druze community against the sect's leaders and its identification with the Zionist establishment (Teitelbaum 1985). In 1977 the DIC joined the national Democratic Front as a member body. Its activities, which received wide coverage in *al Ittihad*, probably enhanced the growth of the CPI vote in the Druze villages in the 1970s, although the vote remained significantly lower than in the other Arab localities.

The most significant outcome of the successful mobilization of the Arab intelligentsia was the setting up of the Democratic Front and the capture of Nazareth by the CPI in 1975. Nazareth is the largest Arab town in Israel and to a large extent the political trendsetter for the entire Arab sector. It had a high concentration of Greek Orthodox and other Christians, which together with the Muslim working-class neighborhood formed a hard-core support of about 40 percent for the CPI in the city council in the 1950s and 1960s (Landau 1969, 171–73). The CPI, however, was not able to win the position of mayor, which required a majority in the council. Attempts by the CPI to capture the mayor's seat through coalitions with other oppositionist lists were frustrated. All the other lists gathered around the pro-government candidate for mayor, Sayf al-Din Zu'bi. His nepotism and his totally inefficient running of the town became a symbol of the government's indifference to and neglect of the living conditions of the Arab population.

The opportunity for a breakthrough for the CPI in Nazareth arose in 1975, when a new law requiring direct election of the head of local government was implemented. The new system of elections favored the CPI, which unlike the accommodationist lists was not split between a number of sectarian lists. Furthermore, the CPI seized the opportunity presented to it by groups of disaffected citizens who organized themselves into action committees in the face of a near breakdown of Nazareth's municipal services. In December 1975 the Democratic Front of Nazareth was set up; it was composed of the CPI-Rakah branch in Nazareth, the Association of Nazareth Academicians, the association of Nazareth students known as Sons of Nazareth, and the Nazareth Chamber of Commerce.[6] The structure of the Democratic Front member bodies (council, executive committee, and secretariat) became a model for the Front's local branches set up later. The principle agreed upon was that decisions concerning the Front were to be unanimous. In Nazareth in 1975, all agreed that Toufiq Ziad would be the Front's candidate for mayor, and the position of deputy-mayor was reserved for the two non-Communist members of the Front. The CPI ran an intensive campaign, using its organizational network of clubs and activists in different neighborhoods, and the result was a stunning success: Ziad was elected by a 65 percent majority, and the Front won eleven of the seventeen seats in the city council. In March 1977, the Democratic Front of Nazareth was one of the member bodies of the national Democratic Front for Peace and Equality.

The Nazareth Front's first year in power was marked by euphoria. Following the mayor's complaint that the central authorities (which financed some 80 percent of the budget of Nazareth) was withholding funds "as a punishment" to the residents of Nazareth (for electing the front), Ziad issued a call for citizens to pay all their taxes at once. The drive was a tremendous success, and citizens stood in line to pay their municipal taxes.[7] The Front-led municipal government organized the first volunteer work camp, which also won enthusiastic response. The capture of Nazareth town hall also helped the CPI mobilize the rural sector.

Sponsoring Arab Professionals

The other important element in the CPI-Rakah's electoral strategy initiated during this period was the scholarships that it awarded for university training in the Eastern bloc countries. Although "Rakah academicians" now account for only a small percentage of the total number of Arab academicians in Israel as a whole, the impact of these scholarships on the Arab sector has been noticeable. Most of those who won the awards studied medicine and dentistry and thus became known as the "Rakah doctors." Besides gaining an avenue of professional and social mobility, many beneficiaries of the awards set up clinics in Arab localities and thus helped to improve access to medical services. In the years 1967–71, 73 Arab students went abroad under scholarships (an average of 15 per year); in 1972–76, the total sent abroad was 144 (an average of 29 per year), constituting some 20 percent of those who passed the matriculation exams;[8] during 1977–81 the total was 297 (an average of 60 per year). By 1986 about 420 Arab academicians, as well as some 25 Jewish scholarship winners, had graduated from universities in the Communist bloc, and 385 students were studying abroad.[9]

The scholarships provided by the CPI (or, more accurately, by the host Communist government) were attractive simply for economic reasons. Besides tuition and travel, students received a handsome monthly allowance and a bonus allowance for excellence, giving them a high standard of living relative to native students in their host countries.[10] It is no wonder, therefore, that the CPI spared no effort to make sure that this investment did not go to waste. Besides the professional curriculum, the students abroad received ideological education in Marxism-Leninism and were under close watch by the local CPI representative. They continued their party activities as members of local chapters in their places of study. A general conference of representatives of the local chapters was held every two years in one of the Easterm European countries, with the participation of a member of the CPI-Rakah politburo.

Before each general election, the students flew back to Israel, in what the Arab localities called the "election plane," to help the party's campaign. They concentrated on the young voters and reminded their families, if they needed any such reminder, to show their appreciation by voting for the CPI. On the whole, the majority of the students remained loyal to the party after their return to Israel even if they became disenchanted with the Communist system. The overall impact of the CPI's scholarship program on Arab youngsters was unmistakable: an alternative avenue of social mobility for the growing number of students about to finish high school in the 1970s and early 1980s who would have had difficulty in getting into university or in financing such studies themselves.

MOBILIZATION OF RURAL LEADERS AND MASS ACTION

The CPI successfully used another sign of politicization in the Arab sector in the 1970s. One of the two most important organizations formed then was the

Committee of Heads of Arab Municipalities (CHAM), set up in February 1974 to bring about the equal treatment of local Arab authorities by government bodies. The initiative came fron Shmuel Toledano, the prime minister's Jewish adviser on Arab affairs, but, once organized, the committee took on an independent course of action. Setting up the committee was part of Toledano's advocacy of a new policy toward the Arab minority and his attempt to create a new basis of support for the Zionist establishment instead of the traditional leadership (Rekhess 1977, 17). But the Labor government's plan to expropriate land, from Arabs, for development in the Galilee, which became known at the end of 1974, led eventually to the tragic events of the Land Day of March 1976 (see following section).

In the following years, CHAM moved considerably closer to CPI tactical and political positions. For a short while, the CPI even seemed to be successful in co-opting the new organization into its orbit. Toward the 1977 elections, the chairman of CHAM, Hana Mois, who had not previously been close to the Communists, was placed high on the list of the newly founded Democratic Front for Peace and Equality. But his successor, Nimr Hussein, did not follow Mois into the Front and instead established a middle-of-the-road stance, emphasizing CHAM's independent role as a municipal and political pressure group, often in cooperation with the Front's representatives in the committee, but not as a follower.[11]

The body that initiated the Land Day strike of 1976 was the National Committee for the Defense of Arab Lands, set up by the CPI in October 1975 but as a nonpartisan body.[12] By February 1976, even accommodationist Arab politicians had joined the committee's militant line against the government's expropriation plan, though such Arab figures tried at the last moment to avert the call for a general strike. By then it was too late: the CPI, which was driving at radical mass action, had set up local chapters of the Committee for the Defense of Arab Lands. The call for a strike to protest the government's unilateral action with regard to Arab land and its disregard for their vital interests no doubt mobilized the entire Arab population despite their political differences.

Since 1976, March 30 is commemorated every year as Land Day, and in many ways it has replaced the First of May rally as the CPI's central mobilizing event among the Arab citizens. But the emergence of new rivals to the CPI on the political scene in the late 1970s and 1980s made the organization of Land Day events a focus of the underlying competition between rival political forces. While the CPI had a decisive say in the forum that planned the events—the Committee for the Defense of the Arab Lands—it required the cooperation of CHAM and the Organization of Heads of Arab Municipal Councils, of which CHAM is the executive body. In the aftermath of the first Land Day and the municipal elections of 1978, the CPI indeed increased its representation in the municipal councils organization and CHAM by forming local Fronts and including more heads of municipal councils in its orbit (see below).

Relying on this institutional base, the CPI was able to put into effect its tactics concerning mass action. For example, in the Land Days of 1977–81, mass protests were toned down, a tactic supported by the moderates in CHAM, probably in order not to endanger the party's legal status. At the same time, to combat the call for massive protests by radical nationalist groups, CPI speakers at the rallies, memorial services, and marches exalted the Land Day as a *national Palestinian* event, while warning against "the 'revolutionary' slogans which have nothing to do with real nationalism."[13] In addition, the CPI made every effort to include sympathetic Jewish public figures and even Zionists in the rallies.[14] Even news of the attempt on the lives of the Arab mayors on the West Bank in June 1980, which caused an uproar in the Arab population, did not move the CPI to a call for a massive strike.[15] Instead, it took another step toward institutionalizing the mass mobilization of the Arab public, playing the leading role in attempts to organize a "Congress of Arab Masses."[16] But authorities viewed the congress as a dangerous move and banned it on security grounds.

The independent stance of CHAM, on the one hand, and radical nationalists' pressure to identify more closely with the Palestinians in the occupied territories, on the other, made it hard for the CPI to maintain its leading role in the "street." The reaction to the Israeli-initiated war against the PLO in Lebanon in June 1982 created some agitation among Arab citizens, but the Arab public was not stirred into mass action, and the demonstration organized in Nazareth by the CPI's Committee Against the War in Lebanon had only a moderate success. Then in September 1982 came news of the massacres in the refugee camps of Sabra and Shatila, where many of the Arab citizens in the Galilee had relatives. Spontaneous demonstrations and violent acts broke out, lasting for three days.[17] All the political bodies of the Arab population again united in a call for a general strike. The CPI, under pressure because of the lack of action on the part of the Soviet Union in defense of the Palestinians, organized a mass demonstration in Nazareth, and it got out of hand.[18]

A year later a new source of conflict with the state on the land issue emerged: the government's inclusion of areas demanded by Arab municipalities within a new "Jewish" municipal region (Misgav) in the Galilee. The National Committee for the Defense of Arab Lands, charging that this was simply a novel way of dispossessing the Arabs, planned protest activities.[19] All the Arab members of Knesset, including those of the two Zionist-Labor parties, were invited to join the struggle in the Knesset, and the Supreme Follow Up Committee was thus established as a high-level, comprehensive forum for discussion of

Arab concerns. The matter was eventually settled without mass protests, helped by the agreement of the Ministry of the Interior to consider Arab demands.[20]

Thus, by the mid-1980s the CPI was no longer the sole initiator and organizer of mass action, though none of its competitors had acquired the same ability to mobilize the Arab "street." But the 1976 Land Day was a political landmark because of the impetus it gave to the establishment of the Democratic Front for Peace and Equality on the national level. Despite the criticism of the CPI's tactics, the protest reflected an emotional consensus on the land issue that cut across party affiliation. The leak of the Kening Memo, which contained an analysis of the events, and proposals of a senior official of the Interior Ministry for underhanded methods against the Arabs strengthened the sense of unity among the Arabs.[21] When unscheduled elections were called for May 17, 1977, the option arose of an independent Arab party, based on the locally elected leaders organized in the Organization of Heads of Arab Municipal Councils. Eventually these efforts were preempted by the CPI and by the Labor party, which both promised to include local leaders in their lists. The CPI offered the Democratic Front as a framework for the inclusion of non-Communists in its representation in the Knesset, modeled after the Nazareth chapter of the Democratic Front. The significance of setting up the Front was the readiness of many of the local leaders to cooperate openly with the CPI, thus acknowledging it as a rival political establishment.

First by winning over many of the accommodationist leaders and then out-maneuvering its radical nationalist challengers (see chapter 9) when it won the implied blessing of the PLO (Shaibi 1976), the Front achieved impressive success in the 1977 elections (table 8.1). Among the Arab electorate, the Front won 50.6 percent of the vote, compared with 39 percent for the CPI in the 1973 elections. Among the Jewish electorate, however, the Front's strategy was a complete failure, leading to the disintegration of its Jewish components, although the party leadership insisted on keeping the Black Panther member, Charlie Biton, in a safe seat on the Front's list for the three next national campaigns. At the same time, the fact that the Front in the 1980s was not able to reproduce its 1977 results indicates that the rate of its success in 1977 was due to the presence of an issue-oriented group of middle-class voters, about 15 percent strong, who were ready to switch their vote from one election to another. Their votes were available to a wide spectrum, from the Communist-led Front to the Zionist Labor party to the small Zionist parties of the center. Unlike the traditional CPI voters, who accepted the party's overriding concern with the solution of the national conflict, these voters had in common the desire to increase their efficacy in making their votes count in terms of their immediate concerns. Al Haj and Yaniv indeed labeled this trend *particularist* (1983, 159). Following the failure of the particularists to organize an indepen-

Table 8.1. Distribution of vote in Arab localities, 1977–81 (percentages)

Year	Participation	CPI-Front	Arab lists	Labor/Zionists	Mapam
1977	75	50.6	21	28	—
1981	69	37.8	16[a]	46	—

Note: The table excludes Arab voters in the "mixed" cities, who constitute about 8 percent of the eligible Arab voters.
a. In 1981 all the Arab lists ran as independent lists.

dent party in 1977, the Front seemed to be the best vehicle for expressing such concerns. In the mid- and late 1980s, other alternatives became available. But there was also an indirect long-term effect from the 1976 events, namely that in the 1978 local elections, the CPI was able to introduce its Front organization on a wide scale at the local level. It thus gained the potential of a steady organizational framework for its supporters. As the next section shows, the results of those efforts were mixed from the CPI's point of view.

The Turn to Pragmatism: The CPI and Local Elections in Arab Localities

The overriding factor in the electoral politics of Arab localities was the division of the locality into kinship groups (hamulas) and religious sects, which were intense rivals. The lack of emigration of the Arab population from their localities preserved this format of local divisions, to the disadvantage of the CPI compared to the Zionist parties. In the 1970s, it became clear that the weakening of the hamula elders' hold on the votes cast in the national elections did not apply at the local level and that the hamula lists were not about to disappear as the dominant form of political contest in the Arab local elections. Rather than disintegrating, the hamula lists changed. The traditional leadership was replaced by younger, better-educated members of the hamula, and hamula identification became a political resource at the disposal of those who aspired to positions of power (Nakhleh 1973). In the 1990s, a few hamulas in a number of the larger localities even held primaries to select the hamula candidate (Ghanem and Ozacky-Lazar 1994, 14).

The CPI realized that if it ignored this reality and continued to denounce "reactionary familism," the new political leaders either would be forged into a potentially rival political party or be co-opted on a new basis by the Zionist parties.[22] Up to the mid-1970s, the policy was to run a local CPI list and if possible enter into a coalition with what it called "independent factors" (i.e., hamulas not identified with Mapai). This policy yielded participation in a small number of coalitions in Arab local councils.

In the early 1970s, the CPI central committee decided to intensify the party's organizational efforts on the municipal level by establishing a municipal department in the party apparatus.[23] The basic idea was to develop organizational ties with the young supporters of the CPI, particularly the educated youth who voted for the party in the national elections but for their hamula representative in the local elections. To repeat the pattern of the Nazareth success among the villages, including the large localities, alliances had to be made with representatives of the local power brokers—the hamulas—most of whom the CPI had denounced in the past.

The CPI's decision to turn to nonideological political alliances, although a necessary condition, was not sufficient to form such alliances on a wide scale. First the CPI had to break the taboo, still widespread, on open cooperation with it on the local level. Although cooperation between the CPI and hamula lists existed in a few villages in the mid-1960s, the entry into more formal alliances on a wide scale came only after the 1976 Land Day. That open challenge to the authorities, led by the CPI, swept away the last psychological remnants of the Military Rule and marked a new era in the relationship of the Arabs to the state authorities. In its new format as the Democratic Front, both nationally and in Nazareth, and as a highly popular organization with the *shabab* (youngsters), the CPI became a legitimate political partner. Open alliance with the Communists, previously unknown, became a legitimate means at the disposal of local political power brokers, either to challenge the political status quo in the locality or to defend it from new challengers.

The first and most obvious political result of the Front's strategy was the increase in the presence of the CPI in local elections. During the years 1978–80, for instance, the CPI itself ran candidates in twelve local contests, and it ran as part of a local Democratic Front list in thirty-two other localities. In other words, through the local Fronts it was able to double its participation, from 40 percent of the contests in the Arab localities in 1973 to 80 percent in 1978. In the 1988 and 1993 local elections, a majority (65 percent) of the local council members in the Arab localities were still elected on hamula lists. But of the party-identified councilors, 43 percent were Front members, making it the single largest *national* political body with representation at the local level (Ghanem and Ozacky-Lazar 1994, 20). In 1993, twelve of fifty-one elected chairmen of local governments were Front members. Thus, through the Front, the CPI became a party in power in several localities, thereby gaining access to resources that could be used to increase its influence.[24] But being in power meant that it also shared the responsibilities for failures and was exposed to setbacks because of poor management.[25]

The second gain for the CPI, and perhaps more significant, was ideological: acquiring legitimacy after years of exclusion from power. As noted in chapter

3, the Front was a political framework, in which non-Communist members agreed to its minimum program. The program constituted the gist of the CPI's integrative ethnonationalist position: its insistence on a solution to the Palestinian national problem and its demands for equal social and cultural rights for the Arab minority in Israel. In the mid-1970s, when the consensus of the Jewish majority was solidly behind the government's total denial of the legitimation of the PLO, the agreement by many former accommodationist local leaders to sign such an agreement reflected the CPI's success in changing the political discourse in the Arab community.

The CPI's hope, however, was that the ideological gain would be accompanied by an electoral gain on the national level. It hoped that if it wooed a large hamula, or a coalition of small families, by helping its candidates win local elections as Front representatives, the CPI would be rewarded by hamula members' votes for the Front in the national elections. In this manner, which resembled the old Mapai tactics, the CPI attempted to expand its organizational backing beyond its traditional bases of support—the Christians—and the newly acquired support of young Muslims. The party officially denied that its considerations were electoral and argued that the major purpose as well as the impact of this massive presence on the local level was programmatic. The turnaround of long-time rivals into allies was similarly explained as the adoption of "correct" attitudes.[26]

Nevertheless, a close look at the political mechanisms of the local Fronts shows the role of pragmatic, some would say opportunistic, electoral considerations. In the 1977 national elections, many of the votes in support of the Democratic Front on the national level were a result of the Land Day events and thus were votes based on an issue. In the 1980s and 1990s, a new organizational basis was added to the CPI vote: political deals between the individual hamula lists and the CPI. A detailed analysis I made of the pattern of hamula votes in four localities (Taibe, Tira, Arabe, and Tamra) in the national elections in the 1980s revealed those deals clearly. However, from the point of view of the local power brokers, the breaking of the taboo on cooperation with the Communists had the effect of normalizing the pros and cons of such cooperation, which could at that point be weighed rationally.

Indeed, "paying" for the CPI's support on the local level by mobilizing support for it in the national elections became easier following the defeat of the Labor Party in the 1977 national elections. On the one hand, the incentives for refraining from alliance with the CPI were reduced, since Labor could no longer threaten retribution or promise government aid. On the other hand, the new ruling party, the Likud, showed a lack of interest in the Arabs and until the late 1980s did not step in to fill the political vacuum.[27] In addition, alignment with the Front in the 1970s became attractive for local leaders aspiring to national prominence when the party decided to reserve the fifth seat on its Knesset list for a non-Communist chairman of an Arab local council. This decision opened a channel for individual political mobility.[28]

However, analysis of the hamula vote in the Arab localities also shows that the CPI's local alliances with the hamula-based lists were not a net electoral success. The wheeling and dealing on the local level necessarily involved the party in hamula politics and made it a target for political revenge. Besides the loss of votes, the ideological image of the party was tainted and its stance against familism lost credibility. Other political aspects of the CPI's local involvement, however, offset the electoral loss: the legitimacy of cooperating with the party and, perhaps most important, the prominence gained in the Organization of Heads of Arab Municipalities and in CHAM, its executive body. For a decade following the establishment of the local Fronts in 1978, about half of the local councils were headed by chairmen identified with the Front, giving the CPI the ability to set the tone in the deliberations and decisions of CHAM.[29] Thus CHAM, which started out in 1974 as an apolitical body concerned with municipal services, adopted in the late 1970s and early 1980s the political line of the Front concerning the Palestinian problem and was influenced by the Front's political style.

The decade of CPI hegemony came to an end in the late 1980s, after it was not particularly successful in running localities and at a time when the Islamic movement had impressed many with its agility and dedication (see chapter 9). All in all, since the local government is the only autonomous organizational body of the Arab population, having a political foothold in the localities was vital for the CPI, despite the price of political opposition.

9

The CPI's New Challengers and Countertendencies in Electoral Support in the 1980s and 1990s

In recruiting the politicized younger generation in the 1970s and 1980s, the CPI encountered competition from groups that challenged its integrative ethnonationalist position. Under the influence of the PLO's activity on the geopolitical scene and the reemergence of Islam as a political force in the region, groups emerged that challenged either the CPI's secular style or its claim of embodying the ethnonationalist Arab Palestinian stand. A long-time rival, the Zionist Labor Party, which after 1977 was in opposition to the governing Likud party, posed a third challenge by addressing its appeal to the floating Arab vote. All three challenges, coupled with the CPI's inflexible organizational style, ended the party's hegemony before the collapse of communism in Europe in the late 1980s. But the party itself did not collapse. In 1992 it became part of the blocking majority of the Labor-led coalition and, indirectly, a participant in the historic process of untangling the national question. In 1996 it even increased its electoral support significantly.

Palestinian Nationalist and Ethnonationalist Challenges

As noted in chapter 3, the CPI's acknowledgment of the PLO as a legitimate movement was gradual and cautious, and it became definite only in 1974. In 1971 a small group of professionals in Um al Fahem organized themselves as Abna al Balad (Sons of the Land) in opposition to the local CPI list, reviving the Palestinian separatist ideas of al Ard. In 1973 they won a seat in the Um al Fahem local elections on the platform of complete political identification with the PLO and disassociation from the Zionist institutions of the state, mainly by abstaining from voting in the national elections.[1] By 1978 similar local groups, some of them named al Nahda (the Awakening), had been established in other villages in the Triangle and the Galilee, with some success on the local scene. In the mid-1970s, their ideas found support among Arab students, particularly on the Jerusalem campus of Hebrew University. The Arab student association, active there since 1964, had a tradition of amorphous nationalist tendencies (Nakhleh 1979, 74–77). In the mid-1970s this trend crystalized into an irredentist Palestinian position.

Thus in 1976 a group of Arab students, which later called itself the National Progressive Movement, challenged the CPI's record of support for the existence of the State of Israel.[2] In 1977 the group won the elections on the Jerusalem campus on a radical Palestinian "rejectionist" political platform (Rekhess 1981, 192). In the period that followed, the political struggle between pro-Front and pro-Progressive students spread to the Tel Aviv, Haifa, and Beer Sheba campuses, with losses and gains for both sides. On the whole, however, with the exception of the Jerusalem campus, the Democratic Front managed by 1981 to win the political battle among the Arab students.

This was the context of the effort to convene the Congress of the Arab Masses in December 1980, as noted. The effort involved a mass signature drive on a covenant, known as the Sixth of June Document, as part of a strategy to create a front of moderates and nationalists, with the CPI in the leading role of the Arab population in Israel. This covenant repeated the position that the PLO was "the representative of the Palestinian people" and that the Arabs in Israel "are the citizens of the state of Israel, and part of the Arab Palestinian People."[3] However, four days before the planned convention, the assembly of the Congress of Arab Masses was banned by the authorities under a military order, on the grounds that it might be the basis for a separatist institution.

The challenge to the CPI received an impetus when the CPI experienced failures as the party in power in Nazareth. The high expectation it had created of a revolutionary change in the running of the town did not materialize. Complaints began to be voiced that the mayor and Knesset member, Toufiq Ziad, was inept and was exercising nepotism and favoritism of his own.[4] The Association of Nazareth Academicians within the Nazareth Front split into two groups, one supporting Ziad and the other demanding that he be replaced with a non-Communist Front member as a candidate in the 1978 elections. Those who supported the renewal of Ziad's candidacy hailed his service to the city in the Knesset Committee for Internal Affairs, as well as his service in CHAM.[5] The attempt to unseat him failed, and the Front proved to be popular still. In the 1978 elections, Ziad won as mayor by a 62 percent majority, and the Front list won ten of the seventeen seats in the city council.[6]

During Ziad's second term, however, the relationship between the partners in the Nazareth Front deteriorated even further, leading to a final break in December 1981 and the establishment of the Progressive Movement of Nazareth. The anatomy of the split is instructive. It reveals the inflexibility of the CPI's organizational culture and the party's overconfidence in its hegemony. The first conflict concerned the establishment of an Arab university. The initiators of the project, some of whom were known for their radical nationalist views, organized the Association for the Development of Culture and Education, which managed to raise funds abroad for the university project. At the beginning of 1980 the CPI was invited to join the association. But a few months later, the party left. According to the CPI's opponents, the Communists had demanded that the project would be under the direction of the Nazareth municipality and that 51 percent of the board of directors of the bodies dealing with the project would be CPI people.[7]

In November 1980 the internal disagreement between leading members of the Association of Nazareth Academicians and the CPI came into the open. The association suggested that the non-Communist members of the Front organize themselves as a united body. The association claimed that in the existing structure of the Front, the parity between the bodies was fictitious and that consequently the academicians were outplayed by the CPI on every issue.[8] The academicians complained further that as members of the national Democratic Front they had not been consulted on the decision to place the Black Panther representative, Charlie Biton, in third place on the Front's list for the Knesset in 1977, and that the CPI had manipulated the confirmation of the decision. On top of that, the candidacy of Biton had proved to be a mistake because the progressive Jewish forces, who supported the Palestinian cause, were not ready to cooperate and vote for the Front. The academicians suggested, therefore, that an Arab, non-Communist body be established and given bargaining power within the Front. These suggestions were flatly rejected by the CPI leadership as coming from "petit bourgeois and sons of the privileged, who look down on the masses, and call them rubble."[9]

In December 1981, therefore, the discontented group left the Association of Nazareth Academicians and established the Progressive Movement of Nazareth. The former partners of the Front were then joined by the remnants of the radical nationalist al Ard group of the late 1950s. Their common political ground, in terms of the pragmatic and ideological elements of the Progressive Movement, was the primacy of the national Palestinian identity and the charge that the Communists put other concerns before the Palestinians' interest.[10] The alternative to the CPI's advocacy of class unity of Arabs and Jews was binationalism. The Progressive Movement's specific binationalist goals were defined as working for "complete equality in the national and municipal rights" of Arabs and Jews but also as seeking "cooperation with Jewish and Arab democratic elements" for achievement of these goals.[11] The list of the professions of the some 120 founding members of the Progressive Movement in Nazareth indeed gives weight to the claim made by the CPI that they were members of the old, well-to-do middle class in Nazareth, along with upwardly mobile professionals. Forty percent were merchants and businessmen, 30 percent lawyers, engineers, and accountants, 13 percent doctors and pharmacists, and only 5 percent listed as workers (including a woman "fortune-teller"). But this class element did not bother the CPI when it applied to membership of the Front, lending credence to the argument that it was political opposition and pluralism that the CPI found difficult to accommodate.

In the 1983 municipal elections, the Progressive Movement of Nazareth ran its own list against the Front and won 20 percent of the vote and four seats in the city council. It was therefore unable to unseat the CPI-led Front in Nazareth. But the 1983 split in the Nazareth Front had national repercussions. The emergence of the Progressive Movement in Nazareth signaled the end of the CPI's exclusive hold on the emerging intelligentsia, who would not accept the CPI's domineering style and self-appointed leading role. Another result was the presence in the 1984 national elections of the Progressive List for Peace (PLP), which was to become the CPI's major political rival on the national scene between 1984 and 1988.

The 1984 national elections were therefore marked by the success of the CPI's various nationalist rivals in organizing at the last moment a list of candidates for the Knesset, the Progressive List for Peace, which won 18 percent of the Arab vote. It was the major beneficiary of the strength of the Arabs' Palestinian identity as a result of the Israeli-PLO clash in Lebanon in 1982. The PLP was a joint list of the Arab Progressive Movement for Peace and the Jewish Alternative group, running on a single-issue ticket: self-determination for the Palestinians in the occupied territories. For the "Palestinians Inside [Israel]"—as the PLP emphatically called the Arab Palestinian citizens of Israel—the demand was national equality with the Jews, or binationalism. The ideological core group of the Progressive Movement for Peace was the Nazareth Progressive Movement, as well as some of the radical nationalist groups in the Galilee and the Triangle (Rouhana 1986, 129–33). However, it was joined also by various activists who opposed the Front. Having the same programmatic component, the PLP challenged the style and slogan elements of the Front's image (see chapter 5). Whereas the Front again ran non-Zionist Jews in first and third place on the list of candidates for the Knesset, the PLP placed a Muslim Arab (Muhamed Mi'ari) at the head of the list and a Zionist Jew (Mati Peled) second. As noted in chapter 3, the PLP also announced its unreserved support of the leadership of the PLO, regardless of the latter's attitude toward the USSR and the Arab regimes.

The appearance of the PLP in the electoral arena probably accounts for the increase in Arab voters' participation in the elections of 1984, from 69 percent

Table 9.1. Distribution of vote in Arab localities, 1984–92 (percentages)

Year	Participation	CPI-Front	PLP	ADP	Labor+Zionists	Mapam
1984	72	33.0	18	—	49	—
1988	71	33.6	14	11	39[a]	3.7
1992	68	23.2	9[b]	15.2	42.6	10[c]
1996	77	36.8	—	25.5[d]	22.8	10

Note: The table excludes Arab voters in the "mixed" cities, who constitute about 8 percent of eligible Arab voters.
a. Labor and other Zionist parties, excluding Mapam.
b. Under the minimum 1.5 percent of the total vote.
c. In 1992 Mapam merged with Ratz to form Meretz.
d. ADP + Islamic Movement = United Arab List.

to 72 percent, and for the overall drop in votes for the Democratic Front, from half of the total in 1977 to one-third in 1984 (see table 9.1). It is instructive, however, that the big losses of the Front and the big gains of the PLP occurred in the Triangle localities where the Front had failed to build strong party organizational links with the electorate. The PLP, through the representatives from the Triangle on its central bodies, was able to collect protest votes against the "Christian-Galilee" image of the Front in the Triangle.

The traditional rival of the CPI, the Zionist Labor Party, then out of the government, reorganized its activities among the Arab electorate in the early 1980s, in view of the changed political map. For the 1981 Knesset elections, it placed two Arab candidates on its list, as did other Zionist parties, and for the first time it did not support an allied Arab list. The Labor Party's strategy was to call on the Arab voters to help it unseat the Likud party from power by voting directly for Labor. The impact of this strategy was particularly strong on the floating Arab vote, since for the first time the Arabs were addressed as an important factor in the rivalry between the two major Jewish blocs. Together, the Zionist parties drew the support of 46 percent in the Arab localities. A close look at several large localities, such as Nazareth, Baqa al Gharbiyye, Taibe, Tira and Tamra (where 25 percent of the total Arab votes were cast) suggests that Labor was successful in drawing voters who in 1977 voted for the Front.

These voters' response to the Labor Party was described as coming from a new particularist attitude toward the political process, which advocated "active participation of the Arab sector in the Israeli political process with a view to maximizing the gains, in terms of the allocation of state resources, for the Arab minority in Israel as a whole, rather than for a handful of privileged individuals and groups" (Al Haj and Yaniv 1983, 149). The stability of the vote for the Labor Party based on this pragmatic attitude depended on the party's willingness to work for implementation of this attitude. The placing of only one Muslim candidate on the list of possible seats, and that one a low-level seat, was not an encouraging sign for the particularists. Nevertheless, the structural change in the Israeli political map in the 1980s to a two-block rival coalition system placed the Arab vote for the first time in a position to decide whether a Labor coalition would come to power.

The Front was therefore faced with a challenge, a dilemma that lasted into the 1990s: if indeed Labor became dependent on Arab voters for getting back into power, the party could increase the chances of promoting Arab collective interests and Arab consensus on the Palestinian issue. The party's own oppositionist stance, however, would not make it a coalitional partner of Labor, and Labor would seek to increase the direct Arab vote to itself. The two parties therefore continued their battle over the Arab vote. In a highly charged political campaign in Histadrut in 1981, each of the parties held to its overall share of the vote: the Front close to 30 percent and the Labor Party 51 percent.[12]

In the mid-1980s the stratification of Arab Palestinian social structure thus had an important impact on the electoral bases of the CPI-Front. Social indicators collected for the forty-four largest Arab localities[13] demonstrate the formation of a politically significant stratum of better-educated, higher-paid, white collar professionals. This trend can be gathered from the correlations between the indicators of education (low, medium, high, median years of schooling of women), of occupation (white collar workers, employees in public services), and income (monthly income per person for an employed family head in the locality) (see table 9.2). The oppositionist trend of Arab opinion started to split in this period between the traditional multiclass supporters of the CPI and the

Table 9.2. Pearson correlation between socioeconomic indicators in Arab localities (N = 44)

Indicators	7	6	5	4	3	2	1
1 Ed. 0–4-.51**	-.41*	-.40*	+	+	+	+	+
2 Ed. 9–12	.35*	.44*	.48**	+	+	+	+
3 Med. wom.	.40*	.52**	.47**	+	+	+	+
4 Academic	.43*	.56**	.66**	+	+	+	+
5 White	.61**	.88**	+	+	+	+	+
6 Pub. service	.59**	+	+	+	+	+	+
7 Income+	+	+	+	+	+	+	+

*Significance = 0.1
** = 0.001

Table 9.3. Pearson correlation of vote for CPI, PLP, Labor, and social indicators (N = 44)

Indicators (a)	Vote for Front 1984	Vote for PLP 1984	Labor vote 1984
1 Ed. 0–4	-.26	-.07+	.31
2 Ed. 9–12	.08	.27	-.42*
3 Med. wom. (b)	.33**	.12	-.40*
4 Academic	.24*	.09++	-.36*
5 White (c)	.07	.49***	-.53**
6 Pub. service	.05	.35**	-.48*

+ The correlation of 5–8 years of schooling with PLP vote is -.46***
++ The correlation of 13+ years of schooling with PLP vote is .39**
Significance = *0.05, **0.01, *** 0.001

Front, on the one hand, and a section of the Muslim and Christian new middle class and intelligentsia, on the other.

The impatience of the newly educated stratum with the Front, as well as the PLP's ability to draw some of them away from the Front, was tested quantitatively on ecological data.[14] Social indicators of the level of education and occupation were correlated with election results for the Front, PLP, and Labor in the forty-four largest Arab localities (table 9.3).

The table shows that the electoral leanings of this stratum in the mid-1980s was clearly against the Labor Party. The higher the social indicators of the population in the locality, the lower the support for Labor. As for positive leanings, the correlations give a somewhat less conclusive picture, probably owing to the split among the Front, the Progressive List for Peace, and other small Zionist parties that recruited Arab candidates high on their lists—hence the lower number of significant correlations with the vote for the Front and the PLP. Nevertheless, the relatively higher success of the Progressive List for Peace in localities with high social status indicators shows that the Front failed to create bonds of loyalty between itself and many members of this stratum, which it mobilized in the 1970s. But neither did the PLP succeed. Its use of the ethnonationalist attribute boomeranged in the 1988 elections, when the new, exclusively Muslim-Arab list, the Arab Democratic Party led by Abd al Wahab Darawshe, also turned the Arab attribute into a political resource and won votes at the PLP's expense. Thus started the process that eventually led to the PLP's demise when it failed to gather the minimum 1.5 percent of the total vote in 1992.

The 1988 general elections were held under the shadow of the Intifada, which broke out on the West Bank and Gaza in December 1987 (see chapters 2 and 5). Six months prior to the outbreak, the informal leadership forum of the Arabs in Israel—the Supreme Follow Up Committee—in which the Front had a dominant voice decided to hold a general strike to mark two days of protest: Equality Day and Peace Day. The purpose was to call the Jewish public's attention to the Arabs' unwillingness to tolerate their inferior status. Equality Day, held before the beginning of the Intifada in December 1987, was a peaceful protest. The planned Peace Day strike was called two weeks after the beginning of the Intifada. As happened during the first Land Day in 1976, the organizers in a number of places lost control over Arab youngsters, who violently expressed their support for the uprising and their sense of pride in and admiration for Palestinians' fearlessness. It therefore seemed in the late 1980s that the line between ethnonationalism and integrative oppositionist ethnonationalism was wearing thin under the pressure of both geopolitical conflict and the subordination of the Arab population.

As expected, the Intifada was the overriding issue in the 1988 campaign, both for Jews and for Arabs. But to the disappointment of the CPI and PLP, its major effect on the Arab electorate was to strengthen the new integrative particularist trend in the form of support for the new Arab Democratic Party (ADP) (see table 9.1), rather than enhancing the ethnonationalist trend. Thus the Front did not increase its one-third share of the Arab vote (33.4 percent), and it maintained its traditional bases of support in the larger localities and those with Christian population. The PLP, despite its emphatic identification with the PLO, lost 3 percent, ending up with 14 percent of the vote. The vote for the Labor Party dropped by 7 percent, to 19 percent of the total, probably due to the unpopularity of Labor Defense Minister Yitzhak Rabin and his handling of the Intifada. The big winner in those elections was the newcomer Arab Democratic Party with 11 percent of the vote. The list headed by Darawshe was made up of Arabs only, but like the Front and the PLP, it called for an independent Palestinian state in its platform, and its slogans denounced sharply the handling of the Intifada by the Israeli government. However, unlike the Front or the PLP, it went further in its integrative message by announcing its goal of becoming part of a coalition government headed by the Labor Party. The two small Zionist parties, Ratz (civil rights movement) and Mapam (Zionist-socialist), which each had an ideological appeal and ran with Arab candidates, won 8 percent of the vote.

Ironically, the similarity in their programmatic components intensified the rivalry between the Front and its competitors and led to an overall loss of two seats in the Knesset and the loss of opportunity to block the Likud coalition from power. This outcome was a result of the CPI-Front's refusal to sign a preelection agreement with the PLP for the distribution of extra votes and the

PLP's refusal to do same with the Arab Democratic Party.[15] The three rivals did cooperate willy-nilly a year later in the elections to Histadrut, out of fear that the new minimum percentage (3 percent) would deprive all of them of any representation. But the lack of enthusiasm among the Arab members of Histadrut for the joint list gave a disappointing result: only one-third of the Arab vote, compared with almost 45 percent when the Front and the PLP ran separately in 1985 (Ghanem and Ozacky 1989). The Front in particular felt pinched between the growing power of the Islamic movement and the weight of global Communism in crisis.

THE ISLAMIC CHALLENGE

Indeed, the challenge to the CPI-Front that emerged in the 1980s and became its most formidable rival in the 1990s was the Islamic movement. It began to grow in the late 1970s and early 1980s in the Triangle region, which is adjacent to the West Bank and later spread to the Galilee (Mayer 1988).[16] Initially, it took the form of a local revivalist group led by the charismatic Sheik Abdallah Nimer Darwish, who preached to the young—many of whom were repentant drug addicts or petty criminals—the virtue of leading an orthodox, pious life and regaining acceptance by Arab society. For a brief period in 1979 and 1980, some of Darwish's followers attempted to operate also as an underground sabotage ring against the Israeli state, similar to some of the radical Islamic groups in the Arab countries, but they were thwarted by the security agencies. The modus operandi of the Islamic movement thereafter followed the open, legal organizational philosophy developed by the Muslim Brothers in Egypt in the 1930s: a spiritual revolution beginning at the grassroots level and working its way up through the Arab community.

The movement was made up of local Islamic charity associations, led by a local charismatic figure who had built a reputation in the community for being honest, devout, and devoted to the public good by having a modest lifestyle, by spreading the word of God, and by setting up the volunteer charity system prescribed by the Koran. The religious leaders preached that young men and women should return to the "right path" and identify themselves fully as Muslims in their appearance (robes and beards) and in their behavior. The ideological message was uncomplicated. It claimed that the ills of Arab Muslim society and the personal hardships of its members resulted from the penetration of materialist, atheist, imperialist Western culture. These foreign influences were held responsible for the estrangement of the Muslims from the just and modest way of life dictated by the religious law, the Sharia. Members were therefore called upon to disassociate from all secular voluntary activities, including voting in the national elections.

In addition to reforming delinquents, the Islamic associations started collecting the traditional charity tax—the Zakaat—during Ramadan and distributed it to the needy. The funds collected were also used with the aid of professional followers of the movement to set up and run low-cost kindergartens, computer classes, and specialized medical services for the community (Mayer 1988, 65–72). Volunteer work camps, rivals to those of the Front, were held to build and renovate mosques. The strong message of self-help, in addition to the directive of returning to modest garb, particularly by women, found resonance in traditional Arab society.

The movement also carried a strong political message, namely that the loss of Palestine—consecrated Islamic land (*waqf*)—to the Jews in 1948 had occurred as a result of the Arabs' loss of their religious faith. The failure of the Arab states ruled by atheist nationalist regimes to defeat Israel in 1967, and the successful rebuff to American interests by the Muslim masses in Iran in 1979, were called the ultimate proof that only return to the Sharia rule in Arab society would remedy the situation. Since Marxism and Zionism were the local agencies of this inimical penetration, they should be totally rejected (Malik 1990; Mayer 1988). Communism, therefore, became a particular target. The Islamic sheikhs depicted practitioners of Communism as enemies of Islam in principle and in practice in Afghanistan and Eritrea.[17] In Israel, the CPI embodied this atheism, which conspired to devoid the Muslims of their identity. In the 1980s, when the CPI and the Islamic movement battled for the hearts and minds of the young Arab generation, violence erupted, mainly in Um al Fahem in the Triangle but also in the Galilee.[18] In Um al Fahem the Islamic association gained prestige and considerable influence through its network of voluntary organizations, which filled the vacuum of social services in this large and underdeveloped locality. It was there that the Islamic movement dealt its direct blow to the Front by winning the local elections of 1989 overwhelmingly.

Surprisingly, the CPI-Front was slow to detect this Islamic danger from the right while busily fighting its rivals on the left, the PLP and the smaller nationalist groups (Paz 1989). Yet the successes of the Islamic movement in several other localities in 1989 had an impact on the Front's hegemonic position despite the former's decentralized structure.[19] (The informal status of the Islamic national leadership was only slightly institutionalized by the decision in January 1992 to set up a loose national organization of the autonomous local associations.) Having won chairmanships of six localities, Islamic leaders entered the Committee of Heads of Arab Municipalities and the Follow Up Committee and created a counterblock to the Front there. The rivalry paralyzed the activities of those bodies and created a crisis of leadership in the organized Arab sector.[20] On the national political scene, the impact of the Islamic movement on the Front has been indirect up to 1996, when the Islamic movement decided to run with the Arab Democratic Party. In the early 1980s, they simply urged their followers not to vote at all.

Right after the November 1988 general elections, a few of the leaders, notably the founder, Darwish, supported entering the national arena, either by publicly supporting a united Arab party (excluding the Front) or by actually running as a senior partner in such a list. But the majority of the Islamic leadership opposed such a move. Instead, prior to the 1992 elections, the leadership issued a vague recommendation to the estimated 60,000 followers on which candidates to support.[21] Although the result was that different religious leaders gave conflicting signals to their followers about how to vote, the clear message was not to vote for the Front. With their growing sense of power, Islamic leaders also began treading on the CPI's political turf by becoming spokesmen of the Islamic Hamas movement in the occupied territories and by posing as mediators between the PLO and Hamas. In December 1992 the Islamic movement took the initiative and organized a protest against the mass deportation of Hamas leaders to Lebanon, and throughout the leaders' forced exile the Islamic spokesmen propagated the Hamas views against the PLO-Israeli peace talks.[22] As the date of the 1996 elections drew closer, Darwish and his followers in the leadership resumed their pressure to enter the election race. Their plea was first turned down by the movement's General Congress in May 1995.[23] Yet in a series of swift moves, Darwish and his followers managed to have the decision overturned in March 1996, and a joint list headed by an Islamic representative was set up with the Arab Democratic Party. The decision to run practically split the Islamic movement, but the United Arab List won four seats with a quarter of the Arab vote. For the first time Islamic movement representatives were elected to the Knesset.

The Fall of Communism

Probably the most devastating challenge to the morale of the CPI and, by chain reaction, to the Front's electoral bases of support in the late 1980s and early 1990s was the collapse of Communism in Eastern Europe and in the Soviet Union. After having exalted the Communist ideology and system as the unquestionable alternative social order and the key to peace in the world, Communist leaders, members, and sympathizers had to face the reality of failure. As noted in chapter 4, the process of glasnost and perestroika in the Soviet Union in the late 1980s gradually unleashed, within the middle and upper echelons of the CPI, criticism of the ideological and organizational mistakes of the leadership, followed by defections and expulsions.

The veteran CPI leadership also reacted with piecemeal reforms and personnel changes within the Front's representation in the Knesset in 1989. These changes entailed a final breakup with the Front's Jewish Black Panther, Charlie Biton, who refused to resign his seat. In a rare occurrence, the leadership admitted that his inclusion on the list for the fourth time in 1988 had been a mistake. The veteran leadership expressed self-criticism for "not listening to the [Arab] partners in the Front and to the public opinion among the Front's supporters" on this matter. Typically, however, the conclusion drawn from this self-criticism was that the Front—not the CPI leadership—should be "democratized."[24]

The efforts of the veteran leadership, specifically of Vilner and Toubi, to control carefully the changes in the party exploded in their faces and almost split the CPI and the Front just before the elections in 1992. In fact, the new democratizing procedures introduced in the Front institutions became a public arena in which Toufiq Ziad, the popular mayor of Nazareth and an old opponent of the Vilner-Toubi leadership, successfully challenged their power. The council of the Front had decided six months before the elections to democratize the selection process and to hold a separate ballot on each of the first eight positions on the list for the 1992 election. A minimum of 50 percent of the votes was needed to be elected.[25] In its customary manner, the CPI's veteran leadership, after its recommended list was approved in the new CPI council, brought the list to the Front's council, which then had the authority to decide. As always, the list was a carefully put together package, which weighed sectarian and regional considerations as well as loyalty to the Vilner-Toubi leadership. At the *head* of the list, the CPI for the first time had put a non-Communist Muslim candidate from the Triangle, Hashem Mahamid. Second on the list was Salim Jubran, a Christian from Nazareth, editor of *al Ittihad* and secretary of the Front. The third, fourth, and fifth places were reserved for the CPI's Jewish and Druze members of the Knesset (Gozanski and Nafaa) and the Jewish trade unionist (Gonen).

But Ziad and his supporters used the new procedures to break the unwritten Communist law by overturning the official CPI recommended list. The Nazareth group objected in particular to Jubran. They argued that the CPI council had no business in imposing on the Nazareth district, the largest in the party, a candidate with no electoral power base in the area. The Nazareth group thus used its influence in the Front's council to pull off a coup against Ziad's rivals in the old guard: putting Ziad at the head of the list and deposing Jubran. Mahamid was placed second. Thus, in 1992, for the first time in the CPI's history, the list for the Knesset was the outcome of a contest worked out in a mixed Communist and non-Communist elected body. The specific results were also unprecedented, since for the first time the first two positions were held by Muslims, a Christian was placed only fifth, and only one Jew was included in the first five places on its list.

A split was avoided and the Front was able to appear united before the electorate in June 1992, but the issue of leadership remained open. The Vilner-Toubi era came to a formal close in the 22nd CPI Congress, held in January 1993, after the elections. The secretary of the party, Toubi, the only one among the leadership remaining from the days of the League for National Liberation (after the break of Emil Habibi with the party) announced his retirement from politics. His Jewish counterpart and predecessor as secretary of the party, Vilner, barely made it into the new secretariat of the politburo.[26] But Ziad's victory in the Front did not earn him automatically the leadership position in the party. Despite his charismatic assets, his fiery temperament and his ideological credentials kept him from the status of possible *party* leadership. Thus his candidacy for the position of general secretary was not even suggested.[27]

Ziad was able, however, to solidify his leadership in the Nazareth Front via the empowerment of the Front institutions, possibly in preparation for a future bid for the party's leadership. Immediately after the 1992 elections he introduced primaries for the Nazareth Front and advocated the same procedure for the national Front.[28] This new strategy of openness paid off in November 1993, when Ziad was reelected for the third time as mayor of Nazareth by a majority of more than 60 percent, and the Front won eleven of nineteen seats in the city council. The Front defeated both the Islamists and the Arab Democratic Party, which had done well in the 1992 national elections. Ziad's death in a car accident in July 1994 dealt a severe blow to the party and left an enormous void in its leadership. In the issue of the party paper dedicated to his memory, the language of the eulogies approached that of a posthumous personality cult.[29]

It is ironic, therefore, that in its severe hour of crisis, after having suffered heavy electoral losses, the CPI found itself for the first time in position to push for the implementation of its integrative ethnonationalist platform. The circumstances were the results of the 1992 elections. During the campaign, the party emphasized its "historic foresight" on the national question and its current devotion to the Palestinian cause.[30] It also stressed that a vote for the Front would help tip the scale against a Likud-Labor unity government, which had resulted from deadlocked elections in 1988. The CPI attempted, however, to prevent Arab voters from taking this argument to its logical conclusion and voting directly for the Zionist "peace camp," and the CPI did so by reiterating Labor's past maltreatment of the Arabs (Ozacky-Lazar 1992, 3).

These efforts were only partially successful. The Front lost one seat compared with 1988, and its share of the Arab vote dropped from 33 percent to

23.2 percent. Proportionally, the largest losses were suffered in the localities where there was a majority of Christians, who may have been disappointed with the reduction in the traditional saliency of the Christian element in the Front. But the PLP, which placed a Christian in second place, did not capitalize on this development and was wiped off the political map.

It therefore seems that a combination of other reasons accounted for the votes lost by the Front: abstention; the vote for the Arab Democratic Party; and the vote for Labor. The Front did remain strong in the urban and larger Arab localities; overall it was the single largest party in the Arab population. Yet the Labor Party trailed the Front by only 3.3 percent in 1992, when it won 20 percent of the Arab vote, and the Arab Democratic Party increased its support from 11 percent to 15 percent. These results showed that the Front's integrative ethnonationalist strategy was difficult to sustain. The more accommodationist alternative—direct voting for the "peace camp," particularly when coupled with hopes of material improvements—had become a more popular alternative.

Yet the significant outcome of the 1992 elections was that for the first time the Front, together with the Arab Democratic Party, formed the blocking majority for a Labor-led coalition government. In other words, without the support of the five representatives of two parties in the Knesset, the Labor coalition did not have the necessary sixty-one-vote majority. In return for their support of the government, the two parties were invited to submit their demands but not to join the coalition, which the ADP aspired to do though the Front did not. The agreement signed between the Labor Party and the Front on July 12, 1992, committed the government to promote the peace process with the Arab countries and the Palestinians and to promote economic and social equality in general and of the Arab population specifically (Ozacky-Lazar 1992, 36–37).

As a result of this agreement, the CPI-Front for the first time found itself in the position of a responsible oppositionist party. The dilemma the CPI-Front faced was how far it could support the government while sticking to its own principles and its image of an antiestablishment party. This dilemma increased as a result of the Oslo agreement and the signing of the Declaration of Principles by the State of Israel and the PLO, which pronounced mutual recognition of the two sides on September 9, 1993. The declaration initiated a long and difficult process of negotiation, with violent opposition to the process on each side. It is no wonder, therefore, that the first time the Front decided to submit a vote of no confidence, at the risk of bringing down the government, was in May 1995, two and a half years after the elections and a year before the 1996 elections.

The issue on which the Front decided to make a stand was the government's decision to expropriate land held by Palestinians in the Jerusalem area—a decision made in the midst of negotiations over the second stage of the Oslo interim agreement. The Front meant to signal to the government that it could not be taken for granted and to the Front's supporters that it had not been co-opted by the Labor government but maintained its independent positions in the political process. The political gamble worked. In the face of the right-wing opposition parties' intention to join the vote of no confidence, the government backed down from the planned expropriation.[31] The prestige of the Front among the Arab public both inside and outside Israel received an enormous boost. The symbolic significance of this minor political incident cannot be overestimated: for the first time the participation of Arab citizens' oppositionist voice in the Israeli decision-making process made a difference.

However, the incremental but growing influence of the Arab vote on the political process met a violent reaction by Jewish right-wing public opinion. On November 4, 1995, a year away from general elections, Prime Minister Yitzhak Rabin was assassinated by a Jewish right-wing activist. In his trial the assassin, Yigal Amir, justified his act by pointing to Rabin's "betrayal" of the Jewish national and religious interests by signing away parts of the land of Israel in the Oslo agreement with the PLO. Amir emphasized that what made the agreement possible was the presence of Arab citizens in the body politic of Israel and declared that it was time to realize that "Israel cannot be both democratic and Jewish." Those words echoed demands from right-wing parties and Likud politicians to disenfranchise the Arabs, either directly or indirectly, by delegitimizing positions that depend on the Arab vote for forming a majority. The approaching talks on the final settlement with the Palestinians and the peace talks with Syria that involved negotiating over the Golan Heights prompted these demands and put the Labor government on the defensive.

Elections were called for May 1996, following a series of events: a stalemate in the Israeli-Syrian talks; terrorist attacks on Israel's civilian population by the radical Islamic Palestinian Hamas, who oppose the Oslo agreement; military pressure by the Lebanese Hezbollah in southern Lebanon; and the shelling of northern Israel. In the period up to the elections, Prime Minister Shimon Peres conducted strong security and military policies, closing off Israel to the Palestinian population on the West Bank and Gaza and launching a military operation, Grapes of Wrath, in Lebanon, in the course of which one hundred civilian refugees were accidentally killed.

To these dramatic events preceding the election, another was added by chance. The election was to be held under a new system. Hitherto the prime minister had been elected indirectly as head of the party that was able to form a coalition government. Under the new system the prime minister was to be elected directly by the people. In order to win, a candidate needed not only over 50 percent of the vote but also the support of a majority in the Knesset in order to form a government. A candidate, therefore, had to appeal to the widest possible range of voters. From the voters' point of view the new system meant that each voter had two votes—one for the prime minister and one for the party list in the Knessset—and these votes could be split between different parties. As campaigning progressed, the focus of the two major parties, Labor and Likud, was on electing their respective candidates, Shimon Peres and Benjamin Netanyahu. The general assumption was that the Arab voters who went to the polls would vote overwhelmingly for Peres. But since Likud had an edge over Labor among Jewish voters, Arab participation in the election for premier became a crucial issue for Labor. Much less effort was invested by Labor in getting votes for the party list for the Knesset.

The Front and the Arab Democratic Party were slow to realize the impact of the new system, particularly the ability of voters to split their votes. Both parties feared a landslide victory for Labor among Arab voters, as a "reward" for signing the Oslo agreement and as encouragement for continuing to reduce inequalities between Arabs and Jews. Both parties also concentrated on trying to head off their new competitor, Dr. Ahmad Tibi, Yassir Arafat's advisor on Israeli affairs, who set up a party and hoped to win the support of the Islamic movement. Tibi announced as his goal becoming the caretaker of Palestinian affairs as the first Arab in an Israeli cabinet. In April 1996, two months before the election, the Arab Democratic Party managed to push Tibi out of the race by signing an agreement with the Islamic movement on a joint list, the Arab United Party. About the same time, the Front succeeded in setting up a joint list with the newly formed National Democratic Alignment (Malad), which consisted of former PMP and Abna al Balad activists and was headed by the charismatic former CPI member Azmi Bishara. In the negotiations between the Front and Malad, the former agreed not to emphasize the Oslo agreement (of which Malad was critical) as the basis for the settlement of the Israeli-Palestinian conflict and to include in the platform the goal of making the state of Israel legally "a state of all its citizens" (rather than a Jewish state). In return Malad agreed to drop the specific demand for cultural automomy for the Arab population. The security policy of Peres toward the Palestinians and Lebanese weeks before the May 29 election enraged Arab public opinion and served as a rallying point for candidates of all the Arab parties and the Front against the Labor party: until about a week prior to the election, they all called on their voters to put blank ballots in the envelope for premier in protest. The most outspoken were Malad's spokesmen, who, unlike the rest of the candidates, did not change their call up to election day. On the other side of the political spectrum, Netanyahu's Jewish religious supporters mobilized Jewish voters with a slogan that Netanyahu was "good" for the Jews, implying that Peres had only the Arabs' interests at heart.

The combined effect of the new electoral system, the participation of the Islamists and the Malad in the process, and the polarized election campaign was manifold. There was a rise in the rate of participation of Arab voters in 1996 to 77 percent after a decade of consistently downward numbers (see table 9.1). There were split votes and a significant shift of votes from Jewish-Zionist parties to the Front and the UAL. Labor's Peres indeed received almost 95 percent of the Arab vote (compared to 44.5 percent of the Jewish vote) but lost the election by 30,000 votes. The call to protest against Peres had a minute but critical effect: In Arab localities 24,000 ballots cast for the premier were either blank or otherwise illegal ballots. The Front-Malad alignment received 37 percent of the vote and five seats in the Knesset, giving the CPI a new lease on its political life.

Conclusion

In this study I have analyzed political mobilization of a population whose ethnic or national affinity is different from that of the majority in the state. As a comprehensive study of minorities in the 1990s shows, it is one of many cases over the globe in which nonassimilated subordinate groups in the modern nation-state ponder their options for changing their social and political circumstances (Gurr 1993). The nature of the modern nation, with its command over power, resources, centralized bureaucracy, and claims to legitimacy, is generally intolerant of such political mobilization. This is especially true of an ethnically defined state, locked in a regional national conflict, of which the indigenous minority is a part. The choice of options for the minorities under these circumstances is limited or risky, though to a lesser extent if the state in question has liberal, participatory electoral politics. The dilemma the minorities face is either acquiescence with subordination on an ethnic and class basis or mobilization on the same basis, in different forms, with uncertain repercussions.

The general conclusions that can be drawn from this case study are that (1) mobilization on an ethnic basis is not an inevitable outcome of the existence of minorities and majorities but rather of the construction of such a dilemma in an environment of social and economic change, and that (2) integrative—that is, nonseparative—ethnonationalism directed at equal participation as a mobilizing strategy is one way of minimizing the costs of making a choice between options. The fact that a Communist party, committed to a non-nationalist class ideology, formulated and led such a strategy among the Arab minority leads to the conclusion that (3) integrative ethnonationalism is likely to be adopted as a strategy of building solidarity and empowerment of a minority whose class vulnerability makes separatist ethnonationalism too risky.

Last, the effects of regional conflict may be paradoxical. This case shows that (4) under circumstances of intense regional national conflict, in which state interests versus stateless national groups are involved, avoidance of a separative ethnonationalist option may be vital part of the solution. No combination of these analyses, of course, leads to any general conclusions on the *results* of such mobilizations. In the case of the Arab-Palestinian citizens of Israel, the results of such mobilization are now only beginning to unfold.

Indeed, some fifty years after being involuntarily included in the Jewish state, the Arab-Palestinian citizens of Israel are on the verge of a new and uncertain era. The process of accommodation between Israel and the Arab states, particularly with the Palestinian national movement, will no doubt undermine the geopolitical condition that has contributed significantly to the Arabs' exclusion from the power structure in Israel—their status as a potential fifth column. Accommodation will also indirectly legitimize in the eyes of the Jewish majority their Palestinian identity. But the settling of the national question of the Palestinians by a territorial compromise will not address directly the question of what role the Palestinian minority could and should play within the ethnically defined Jewish state. The Jewish majority will have to confront this question, which it has tended to avoid throughout the years of conflict with the Arab world. For the Arab-Palestinian minority this is a central issue that is likely to engage them actively, unlike the situation in 1948.

The change from acquiescence to activism as portrayed throughout this book is far from being univocal. Political activity of the Arab-Palestinian citizens is a dynamic field divided by local and national politics, split between antagonism and acculturation, in which multiple parties—the CPI being only one of them—compete by presenting various ethnonationalist images, identifications, and paths of activity. This dynamic contradicts the prediction of the "internal colonialist" approach: that a uniform political separatist tendency would emerge after the diminution of control by Israeli authorities and after the disappearance of the traditional pro-Zionist Arab lists.

The dynamics of political activity of the Arab minority in the 1980s and 1990s also run counter to the main thrust of the cultural modernization approach. In the cultural modernization analysis, the given of the national Arab—and later Palestinian—identity is an overriding factor in explaining the political reaction of the Arab citizens to the geopolitical conflict. The conflict's cumulative effect, according to the analysis, has been to change progressively the political tendencies of the Arab citizens of Israel, from an accommodationist attitude toward the Jewish state to a nationalist oppositionist trend. Thus, the CPI's electoral success, the springing up of the essentially Arab Progressive List for Peace in the early 1980s, and the origins of the Islamic movement and the Arab Democratic Party in the late 1980s all signify a growing alienation between the Jewish majority and the Arab minority and raise the prospect of irredentist ethnonationalism. That is the gist of the radicalization thesis.

The alternative interpretation, politicization, is followed in this book. The cumulative impact of the geopolitical conflict on the political tendencies of the Arab-Palestinian citizens in Israel, according to this interpretation, has gone in the opposite direction—toward accommodation to their existence as a minority in a Jewish state. However, the conditions underlying the incorporation of the Arab minority into the Jewish state have produced politicized Arab ethnicity, or ethnonationalism. In an ethnically defined state, national identity—whether of the majority or of the minority—becomes the only legitimate basis for making collective political demands. The outcome of these cross-pressures is an overriding tendency of integrative ethnonationalism. The Communist Party was the mobilizing agency in the oppositionist version of this trend in the 1960s and 1970s. While some of the undercurrents in the ethno-nationalist trends were irredentist (especially in the Abna al Balad, PLP, and the Islamic movement), they are basically Arab autonomistic alternatives to the status quo within the system. The specialty of the CPI is that it charted the way for the Arab minority to find alternatives to the Zionist framework. Its more recent Arab rivals should be seen as the dialectical fruits of its success.

This conclusion was reached by charting the sociopolitical and economic changes among the Arab minority. The immediate, almost instinctive reaction of the fragmented, rural remnant of the Palestinian population in 1948 was to demand their citizenship in the new state as a way to protect themselves from expulsion. This impetus to cling for survival to whatever the new political reality had to offer grew stronger as it became apparent that the State of Israel is a viable and strengthening political entity. Yet no role in the public sphere was allotted to the Arab minority in the Jewish state, and the only demands made of them were rejection of subversive acts, proof of loyalty by means of votes for the establishment Zionist parties, and acceptance of a disjointed, exclusionary process of incorporation, which kept them in a subordinate position in society.

The ruling Zionist Mapai Party was frustrated in its expectations that these incorporation processes were working to ensure the attachment of the Arab citizens to the establishment. On the contrary, the more those processes intensified, the larger was the opposition within the Arab minority to the mixture of exclusion, control, and "benign neglect" that made up the policies of the state toward the Arabs. The traditional social structure on which the Zionist parties relied was undercut by the process of social and economic change, and no alternative new political basis of cooperation with the establishment emerged. The Arabs' irrelevancy to the Jewish national ethos and system of priorities, on the one hand, and the emergence of the Palestinian national movement, on the other, raised the issue of identity. Under those conditions, continued reliance by the Zionist establishment on the traditional leadership depended both on greater material incentives to individuals and on threats against the vote for the Communists. These tactics, in turn, bred cynicism and alienation from the Zionist ruling party on the part of the younger generation. While part of the electorate sought to transform the terms of identification with the Zionist establishment into a particularist, narrowly defined ethnicity, others turned to an alternative party—the Communists.

The Significance of the Arab Vote for the CPI

The contention of this study is that the CPI suggested to the Arab national minority an oppositionist, alternative means of integration into the Jewish state. Through its resources—leadership and organization—the CPI was in a position to draw on the growing detachment from traditional leadership and the Zionist establishment and to use this detachment in making itself into a hegemonic, rival political establishment. The social order the CPI presented was oriented toward class interests, but the Jewish and Arab working classes were totally split along national lines, and the Islamic cultural heritage impeded the acceptance of an outright secular materialistic ideology. Hence, the only realistic means of solidifying support against the Zionist establishment was reliance on the Arab ethnonationalist attribute. This itself had to be molded in a manner that would take into account both the interests of the Arab population and the political interests of the pro-Soviet Communist Party in the region. The main strategy that the party had employed, especially since 1965, was cultivating among the Arab citizens, who were split along regional and sectoral lines, the sense that they were united by a common destiny, which was threatened by the authorities, and that the party itself embodied their aspirations for equality and national honor.

The basic argument that the Communist Party presented to the Arab voter, therefore, was that the Zionist establishment was hostile and scornful toward Israel's Arabs, held them as hostages in the Zionists' conflict with the Arab states, and prevented their equal integration into the State of Israel. On the other hand, the party—in its Jewish-Arab composition, its nontraditional and fearless political style, its insistence on a just solution for the regional conflict, and its international backing by the Soviet Union—exemplified the only way of achieving the Arabs' goal of equal integration. Hence, only by solidifying the Arabs into a united political force under the leadership of the party, outside the Zionist establishment, could the Zionists' power be curtailed. Faced with the opposition of non-Zionist Jews and the Soviet Union, the establishment would eventually disintegrate from within.

The success of such a strategy was predicated, first, on the detachment of the Arab electorate from dependency on the traditional structure and, second, on the lack of a new basis on which the Zionist parties could enlist support. This study has provided support for the hypothesis that the success of the Communist Party in winning votes in the Arab sector is indeed related to the reduction of direct control through the abolition of the Military Rule; the process of social change, which undermined the traditional structure; and the stratification process that characterized the population in the 1970s.

However, the relationship between the process of socioeconomic change and support for the Communist Party is not a simple, linear one, nor is it the only explanatory factor. Rather, it is the interaction of this process with cultural factors and strategies of political mobilization that explains the electoral outcome. The increase in the electoral support for the Communist Party among the Arab citizens in Israel was a result of the development of different kinds of links with the Arab electorate.

In the 1950s the Communist Party was able to recruit grassroots support mainly by reliance on its pre-state image as the party of the nontraditional, left-wing part of the Arab national movement. The Arab Communist leaders, who had their roots in the pre-state Palestinian society, held cultural links with segments of the secularized Christian population and with small sections of the Muslim working class. The purpose of the Arab-Palestinian Communists during the mandate period was to ensure that the future Arab state in Palestine would be pro-Soviet. After the establishment of the State of Israel, a large segment of this elite, out of loyalty to the Soviet Union and commitment to the progressive Arab cause, was ready to continue that mission as the minor partners of the Jewish Communists in the framework of legal opposition to the Zionist ideology and foreign policy. In the absence of any nationalist organization, they were in a better position to recruit support among the Arabs in opposition to the traditional leadership, which cooperated with the discriminating Zionist establishment.

However, the Arab-Palestinian Communists had to fight the survival instinct of the fragmented traditional minority, which directed it to go along with the authorities and adapt passively to their policies. In addition, since the Communists had lost their urban trade union organizational base as a result of the 1948 war and were unable to rebuild it in competition with the powerful Histadrut, the only basis of popular support was the leadership's cultural links with the secularized Greek Orthodox population. These links were indeed the traditional basis of support on which the Arab Communists could rely for membership and voters, but they were a minority among the mostly rural traditional Muslim population.

The stumbling block for wider recruitment, encountered by all segments of the Communist Party in the Middle East, was the secular European nature of the Communist ideology, which ran counter to the religious outlook and customs of a Muslim peasant society. Moreover, the highly centralized Soviet style of party was not attractive to segments of the Christian intelligentsia. The logic of this situation called for a strategy that would emphasize the Arabs' common ethnonational attribute and encourage identification on that level. Such an ethnonationalist line dictated solidarity rather than class politics: an alliance with Arabs of all denominations and classes—peasants, workers, and intelligentsia—who were ready, for whatever reasons, to oppose the Zionist political establishment. At the same time, Israel's international legitimacy, its existence as geopolitical reality, the ideological and political guidelines of the Soviets, and the survival needs of the population all dictated the formulation of a basically integrationist position. Only such a position could justify demands to open the job market to the Arab population, and only it could refute the suspicion that the Arab minority was a fifth column in the Jewish state.

The political and ideological solution to the contradiction between these two political lines was to challenge the Zionist, but not the Jewish, character of the state. This approach would entail opposition to national Jewish priorities as formulated by the regime and to its outlook on global and regional conflicts, demands for equal civil rights for the Arab citizens, and advocacy of unspecified Arab "national rights." Yet the second condition for the success of this strategy was an "alliance from below" with the Jewish working class on the basis of class solidarity. But given the conditions of the Arab-Israeli national conflict in the region and the different trajectory of the socioeconomic changes in the class structures of the two communities, the two strategies were pulling in opposing directions: the Arab ethnonationalist line was alienating the Jews, and the attempt to forge a direct alliance "from below," with the Jewish working class, faltered. The majority of the Jewish Communists demanded that the strategy be changed to one of alliance "from above," with Zionist leftist parties, a demand that the Arab Communists rejected, and the party split between its two national components.

Those developments in the mid-1960s to the mid-1970s coincided with the disappearance of the Arab peasant class as a result of the proletarization of the Arab sector. The CPI-Rakah was thus in a position to push aggressively for the party's embodiment of both the working class and the national attributes of the Arab minority. It accentuated its position that the way to resolve the subordinated position of the Arab minority within Israel was to solve the national question of the Palestinians outside Israel. This line, again, was pursued at the price of alienation from the Jewish electorate. But a growing number of Arab youth, whose allegiance to the traditional structure was weakening and who had been incorporated into the Israeli economy, were won over to the CPI through its slogans. The young Arabs saw the CPI as the embodiment of their desire for greater acceptance within the system, based on recognition of their identity as Arabs. Such supporters did not necessarily share the party's Communist ideology and only a small number of them actually joined the party. Instead, these voters supported the party because of its oppositionist, antiestablishment "Arabness."

The peak of the CPI's success among the Arab voters in the mid-1970s was due to a number of factors.

(1) The party readjusted its program to support explicitly the Palestinian national aspirations on the West Bank and Gaza, which became popular among the Arab electorate.

(2) The party succeeded in enlisting the support of non-Communists in the Democratic Front for a platform that excluded the party's ideological components but included its social and political tenets. In doing so, the CPI had to come to terms with the local hamula splits and attempt to use them for the party's advantage.

(3) By launching a new organizational strategy, the CPI succeeded in institutionalizing the support it had gained on the basis of its slogans alone. Although the party's bureaucracy at the middle and top levels remained centralized and closed, on the local level its organizational activity, geared specifically to the youth, developed an open and mobilizing style. The cultural figures active within the party, its publications, youth clubs, volunteer camps, and festivals all became part of the Arab youth counterculture. Its university scholarships were an additional incentive for joining the ranks of its youth organization.

(4) The party's organization of the first Land Day in 1976, in defense of what was seen as a vital Arab interest, won it ad hoc support from voters who otherwise were put off by the party's political style. This Arab "floating vote" apparently shifted, from one election campaign to the next, among parties within or outside the Zionist establishment, according to the voters' perception of the immediate national or local interest.

The threat to the CPI's embodiment of the antiestablishment Arabs in the 1970s was the radical nationalist groups, which identified ideologically with the Palestinian nationalist movement. In the late 1970s and early 1980s, the CPI leadership feared that the PLO itself was such a challenge—that its voting directives to the Arab population would be heeded by the CPI's own voters. This fear turned out to be misplaced; the threat sprang from within the Arab population in Israel, in the form of the Progressive Movement for Peace, the Islamic movement, and in the 1990s the Labor Party itself.

The decline of the CPI's electorate in the 1980s and the success of the Progressive List for Peace in 1984 stemmed partly from the latter's challenge to the CPI's embodiment of the Arab-Palestinian identity, but the main reason for decline was its challenge to the CPI's political style. The CPI also had no impact on the Jewish majority. Not only did the party fail to forge an "alliance from below" with the Jewish working class, but the Jewish majority, particularly the workers, in fact moved to the right. The government in power in the 1980s was even less likely than its predecessor to follow the policy advocated by the CPI.

The CPI-Front's promises to the Arab voters to increase their political efficacy remained unfulfilled. The party's success in capturing half of the Arab vote and the city of Nazareth did not change the official state policy toward the Arabs up to 1992: no steps were taken for incorporation of the Arab educated stratum, and no special programs were designed for development of the backward infrastructure of Arab localities. The conflict with the Palestinians in the region was escalating, as exemplified by the Lebanon war and the intensification of the settlement policy in the occupied territories, and the promised help of the Soviet Union was not forthcoming. The CPI itself no longer seemed in the vanguard: its bureaucratic, overcentralized, Soviet-style organization, which was progressive in comparison with the traditional political style, proved too inflexible both organizationally and ideologically when compared with the pluralistic nature of the Jewish political parties. The party's insistence on having a political leading role, dominating the decisions of the Democratic Front and other Arab organizations, was seen by many as the action of a monopolistic establishment. Thus, the CPI in the 1980s became the target of antiestablishment feelings of all sorts, much as the Zionist Labor party had been for large sections of the Jewish public a decade earlier. The PLP first, and the Arab Democratic Party later, used the ethnonationalist attribute as a resource for political mobilization. In both sectors, part of the antiestablishment reaction was to turn to religion.

Indeed, the most successful challenge to the hegemony of the CPI-Front in the late 1980s and early 1990s proved to be the Islamic movement. At its disposal were two important advantages: a simple ideological message and a proven organizational model rooted in the religious mores of the Arab society. The CPI, for its part, had attempted to mold Arab society in Israel into a politicized ethnonational group that could be integrated into the state and civil society; it invested in building an educated intelligentsia to lead this effort. In the process, however, the CPI took for granted the support of the Arab lower strata. The Islamic movement, on the other hand, concentrated on helping the poorer sections and on mobilizing grassroots support. On the ideological level, it targeted the CPI-Front by accusing it of collaborating with the state in robbing Arab civil society of its true identity. The movement exalted Muslim identity and relegated national identity to the status of a derivative (Malik 1990; Paz 1989). In contrast to the Front's protests against the establishment, the Islamic movement propagated self-help and independence from the establishment, demanding to have the Sharia implemented locally.

Several other local and global developments in the late 1980s and early 1990s were to have a profound effect on the Arabs in Israel in general and on the CPI in particular: the outbreak of the Intifada among the Palestinians on the West Bank and Gaza in December 1987; the breakdown of Communism and of the Soviet Union; and the accord on the Declaration of Principles between Israel and the PLO in September 1993. The accord was an outcome of the June 1992 formation of the Labor coalition government, which for the first time in the history of the state relied on the outside support of the non-establishment Arab Democratic party and the Communist-led Democratic Front. As a result of these developments, the CPI lost its hegemonic position among the Arab population, which arrived at a new crossroads in the history of its evolvement as a political community.

The Intifada and Future Political Trends among the Arabs in Israel

The reaction of the Arab citizens in Israel to the Intifada can serve as a test case for the competing interpretations of basic political tendencies so far and of those likely in the future. The Intifada posed for the Arab citizens of Israel a sharp dilemma of identity and loyalties. As Palestinians, they were impelled to join the uprising and actively help their brethren across the Green Line free themselves from Israel's rule. As Israeli citizens, they had to abide by the law and were restricted to legal means in fighting Israel's policy of putting down the Intifada by force. Which way did they choose?

The radicalization school of thought, which argues that the Arabs in Israel are gradually but steadily moving toward total Palestinization through the reestablishment of cultural and political ties with the West Bank, Gaza, and the PLO, sees the Intifada as another catalyst in this process (Rekhess 1989, 119–54; 1992, 99–112). As indicators of the process, proponents point to statements in support of the Intifada by Arab leaders of all political tendencies; an increase in mass protest, sometimes violent, and sporadic acts of sabotage, such as arson and fire-bombing of cars, during the first year of the Intifada (1988); and one murderous attack on soldiers by Israeli Islamic fundamentalists in March 1992. On the political level, the same thesis points to the Arab M.P. Darawshe's breakaway from the Zionist Labor Party and the use of the Intifada as the major campaign issue in the 1988 elections by the Arab parties and the Front (Al Haj 1989, 35–49; Reiter 1989, 63–84). The fact that in the 1988 elections these parties gathered almost 60 percent of the Arab vote was seen as a further indicator of the process of radicalization. Above all, the success of the Islamic fundamentalist movement in the local elections of 1989 attested to the impact of the Intifada within the Green Line. The fact that all political movements refrained from openly calling for active participation in the violent aspects of the Intifada is attributed to the fear of being outlawed by the authorities.

The politicization and disjointed modernization hypotheses, alternatives to the radicalization school, argued that reactions to the Intifada should be seen in the context of a stronger assertion of the Arabs' political role *within* the state. The especially militant yet integrative position of the CPI on the Palestinian question became the consensus of all the other political stands. The Intifada had a paradoxical effect on the Arabs in Israel; whereas it strengthened their identification with the goals of their Palestinian brothers, it also accentuated the difference between themselves as citizens and the Palestinians who were under military occupation. With the exception of a small minority who actually participated in acts of sabotage, Arab-Palestinian citizens reacted to the Intifada by expressing political solidarity and supplying humanitarian aid, not by participating in it. The bloody struggle redrew the Green Line, which had become somewhat blurred over the course of twenty years of occupation, and it sharpened the difference in the political agenda and political fate of the two Palestinian communities. Those living in the West Bank and Gaza, fighting for national liberation, were ready to pay the price that such a struggle entailed. The Arab-Palestinians in Israel, however, took a different route, seeking to press further their demands to be recognized as truly equal in the Israeli system—both as a collective and as individuals. Unlike the Palestinians in the territories, they had the legal means to protest their exclusion from the system and to oppose occupation of the territories, and they had much more to lose by joining the Intifada.[1]

As the Intifada dragged on and political deadlock continued, frustration among the Arabs in Israel was growing because they were neither part of the heroic struggle on a day-to-day basis nor effective in changing the political status quo. This was made patently clear in March 1990 when the Labor Party shrank from forming a coalition based on the outside support of the Arab parties and the Front.

The frustration was vented in May 22, 1990, after a Jewish youngster massacred six Palestinian workers from Gaza who had come to look for work within the Green Line. The attack provoked an outpouring of rage and clashes with the police in Nazareth and several other Arab localities and in neighborhoods of mixed cities in a manner that resembled scenes in the West Bank and Gaza. Outrage was similarly expressed on the streets after the massacre of thirty Palestinians in Hebron by a Jewish settler in February 1994. While these outbreaks did not develop into any kind of sustained effort to join the Intifada, the unprecedented outbursts of the Arab residents in Jaffa and the Bedouins in the Negev signifies that the politicization process is intertwined with the process of socioeconomic stratification. Jaffa and the Negev were the most disadvantaged communities and, hitherto, the most compliant with the political status quo. That their citizens took to the streets is a sign that the Arab-Palestinian citizens in Israel are forcing the issue of their place in society onto the public agenda, lest they be forgotten by both the Jews and the Palestinians in the era of peace.

The most intriguing question regarding the Front and the CPI has been the effect on their ideological and organizational profile brought about by the changes in the Soviet Union and the eventual fall of the Communist regimes in Eastern Europe and Russia. The prospects for an orthodox pro-Soviet party are not good, judging by the internal upheaval and electoral decline of the French Communist Party.[2] Mikhail Gorbachev's glasnost and acknowledgment of Western superiority in the implementation of democratic values has caused uneasiness, confusion, and demoralization in both the leadership and the lower party ranks. The eventual fall of the Soviet Union and the resulting termination of the Communist Party's fellowships for Arab students were a severe blow to the party's political leverage and image. The damage was reflected in internal bickering among the leadership. Yet the majority in the leadership stuck to the old line, admitting only the party's negligence of the socioeconomic struggle, which it claimed arose out of its focus on the Israeli-Arab-Palestinian conflict.[3] Paradoxically, this focus also prevented the party from collapsing. Perhaps this is the reason why the party leadership is adamant about preserving its binational structural uniqueness, refusing to become just another Arab party.

But it has yet to be seen how the party can cope with the ideological crisis. No less of a challenge is the historic breakthrough after the 1992 elections, namely the decision of the Labor Party to form a government based on the Front and the Arab Democratic Party as a blocking majority. The CPI-Front's dilemma in the four years of the Labor-led government was whether to preserve its image as the promoter of Palestinian independence and use its newly acquired political muscle or to support the Zionist establishment that seemed to be moving only hesitantly in that direction. The lack of consensus on this matter in the enlarged Front prior to the 1996 election may have been critical in Labor's loss of power. The results of the 1996 election—increased representation of the Front in the Knesset and victory of the Likud-led Jewish ethnocentric coalition—may sharpen the internal debate within the Front on its future strategy.

The political behavior of the Arab-Palestinian minority in the next decade will be constructed along the lines of three major options. The first calls for promoting autonomous community institutions that are exclusively inward-oriented based on the hope that in the long run Israel will eventually disappear as a political entity. This option is supported by sections of the Islamic movement and their ideological rivals, sections of the radical socialist Palestinian nationals. Its social basis seems to be the alienated intelligentsia, either radical nationalist or radical Islamic, and workers who adopted the call of the charismatic Islamic leaders to identify in terms of their Islamic attribute. Holders of this position would probably promote, in the short term, the cultural integration of the Arab-Palestinian citizens within the emerging Palestinian entity on the West Bank and Gaza (Ozacky-Lazar and Ghanem 1993, 18). It could therefore be termed the separatist trend. The peace negotiations in Madrid and the accord with the PLO did not seem to affect the amount of support for this stance. It remained small—10 percent by one estimate—and the political movement that represents the secular version of this position remained an insignificant force on the local level.[4]

The second position, which might be termed the semiautonomous option, has a number of versions, none of which have been clearly spelled out. In general it argues for institutionalized cultural pluralism, or binationalism. It calls for the creation of Arab autonomous institutions that would be the primary affiliation of Arabs, who would also participate as citizens in the state and public organizations of Israeli society. This position shares with the separatist trend the assumption that real integration with the ethnically defined Israeli state is impossible, but it also sees as unrealistic or not necessarily desirable the prospect of forging a common political fate with the Palestinian sovereign entity. As a short-term political strategy, it calls for the mobilization and consolidation of Arab political and economic resources on all levels outside the Zionist establishment, as long as the establishment continues to deny Palestinian self-determination and Arab collective identity within Israel. In the long run, Arab political power should be used in combination with Jewish political allies to bring about Palestinian sovereignty and recognition of the Arabs in Israel as a native national minority having extraterritorial political bodies and equal title to the land. Sections of the Islamic movement, the PMP and the Democratic National Alignment (Malad), are the political movements that come closest to representing this trend. The split between the more proletarian Islamic supporters of this trend, on the one hand, and the secular Muslim and Christian intelligentsia and middle class of the PMP and Malad, on the other, seems to lessen the prospects that this position might win a hegemonic status. It is yet to be seen whether the decision of both of these groups to run in the 1996 elections—the Islamists as part of an alliance with the ADP and Malad as part of the Front—will increase their impact on their respective political allies and on Arab political discourse.

The third position, which might be termed integrationist, argues—in contrast to both the separatist and the semiautonomous—that Arab political and cultural institutions should be an integral part of an Israeli political structure that should be forced open for equal participation of Arab citizens. Its representatives are the CPI, the Arab Democratic Party, and various Arab activists within the Zionist parties. It is this position that has been emphasized throughout this book. The tripartite analytical distinction sketched in this chapter becomes blurred, however, when considered against the following paradox. It was found that both the idea of autonomous Arab institutions and the professed desire for full integration into the Israeli system were equally popular among Arabs.[5] How can this be explained?

The key to this riddle seems to be the ambiguous manner in which the concepts "autonomy" and "integration" are perceived and used. The ambiguity stems from the mixture of conflicting symbolic and economic concerns of the different socioeconomic strata of the Arab community. The CPI-Front exemplifies this ambiguity more than any other body. It supports both the recognition of the Arabs as a national minority and the establishment of autonomous *cultural* institutions as well as Arab mass organizations. But at the same time it strongly opposes both *economic* autonomous bodies and a set of separate *political representative* bodies, as have been suggested by spokesmen of the semiautonomous trend. The Front's spokesmen argue that autonomy will marginalize the Arabs even further and weaken their demand for equality with the Jewish majority. The CPI-Front therefore tries to cater to the common sentiments and conflicting concerns of the professional stratum and the workers.

The assessment of the semiautonomous spokesmen, many of whom belong to the professional stratum, is that equality with the Jewish majority can be achieved only through separate institutions that would legitimately express the Arab community's collective memory and particular concerns. This stratum (in which Christians are overrepresented) suffers more than blue-collar workers from job market discrimination in the Jewish sector and from low returns for their education.[6] Hence, at least in the short run, they will benefit more than any stratum from an increased number of autonomous Arab bodies. Because the Arab sector is underindustrialized, the less educated particularly are almost totally dependent on the Jewish private sector, and because of their lower level of schooling they suffer less, in comparison with professionals, from educational-occupational mismatch on job market. Under current conditions, disengagement from the Jewish sector would spell disaster for them, even though they may be more exposed to unemployment and more comfortable working for an Arab employer.

The CPI-Front position, at least up to its alliance with Malad in 1996, seems to argue for challenging the current ethnic division of labor and exclusion of professionals. The semiautonomous stance, on the other hand, argues for developing the nascent "enclave economy" of the Arabs and for setting up corresponding cultural and political institutions.

The fact that the Arab workers remain the economically weakest and most vulnerable category in Israeli society, as evident in the period of economic decline in the 1980s, infuses the struggle for equality but also strengthens the avoidance position of religious and nationalist radicalism. Relief of this tension will require a mutually acceptable definition of the rights and duties of the Arab citizens and a recognition of the national dimension of their heritage. If, on the contrary, extreme right-wing Jewish nationalist attitudes gain prominence and the peaceful settlement between Israel and the Palestinians on the West Bank and Gaza falters, there is danger that the general trend will change in the direction of widespread support for underground activities of sabotage. The solution of the Palestinian national issue outside the borders of Israel, without tackling the internal issue, will lay the basis for irredentism.

Notes

Introduction

1. The official statistics include the Arabs who are residents of East Jerusalem but are not citizens. After their estimated number was subtracted, there were 863,000 non-Jewish citizens in 1994. Central Bureau of Statistics, *Population in Localities*, 1996.

2. The choice of a term to designate this group is itself part of the politics of identity. The official Israeli reference to this population is either "non-Jewish minorities" or "Arabs with Israeli citizenship" or, in short, Israeli Arabs. Large sections of the Arab public in Israel, however, reject the official designation and prefer to use "Palestinian," with or without additional reference to their Israeli citizenship. For purposes of clarity, and without intention to obliterate the Palestinian identity of this population, the designation used in this study is "Arabs in Israel."

Chapter 1. Ethnonationalism

1. The classical statement of the primordial argument is that of Clifford Geertz (1963, 105–57). A later application is Anthony Smith's (1986).

2. I include in the constructionist group, for example, Gellner (1964; 1983), Tilly (1990), Hobsbawm (1992, 80–101), Anderson (1991), and J. Breuilly (1985).

3. A classical statement of the plural argument is Smith's (1969). For a critique, see Brass (1985, 10–14). Examples of later applications are Enloe (1973) and Horowitz (1985).

Chapter 3. The Programmatic Component

1. On Lenin's Resolutions in the Second Congress of the International, 1922, see List (1964, 157–58). On the acceptance of this line by the PCP, see Ben Avram (1978, 83).

2. The number is quoted in M. Vilner in his booklet "CPI: Fifty Years of Struggle of Our Communist Party" (April 1970), 29. A small number of Arabs were recruited into the party in the late 1920s and early 1930s.

3. Budeiri (1979, 165) writes that the advice to keep the split and to deemphasize the Communist nature of the league was given in the summer of 1943 by the secretary of the Syrian Communist Party, Khaled Bakdash. His eminent position in the Communist movement made his guidance suitable to replace that of the Comintern.

4. Up to 1945, the slogan was "A Free Arab Palestine," which the league thought would be more agreeable to the traditional Arab national leadership (Budeiri 1979, 217).

5. The Congress of Arab Workers claimed to represent 20,000 workers, but observers estimate the real figure to be 10,000 (Nevo 1977, 346).

6. Nevo 1977, 354; *al Ittihad* claimed that 12,600 of its supporters protested the league's exclusion in late 1946 by sending their membership certificates to the Arab High Command (see Samara 1980, 285).

7. The figures are based on the censuses of 1922 and 1931 and on an estimate of the government in the *Statistical Abstract* of 1944.

8. They were Halil Shnir, Mulis Amru, and Salim al Qassem. Interview with Qassem, August 8, 1986. See also Nevo 1977, 344.

9. Quoted in *Kol Ha'am*, June 11, 1947, as cited in Frankel (n.d., 227). See the testimony of Mikunis and Vilner before the UN Special Commission on Palestine, "The PCP Testimony Before the UNSCP" in Frankel, 216–21.

10. *Kol Ha'am*, Oct. 15, 1948; quoted in full in Frankel (n.d., 244–45).

11. Frankel, 244–45.

12. In his 1946 appearance before the UN Special Commission on Palestine, which eventually recommended partition, the Jewish Communist leader, Schmuel Mikunis, was put on the spot when questioned about the split. At that time, the PCP opposed partition and recommended a "unitarian binational state." Mikunis was asked whether the split did not show the unwillingness of the Arabs to cooperate with Jews in a political organization (Frankel n.d., 216).

13. Ibid.

14. According to Toufiq Toubi, in an interview with Tom Segev (Hebrew), *Koteret Rashit*, Nov. 12, 1985.

15. Sections 2 and 4 of the statute of CPI-Maki, 13th Congress, 1957, 214; statute of CPI-Rakah, 19th Congress, 1981, 196. In the 21st Congress, held in May 1990, after the fall of Communism in Eastern Europe, the phrase was eliminated.

16. Ibid.

17. CPI, 21st Congress, 1990, article 5, 105.

18. This was the wording of the 1969 statute. The 1990 statute read "on the basis of two states for the two peoples." CPI, 21st Congress, 1990, article 4, 105.

19. Ibid.

20. The statute of the CPI as approved in the 13th–19th Congresses, 1957–81.

21. 18th Congress, 1976, 132.

22. Statute of the CPI-Rakah, 19th Congress, 1981, section 8. In the 21st Congress, 1990, the specific reference to the CPSU was dropped from this section.

23. CPI-Maki, 14th Congress, 1961, 61. Also "The Jewish Question and Zionism at Our Time" (Hebrew), in CPI-Rakah, 16th Congress, 1969, 372–96.

24. CPI, 20th Congress, 1985, 135.

25. CPI, 21st Congress, 1990, 20–23, 91–94.

26. Toubi, Vilner, and Gozanski justified the coup. *Hadashot*, Aug. 23, 1991; *al Ittihad*, Aug. 20–21, 1991; *Zo Haderech*, Aug. 20, 1991.

27. Toufiq Toubi and Meir Vilner in CPI, 22d Congress, 1993, 11, 25.

28. CPI-Rakah, 17th Congress, 1972, 65.

29. See the article by the general secretary of the CPI-Maki, S. Mikunis, *Kol Ha'am,* May 16, 1952.

30. See Vilner's angry reply to attacks on the CPI by the Zionist parties, *Kol Ha'am,* June 11, 1952.

31. This assessment by the party leaders included also the Arab peasants who were members of the party. See Toufiq Toubi's reference during the 12th Congress, *Kol Ha'am,* July 4, 1952.

32. See *Kol Ha'am* during July 1952.

33. British embassy secret dispatch, "Communist activities in Israel, 13th December–28th February, 1953" (F.O.371/10474/98790 no.99).

34. Lecture of CPI-Maki secretary, Schmuel Mikunis, 13th Congress, 1957, 28.

35. According to B. Balti, a Jewish member of the CPI-Maki central committee at the time, who later, at the time of the split, opposed the Arab faction (quoted in Balti 1981, 50–51).

36. CPI-Maki, 13th Congress, 1957, 29.

37. Ibid., 31.

38. Emil Habibi, in his lecture (CPI-Maki, 14th Congress, 1961, 131); the same version was repeated to me by Saliba Khamis, who argued that it made no sense then to set up an underground; if those were their intentions, he argued, they would have done so immediately following the end of the 1948 war (interview, July 1987).

39. Uzi Burshtein, interview, May 1988.

40. CPI-Maki, 14th Congress, 1961, 36.

41. CPI-Rakah, 15th Congress, 1965, 107.

42. Emil Habibi, one of the two top Arab members of the politburo and a member of the Knesset, said that some concessions were made in order to prevent the split (CPI-Rakah, 15th Congress, 1965, 101).

43. CPI-Rakah, 15th Congress, 1965, 101.

44. Ibid., 57.

45. CPI-Rakah, 16th Congress, 1969, 24.

46. Ibid., 347.

47. Ibid., 309.

48. See the indirect, critical reference by Emil Habibi, ibid., 161.

49. See the complaint on this point by Muhamad Haas in the course of the 16th Congress (ibid., 149–50). Hass eventually moved back to Gaza. Emil Habibi in his speech emphasized that "we are an Israeli party" and "we object to every adventurous act or slogan" (160–61).

50. Ibid., 314.

51. Ibid., 316.

52. CPI-Rakah, 17th Congress, 1972, 294–95.

53. Ibid., 295.

54. CPI-Rakah, 18th Congress, 1976, 109.

55. Ibid., 128.

56. Ibid., 131.

57. Ibid., 132.

58. CPI, 19th Congress, 1981, 137–38. However, the first test of the political unity of the Front was not successful, when the Black Panther member of the Knesset supported the Camp David accords, which the party denounced. However, this misunderstanding, which could be attributed to lack of political experience, was settled. See ibid., 35.

59. See the book written by the CPI ideologue Emil Touma, published by the party in Arabic in 1986 as *The Palestinian Liberation Organization* and in Hebrew in 1990 as *The Palestinian National Movement and the Arab World* (Touma 1990, 116–22).

60. CPI-Rakah, 19th Congress, 1981, 31–49, 100–108.; 20th Congress, 1985, 44–48.

61. CPI, 20th Congress, 1986, 39–41.

62. Touma, ibid., 123, 130.

63. Ibid., 34.

64. Ibid.

65. CPI, 21st Congress, 1990, 60–61.

66. See the editorials in *al Ittihad*, Jan. 15, 22, 1991.

67. See, for example, *Ha'aretz*, Jan. 23, 1991.

68. See N. Athmana in *Davar*, Feb. 12, 1991; M. Ali Taha (the editor of the party monthly *al Jadid*) in *al Ittihad*, March 8, 1991.

69. *Zo Haderech*, Sept. 14, 1993.

70. CPI-Rakah, 19th Congress, 1981, 167.

71. Ibid., 53.

72. Salim Jubran, "Self Administration or a Narrow Political Interest?" (Hebrew), *Zo Haderech*, July 24, 1991; CPI, 22d Congress, 1993, 52–54.

Chapter 4. The Style Component

1. The Cominform was founded in September 1947 as part of the Soviet postwar view of the division of the world into "democratic" and "imperialistic" blocs.

2. See, for example, the party statute, CPI, 13th Congress, 1957.

3. This position was taken by one of the important figures in the party, Muhamad Haas, originally from Gaza (CPI-Rakah, 16th Congress, 1969, 150). Those opposing the party's adherence to the 1967 borders were accused by the leadership of holding a nonproletarian, that is, nationalist, position (18th Congress, 72–73).

4. See the speech of the Jewish member Abraham Rorlich on Czechoslovakia in CPI, 16th Congress, 1969, 164–65; on the support of Nasser, see critical remarks by two members (one Jewish, one Arab) in CPI, 17th Congress, 176–77.

5. CPI, 17th Congress, 1972, 176, 224.

6. See critical remarks by various members, Arabs and Jews, in CPI, 20th Congress, 1985, part 2, 75–77, 107, 111.

7. See Vilner's reply to the criticism made by Azmi Bishara in the 19th party congress, 1981, 73–74.

8. See reference to this criticism, ibid., 75, and in Saliba Khamis' book review in *A-Sinara*, June 25, 1993.

9. Throughout its history, the party would not reveal its financial situation or its sources of funding, beyond party dues and occasional fund raising. Indirect sources,

however, indicate that the finances of the party after 1948 were linked to trade relations between Israel and the Communist bloc countries.

10. *Ha'aretz*, Oct. 9, 1987. The estimated total membership for 1990 was 3,000. A. Mansur, *Ha'aretz*, May 31, 1990.

11. In Abu-Gosh's study of the village of Qalansawa in 1963, no villagers identified as the intelligentsia (high school graduates) were members of the party (Abu-Gosh 1973). In the late 1970s, when the standard of education was higher, membership in the youth movement (Banki) became fashionable among Arab high school graduates. But as explained by one of my informants, Abdalla Naamneh of Arabe, twenty-seven years old, who became a member of Banki during his last two years of secondary school: "I was a reader of the party paper, and I joined Banki because of the Ping-Pong table at the Banki club and because I had entertained the idea of getting a fellowship from the party to study at the university; but I did not want to be a party functionary, and none of the educated were attracted by the bureaucratic work. The secretary of our cell was neither educated nor intellectual."

12. For instance, Ahmad Hamdi, a member of the committee of the Shefaram branch, had eight years of primary schooling and two years of high school evening courses. By profession he was a carpenter. He began to participate in youth organization activities at the age of fourteen as a party sympathizer. In 1974, at the age of twenty, he became a full member of the party, and three years later he was sent by the party to the Soviet Union for a one-year course on Marxism. At the age of twenty-six he became a functionary in the party (interview, June 1983).

13. The most famous of them is Mahamud Darwish, who became a well-known poet in the Arab world. He began his career working for *al Mirsad*, the Mapam paper in Arabic, and, after it closed, as a regular writer for *al Ittihad*, where his talent was recognized. In early 1971 he shocked the party by deserting to Egypt and joining the PLO, for which he later became unofficial minister of culture.

14. Saliba Khamis, a dissenter in the party leadership, interview, July 1987. (For rumors that the Muslim cadre categorically demanded such representation, see *Ma'ariv*, Sept. 19, 1969; for denials by the party leadership, see *Zo Haderech*, March 28, 1973.)

15. During 1948–65 the general secretary was Shmuel Mikunis; the general secretary of Rakah from 1965 to the 1990 was Meir Vilner. He was replaced in 1990 by Toufiq Toubi, a Christian Arab, who had been his deputy for all these years.

16. The Christian League activists were Emil Habibi, Toufiq Toubi, Saliba Khamis, Fuad Khuri, Emil Touma, Zahi Karkabi, Hana Nakara, and Mun'am Jarjura. The two Arab Union activists were Jamal Musa and Salim al Qassem, the only Muslim in the party leadership up to 1965.

17. Touma, who was the founder of the *al Ittihad* newspaper in 1945, was a prolific historian who wrote a dozen books. He would not accept the partition decision in 1947 but repented and returned to the CPI. Especially after the split in 1965, he was again considered an ideological authority in the party, and he served as editor of *al Ittihad*. He died in 1985 (*Ha'aretz*, Sept. 8, 1985); see an interview with him in *Leviathan* 3, no. 1 (Fall 1980): 39–44.

18. On the hope of mobilizing workers and the attendant difficulties, see T. Toubi,

Kol Ha'am, July 4, 1952. On the sacking of Communists from government offices by the Israeli security authorities, see the British embassy reports for the period December 13, 1952–February 28, 1953. The same reports also estimated that 25 percent of the Arab workers at the end of 1952 were adherents of the Communists; when the Congress of Arab Workers was dissolved in July 1953, the British report (June 1–August 31) estimated their number as 4,000. Only a handful of them, however, were actual members of the party (F.O. 371/10471/122057).

19. Saliba Khamis confirmed that he had made preparations for setting up an underground press in the event that the party was outlawed (A. Mansur, *Ha'aretz*, Jan. 23, 1987).

20. These are intelligence sources that publish estimates on the strength of Communist countries around the world in the *Yearbook on International Communist Affairs;* other sources are journalists' assessments. For the 1950s and early 1960s, see CPI-Maki, 14th Congress, 1961, 110–18; Czudnowski and Landau (1965, 95).

21. Abu-Gosh 1965, 60; Nakleh 1979, 96.

22. "Banki Between Congresses," *Arachim* 23, no. 1 (Feb. 1973): 101. CPI-Rakah, 16th Congress, 1969, 66.

23. *Yearbook on International Communist Affairs*, 1968, 330.

24. T. Segev, "Between Moscow and Nazareth—A Profile of Vilner," *Ha'aretz* (supplement), Feb. 22, 1980; *Yearbook on International Communist Affairs*, 1980, 415; according to Attala Mansur, who quotes an internal party report in 1982, the number of members in the largest district—Nazareth—alone was 1,500 (*Ha'aretz*, April 15, 1982).

25. CPI-Rakah, 15th Congress, 1965, 134; CPI-Rakah, 22d Congress, 1993, 79.

26. CPI-Maki, 14th Congress, 1961, 110.

27. In his speech the poet Hana Ibrahim charged that "there is a gap between the leadership and the rank and file" and that "the standards of the party activity are deteriorating. Responsibility, for sure, does not lie only with the rank and file. . . . In my opinion, there are too many functionaries in the party. It is not the way to strengthen it and forge it." Another member, Amin Ubeid, complained that in the distribution of scholarships for study abroad "there were acts not according to principle" and that decisions should be based on merit "rather than on family considerations." CPI-Rakah, 17th Congress, 1972, 128, 237.

28. General Secretary Vilner quoted Azmi Bishara's accusation that the leadership "promotes young cadre who agree to everything they [the leadership] say" (CPI, 19th Congress, 1981, 73). Charges of favoritism were made by Sami Gitas (CPI-Rakah, 20th Congress, 1985, 91; see also Samih Sabag, 97). For the same charges made in the 21st Congress, 1990, see A. Mansur, *Ha'aretz*, May 31, 1990.

29. See the interview with central committee member Nazem Bader in *Ha'aretz*, Sept. 1, 1991, when he revealed that during 1991 he was in the minority in support of a multiparty system in the Soviet Union. The party line was expressed as vague support for the reforms in the USSR, for example, the article by the editor of *al Ittihad*, Salim Jubran (May 16, 1989) in which he praised the "rebuilding of the revolution"; Jubran's deputy, Ali Ashur, commented that the CPSU voted for Gorbachev's plan because it had no choice other than to "give up the Stalinist way" in the future multiparty system (Aug. 7, 1991).

30. The most prominent figure, Emil Habibi, the well-known writer, was deposed on April 28, 1989, as the editor of the party paper in Arabic, *al Ittihad,* which he had helped found in 1944. He resigned from the politburo on May 8 and made his views public in the nonparty media, a breach of the Communist code of behavior (e.g., *Ha'ir,* Sept. 1, 1989). He later left the party. A well-known poet, Sammih al Qassem, resigned from the central committee the following February and established a weekly, *Kul al Arab.* Yossi Algazi, a prominent Jewish functionary who in the mid-1980s had criticized from within the party its total backing of the PLO, in 1990 made an outright attack in a nonparty paper on the "conservative Communist outlook and oligarchic practices" of the party leadership (*Ha'aretz,* May 18, 1990). He was ousted from the party. Uzi Burshtein, the spokesman of the Front, who suggested to the party conference in May 1990 that it drop democratic centralism, was demoted and lost his seat on the politburo (A. Mansur, *Ha'aretz,* May 31, 1990).

31. CPI, 22d Congress, 1993, 68. According to one report, in 1990 the party laid off 40 percent of its apparatus and stopped the publication of its ideological journal. Only one-third of the membership took part in the traditional volunteer camp in Nazareth (*Davar,* Aug. 5, 1990). In the Nazareth regional convention that year, only half the membership took active part, and the circulation of the party newspaper dropped considerably (*Ha'aretz,* Dec. 12, 1990).

32. *Zo Haderech,* Feb. 17, 1993.

33. The number is estimated by counting the number of localities in which protest rallies were held (*Kol Ha'am,* July 2, 1952). For the number of cells in workplaces, see CPI-Maki, 13th Congress, 1957, 207–9. For the 1980s, see CPI, 20th Congress, 1985, 15; the figure for 1995 was given by the general secretary, Muhamad Nafaa (interview, Aug. 21, 1995).

34. The central committee report in 1957 revealed that the CPI devoted 80 percent of its expenses to the party newspapers (CPI-Maki, 13th Congress, 1957, 115).

35. See *al Ittihad,* May 6, 1955.

36. See the comparison of the reporting by *al Youm* and *al Ittihad* in Abu-Gosh 1973, 198–202.

37. See the speech made by Abdel Qader Dahr, CPI-Rakah, 17th Congress, 1972, 195. In the 20th Congress, Y. Algazi criticized the party papers for "covering up for Arafat over a long period of time" during his approach to King Hussein (20th Congress, 1985, 76).

38. For instance, the editorial "Her Father Is Pleased, I Am Pleased, So Why Do We Need the Judge [for the marriage]?" The article attacks Sadat for coming to Jerusalem, thereby dealing a death blow to the Geneva Conference of 1977, with the participation of the Soviet Union. By doing so, Sadat, who claimed to be speaking for the Palestinians, let the United States off the hook for its implied recognition of the PLO which could dispense with the services of the "Judge"—the Soviet Union (*al Ittihad,* Jan. 29, 1982). The background for this commentary was the moves, not approved by the CPI, of the right-wing circles in the PLO to find a way to win American recognition.

39. David Ben-Gurion coined the expression, and set the precedent, that coalition governments in Israel would be "without Herut and without Maki." The boycott on Herut was lifted by Levi Eshkol in 1967. After the 1992 elections, for the first time in

Israel's history, a Labor-led coalition relied on the Front and the Arab Democratic Party as a parliamentary bloc for a majority.

40. See M. Vilner, "The Crisis in 1965" (Hebrew), *Arachim* no. 1 (1986): 16–17.

41. *Divrei Ha'Knesset* (The Knesset Proceedings), vol. 6, 1950, 2122–23, 2106.

42. See Toubi's question to Golda Meir, the minister of labor, on the workers in the quarry of Teibe, March 6, 1950 (*Divrei Ha'Knesset*, vol. 4, 1950, 924); during the second Knesset, 1951–55, Emil Habibi submitted numerous such questions. See Index to *Divrei Ha'Knesset*, vols. 10–12.

43. *Divrei Ha'Knesset*, vols. 10–12, 346.

44. *Zo Haderech*, March 23, 1983.

45. An example is a question to the minister of education on a dangerous school building in Acre; it was submitted by M. Miari of the PLP, on October 23, 1984; on October 31, T. Toubi submitted the same question to the minister (*Divrei Ha'Knesset*, vol. 100, 1984–85, 320). In the first sitting of the 11th Knesset the Front submitted forty-nine questions, most of them "instrumental." During the same period it submitted only four no-confidence votes, compared with seven from the Progressive List for Peace.

46. For example, between June 1992 and July 1994, the Front submitted 37 questions to ministers, passed on 200 requests of individuals to ministers and other governmental institutions, and introduced numerous bills. *Report by the Front in the Knesset*, July 27, 1994.

Chapter 5. The Slogan Component

1. *al Ittihad*, June 10, 1955.

2. Mansur 1975, 47; *Ha'aretz*, May 3, 1958.

3. *Ha'aretz*, May 3, 1959. According to the report, in the Mapam demonstration in Nazareth the slogan "Long live Nasser" was heard repeatedly.

4. The slogans carried in the First of May demonstrations in Nazareth, 1959. *Kol Ha'am*, May 3, 1959.

5. Ibid.

6. Al Ard, "Memorandum on the Arabs in Israel," sent to the secretary of the UN, July 1964; in Landau 1969, appendix D, 229.

7. Toufiq Toubi, in a speech outlining the campaign strategy in the 14th Congress, two months before the 1961 elections. CPI, 14th Congress, 1961, 158, 162.

8. Toubi, ibid., 161.

9. See the report in *Kol Ha'am*, Aug. 9, 1965. In the final official version, this slogan included the choice between return or receiving compensation. According to Habibi, this was a concession to the Mikunis group in an attempt to prevent the split. It nevertheless remained as the official Rakah line after the split.

10. CPI-Rakah, 16th Congress, 1969, 37.

11. *Ha'aretz*, May 2, 1976.

12. E. Touma explained the use of "Arab Masses" or "Arab Palestinians" rather than simply "Palestinians" as connoting the national-cultural relationship of the Arabs in

Israel, as opposed to their political allegiance; interview, *Journal of Palestinian Affairs*, quoted in *Leket*, nos. 35–36, December–January 1984.

13. The attributes used by CPI speakers in rallies and in leaflets; for example, leaflets published before the 1981 elections to the Histadrut and the Knesset (see n. 14) and for the Land Day rally in 1982 in Taibe, which I attended.

14. *al Ittihad*, April 24, 1981.

15. *Ma'ariv*, May 20, 1977.

16. *al Ittihad*, May 10, 1977.

17. *Ha'aretz*, April 24, 1977; *Ma'ariv*, May 20, 1977.

18. *Ma'ariv*, Sept. 26, 1980.

19. For the slogans used in Nazareth, see A. Mansur, "The Struggle for the Arab Vote," *Ha'aretz*, March 29, 1981.

20. PLP Platform 1984, which demanded a complete withdrawal from the 1967 occupation and the return of Arab refugees or compensation. The platform included a solution for the "internal" refugees (which the CPI lacked); it provided that peace negotiations were to be held with the PLO without mentioning an international peace conference as a necessary condition (as the CPI did).

21. See E. Touma, "Claims On the One Hand, and Reality on the Other," *al Ittihad*, July 13, 1984.

22. The slogans prepared for the First of May celebrations, 1952, *Kol Ha'am*, April 28, 1952.

23. For instance, the slogan two weeks before the elections to the Seventh Knesset, 1965: "With the 'Wau' [the letter of Rakah] we will break the head of the Reaction, Say al-Din Zu'bi [the mayor of Nazareth and head of one of the pro-government Arab lists]." *Al Ittihad*, Oct. 19, 1965.

24. In E. Habibi, "Proletarian Internationalism versus Social-Chauvinism" (a rebuttal to the incitement of Al Ha'mishmar on the CPI-Maki's struggle against the national suppression); Givaat Haviva booklet, n.d.

25. During the campaign to the 7th Knesset 1965; *al Ittihad*, Sept. 10, 1965.

26. *al Ittihad*, Dec. 14, 1973.

27. For instance, during the campaign to the 7th Knesset; *al Ittihad*, Oct. 1, 1965.

28. During the campaign for the 4th Knesset; *al Ittihad*, June 17, 1955.

29. *al Ittihad*, Oct. 8, 1965.

30. *al Ittihad*, March 31, 1981. The massacre in the village of Dir Yassin was perpetrated by the Etzel organization in April 1948, after the outbreak of hostilities but before the State of Israel was declared. After independence Etzel turned into the Herut party.

31. *al Ittihad*, July 15, 1955.

32. *al ittihad*, Oct. 8, 1965.

33. *al Ittihad*, Oct. 19, 1965.

34. *al Ittihad*, Dec. 2, 1966; Toufiq Toubi, in *al Ittihad*, Nov. 11, 1966, quoted in Geffner 1973, 99.

35. *al Ittihad*, Nov. 11, 1966.

36. With this slogan, Nasia Shafran (1983, 153–74) heads the chapter on the Jewish-Arab relationship in the CPI-Maki. As a Jewish youth affiliated with Maki, however, she sees the split in 1965 as the total collapse of the "Jewish-Arab Fraternity." Nevertheless, in almost every demonstration Rakah organizes, especially the First of May demonstrations, this slogan is not only carried on signs but also called out by the demonstrators.

37. *al Ittihad*, Sept. 9, 14, 1965.

38. *al Ittihad*, Aug. 12, 1969, March 24, 1981.

39. In the 1979 Land Day rally a squabble developed between the radical nationalist Abna al Balad and the CPI demonstrators. The former called out nationalist rejectionist slogans ("The Galilee is like Hebron") and were answered with "Jewish-Arab Fraternity" (*Ha'aretz*, Feb. 18, 1979).

40. *al Ittihad*, Sept. 17, Oct. 22, 1965, Aug. 12, 1969.

41. See for instance, *al Ittihad*, June 29, July 2, 3, 1984.

42. *al Ittihad*, July 2, 1984. The CPI continued to call the party Ma'arach even though its name was changed to Labor. The reason is probably the desire to keep the negative association that Arab voters may identify with the "old regime."

Chapter 6. Social and Economic Change

1. Carmi and Rosenfeld refer to them as "peasant proletarians" because of the casual nature of their out-of-village employment and their lack of urbanization. They estimate that during the height of the war economy in the 1940s, half of the peasant labor force was employed as wage earners outside the villages (1974, 477).

2. This line of analysis follows Rosenfeld's studies of the rural social and occupational change among the Arab-Palestinians, particularly his 1978 work.

3. Figures for 1956, *CBS Labor Force Survey*, special series no. 68, table 3; for 1965, Israel's *Statistical Abstract* 1968, table K/9.

4. For 1963, *Statistical Abstract* 1964, 317–19; for 1976, *Statistical Abstract* 1978, 351.

5. *Statistical Abstract* 1970–1981, tables "Income and Expenditure and Savings Per Urban Households." For 1989, see Faris 1993, 49.

6. For income, see Ginnor 1980, 134, 195. Data on appliances are given in the *Statistical Abstract*.

Chapter 7. Oppositionist and Electoral Politics

1. Mapai was the chief Zionist party that sponsored a number of allied Arab lists but was not the only one. None, however, was successful in entering a representative to the Knesset (Landau 1969, 121–39).

2. *Divrei Ha'Knesset*, index to vols. 10–12, 101–209.

3. Mun'am Jarjura, Fuad Khuri, Hana Nakara, and Saliba Khamis.

4. See, for example, the involvement of the local Ramle CPI cell in agricultural workers' pay dispute against Arab landowners (Nakhleh 1979, 97–98). Jamal Mousa, as a functionary of the Mu'tamar in the early 1950s, organized a demonstration of workers in the village of Dir al Asad demanding "bread and work" and strikes in the Haifa

area seeking better conditions for the Arab workers. Cooperative food shops of the Mu'tamar were set up when food shortages occurred in several villages in the years 1949–52. Interview, August 1988.

5. Interview with Arna Mer, July 1986. Mer, a Jew, was a member of the CPI until 1974 and the ex-wife of Saliba Khamis, one of the Arab Communist leaders; although Mer was a rank and file member, she was heavily involved in the cultural and political activities of the party.

6. Saliba Khamis lamented this historical decision as a mistake (interview, February 1987).

7. Regarding Kfar Yassif, see Nakhleh 1979, 94; Dir al Asad, according to Jamal Moussa, interview 1985.

8. For instance, the secretary of the CPI branch in Um al Fahem and other members were banished in 1950 to the village of Bartaa after they organized the demonstration against the Military Rule. Interview with Abu Afuwi, July 1983; see also Jiryis 1976, 29.

9. State Controller's Report on Security, 1957/8, February 1959, 57–58.

10. The quote is by S. Divon, the former adviser to the prime minister for Arab affairs (Shwartz 1959, 141).

11. For example, see the report on the speech of Emil Habibi to a mass rally in the village of Rame (Ha'aretz, April 30, 1954).

12. See Habibi's protest, Knesset Debates, July 31, 1957, p. 2625.

13. For instance, after a demonstration organized by the party cell in Um al Fahem in February 1950, a petition denouncing the Communists was signed by villagers; the Communists claimed that the military governor was behind it (interview with Abu Afuwi, the late secretary of the party branch, in Um al Fahem, May 1983). A similar petition was signed in Taibe in August 1954, and in Nazareth Communists were harassed by political rivals. Emil Habibi, "Proletarian Internationalism vs. Social Chauvinism," n.p., n.d. (a polemic for the Mapam party).

14. The coherence and strength of the traditional leadership are relative matters and subjectively determined. The categorization of villages as having "strong" or "weak" leadership is based on discussions with inhabitants and local officials, as well as on a few academic works related to a number of localities, e.g., Habash 1973 (on Kafar Qara and Baqa al Gharbiyya), 1977 (on Kafar Qasem); Abu-Gosh, 1965 (on Qalansawa).

15. See Davar, May 2, 4, 1958; Al Hamishmar, May 4, 1958. Party spokesmen presented the clash as resulting from the attempt by the police to prevent the CPI demonstration. But this motivation was affirmed by the late party secretary in Um al Fahem, Abu Afuwi; interview, May 1983.

16. In the two days of riots that followed, twenty-eight people were injured and mass arrests made.

17. While it politicized the high school students, it did not necessarily lead them to the Communist Party. Nawaf Massalha, later a Labor party activist in Histadrut, member of the Knesset, and deputy minister representing Labor, described the strong impact of this period on him as a high school student in Nazareth; radio interview, Galei Zahal, Aug. 13, 1983. Ibrahim G'anaim of Baqa al Gharbiyya, on the other hand, be-

came a Nasserist as a young student living in Nazareth at this period. He was active in the circle of the CPI sympathizers until 1958. He subsequently became involved in al Ard and Palestinian underground activity and was detained by an administrative order. After being freed, he identified with the Islamic fundamentalist movement. Interview, June 1983.

18. The figures are computed from the election results (Harari 1981, 69).

19. It is estimated that by 1963, a total of 1,500–2,000 Arabs were high school and college graduates, out of a total of 20,000–25,000 in that age group (Mansour 1964, 26–31).

20. Mansour estimated that of the 6,000 graduates of elementary schools in 1964, 5,000 went on the job market, and despite the increase in job opportunities in the public sector after 1958, 20 percent of the high school graduates had to turn to manual labor (Mansour 1964, 28).

21. Between the middle of March 1968 and the end of October 1969, there were eleven terrorist attacks in which civilians in Israel were killed and injured. In this period at least six Arab citizens were tried and sentenced for direct involvement in some of the bombings. See *Davar*, May 21, 1985. By 1972, a total of 320 Israeli Arabs had been tried for involvement with subversive organizations (Jiryis 1976, 67).

22. See the results of a small survey on the attitude of Arab youngsters to religion in *Hamizrach Hachadash* 15, no. 1 (1965): 87–90.

23. The text of the lecture given in Haifa on Nov. 11, 1969, appeared in the party monthly, *Arachim* no. 4 (Jan. 1970): 21–30.

24. According to the 1972 Census data, 30.2 percent of the men between the ages of eighteen and twenty-four had nine to twelve years of schooling, compared with 17.2 percent of the age group twenty-five to twenty-nine. Of the first group, 47.7 percent had five to eight years of schooling. Quoted in Shmaltz 1978, 50.

25. The data on Arab membership supplied by the Institute for Economic and Social Research of Histadrut to the delegates of the 15th Convention, October 1985. Almost all political parties that run for the Knesset run in Histadrut as well. Before Labor's loss of control of Histadrut in 1994, which brought about major organizational changes, 60 percent of the adult population in Israel was organized by Histadrut. Hence, the results were often looked upon as the results of a by-election.

26. In 1989, the CPI ran an ad hoc joint list with its Arab rivals, the PLP and the Arab Democratic Party. The list received 33 percent of the vote, 12 percent less than the separate lists in 1985. In the 1994 elections, the CPI ran again with the PLP and received only 22 percent. The Arab Democratic Party ran with Labor, winning together about 50 percent—a significant increase (Ghanem and Ozacky-Lazar, 1994).

Chapter 8. Instituting a Rival Political Establishment in the 1970s

1. CPI, 19th Congress, 1981, 137.

2. See the reply of the general secretary, Vilner, to Azmi Bishara's criticism of the inclusion of Black Panther Charlie Biton in a safe seat in the Front's list for the Knesset (CPI-Rakah, 19th Congress, 1981, 75). Bishara, a young academician, voiced in public

the opinion held by Saliba Khamis, at the time a member of the secretariat and in the process of demotion from the party's central bodies for his oppositionist views on a host of other matters. In 1987, Khamis was expelled from the party.

3. Nakhleh 1979, 57–62; interview with Johnny Jahchshan, secretary of the Front 1979–80, July 1983.

4. Bishara's father was a member of the League for National Liberation and for a number of years a member of the CPI-Maki; interview, June 1988. See also *Ha'aretz*, March 3, 1979.

5. Yet Bishara, while a student under a party grant in East Germany, was also one of the outspoken critics of the party leadership in the early 1980s, and he eventually left the party. In April 1996 he returned to the Front as the representative of a coalition, the Democratic National Alliance, and was elected to the Knesset on the Front's slate.

6. They organized themselves when the nominated city council, which replaced the elected one in 1974, began to raise drastically the low rates of municipal taxes; interview with Ramez Jerisi, acting deputy of the mayor of Nazareth, July 1983. In 1994 Jerisi became mayor following the death of Ziad.

7. The authorities blamed the city's financial difficulties on the ignorance of the new administration. See *Los Angeles Times*, May 2, 1976.

8. In 1969–70, a total of 212 Arabs passed the matriculation exams; in 1974–75, the number was 780. CBS *Statistical Abstract*, 1985, 629.

9. Figures provided to me by Salim al Qassem, member of the CPI politburo and head of the committee on scholarships in the CPI central committee.

10. Based on a discussion in March 1986 with one such scholar, who had graduated from the Soviet Union in 1985 and who asked not to be identified because of his critical views of the Soviet Union. See also *Ma'ariv*, October 1980.

11. A. Mansour, *Ha'aretz*, Feb. 14, 1984.

12. According to Saliba Khamis, it was his idea to set up such a committee, and he indeed was active in it until his break with the party in 1986 (interview, January 1987). See also Memorandum submitted by the National Committee for the Defense of Arab Land—Israel, to the UN Committee on Human Rights, Feb. 17, 1979.

13. *Zo Haderech*, April 5, 1978. This was a response to the attempt by the nationalist Abna al Balad to call a general strike during the 1978 Land Day. See *Zo Haderech*, March 15, 1978.

14. For instance, in the 1979 and 1981 Land Days; *Zo Haderech*, March 21, 1979, April 1, 1981.

15. This was suggested by some of the more radical members of the National Committee for the Defense of Arab Lands, probably including the Communist Saliba Khamis. A. Mansur, "Rakah Blows Slogans and Confusion" *Ha'aretz*, Oct. 10, 1980.

16. See *Davar*, Nov. 9, Oct. 27, 1980.

17. *Ha'aretz*, Sept. 21, 1982; *Davar*, Sept. 26, 1982.

18. The Committee against the War in Lebanon was the first to call for a strike, and the CPI suggested that the Committee of Arab Municipal Heads would "join that call." But the latter, calling itself a "more representative body," decided that it would call for

a general strike and would offer any other body to join. See A. Mansur, "The Violent Rage of the Arabs of Israel," *Ha'aretz*, Sept. 24, 1982.

19. *Ha'aretz*, Jan. 3, 1983.

20. A. Mansur, "The Lesson of the 'Land Day,'" *Ha'aretz*, April 3, 1983.

21. The Kening Memo, written by Israel Kening, head of the Northern Region in the Interior Ministry, was published in *Al Hamishmar*, Sept. 7, 1976. It was never adopted as an official document by the government. For a profile of Kening, see R. Pedatzur, *Ha'aretz* (magazine), Feb. 4, 1983.

22. See Toufiq Toubi's lecture to the 10th meeting of the central committee, Jan. 29, 1982, quoted in *Arachim*, Feb. 1982, 26.

23. Toufiq Toubi, "Toward Progress in Our Party Work," a lecture to party activists, Nov. 11, 1969, as it appeared in *Arachim*, Jan. 1970, 28.

24. As a rule, the CPI representatives ask for the culture and education portfolios in the local councils in which they are part of the coalition.

25. The local councils in two Front-controlled villages—Mgar and Eblin—were suspended by the Ministry of Interior in 1981 because of mismanagement (*Arachim*, Feb. 1982, 14). In Um al Fahem, the least developed of the large localities, the Front-led council was unable to overcome the huge infrastructure and financial problems and lost the elections there to the well-organized Islamic movement in 1989.

26. CPI-Rakah, 19th Congress, 1981, 137–38.

27. The only community in which the Likud showed some interest was among the Druze.

28. In the 1984 and 1988 campaigns, the fifth place was allotted to the Front chairman of Um al Fahem, Hashem Mahamid. By the time he entered the Knesset, in 1989, he had lost his position in Um al Fahem. Nevertheless, he was placed second on the list in the 1992 and 1996 elections to the Knesset because he represented the Muslim Triangle area.

29. In the 1978 local races for the chairmanship, eighteen municipalities were won by the Front candidates; in 1983, twenty of a total of forty-six municipalities; in 1989, fifteen of forty-seven; and in 1993, twelve of fifty-six. *Ha'aretz*, Oct. 24, 1983; CPI, 20th Congress, 1985, 60; Ghanem and Ozacky 1994, 19.

Chapter 9. The CPI's New Challengers

1. Z. Askander, "Sons of the Village" (Hebrew), *Bamerhav*, Jan. 6, 1979.

2. See the public statement put out by the group during the convention of the Palestinian National Council in January 1979, in which they denounced the leadership of the CPI for recognizing the "Zionist entity." *Ma'ariv*, Feb. 2, 1979.

3. According to newspaper reports, there were two versions of the covenant: the first, which was closer to the radical nationalist position, stated that "Arabs living in Israel are an inseparable part of the Arab Palestinian people, and that the PLO is the sole representative of that people." The second and final version was the same as the CPI's official position. See *Davar*, Oct. 27, Nov. 9, 1980.

4. See A. Mansur, "The Revolution Has Not Come to Nazareth," *Ha'aretz*, Dec. 9, 1977; "Nazareth Without Illusions," *Ha'aretz*, Oct. 18, 1978; *Ha'aretz*, May 12, 1978.

However, the spokesman for the Nazareth municipality, Ziad Fahum, denied the charges of nepotism and claimed that of the 380 workers of the municipality in 1983, only 5 percent were members of the Front. Interview, July 1983.

5. Interview with Ramez Jerisi. See also the Nazareth Front publication "Voice of Nazareth" (Arabic), June 1983.

6. *Ha'aretz*, Nov. 8, 1978.

7. A. Mansur, "The Dream of a University of the Arabs of the Galilee" *Ha'aretz*, March 11, 1981.

8. In the manifesto explaining why the Progressives left the academicians and the Front, it is claimed that the Communists were represented, both in their party capacity and as individual members, in the academicians' association. "The Progressive Movement—Nazareth" (Arabic), 1981.

9. A. Mansur, "Rakah Is Looking for an Alternative to the PLO," *Ha'aretz*, Nov. 30, 1980.

10. Article 1 of the Progressive Movement manifesto defines the Arabs as "citizens in Israel who are part of the Arab Palestinians who insist on their identity." It calls for the "just solution for the two sides, by carrying out the U.N. Resolutions . . . and recognition of its right for determining its own fate." "The Progressive Movement—Nazareth" (Arabic), 1981.

11. Ibid.

12. Results of the Histadrut elections are based on figures supplied by the Vaad Hapoel (the Executive Committee); for information on the campaign, see A. Mansur, *Ha'aretz*, April 13, 1981.

13. Central Bureau of Statistics, "The 1983 Census of Population and Housing," publication nos. 3–5, Jerusalem, 1985. Socioeconomic data are available only for localities where the population exceeded 2,000.

14. The independent and dependent variables are averages of various indicators that characterize the population in a locality. The justification for using ecological variables in this case is that the arguments presented in this study are contextual in nature. The assumption of such arguments is that social contexts within which a person lives—the community, the neighborhoods, the ethnic or class ties—have an independent effect on the electoral behavior of the individual. This study hypothesizes that the Arab locality, where social boundaries remained defined over the entire period, constitutes an important intervening variable in the political mobilization or politicization process. The effects of the general process of change on people are mediated by the social dynamics that characterize the locality in which the people live; in turn, these social dynamics are influenced by the political tradition, by the social structure, and by the personalities active in the public arena of each locality. Thus, people in the same locality who have different personal attributes (level of education, political interest, religion, etc.) may behave electorally in a similar way, owing to the political atmosphere and political dynamics of their locality.

15. See the detailed account of the failed negotiations on this matter between the Front and the PLP in *Smoll*, no. 42, Oct. 1988.

16. Because there is no Islamic seminary college in Israel, those who wanted to

specialize in Islamic religious studies had to study in Hebron in the West Bank. There they were usually "converted" to fundamentalist Islam. See "From Hebron without Love," *Ha'aretz* (magazine), November 1980.

17. A. Mansur, "The Hamulas Are Dead, Long Live Khomeini," *Ha'aretz*, Jan. 25, 1980; Y. Bitchkov, *Ha'aretz* (magazine), Nov. 20, 1981.

18. In the Land Day rally in the village of Dir Hana in 1989 and in the town of Shefaram in 1994, supporters of both groups clashed.

19. It won the race for head of the locality in five places and 10 percent of the seats in the local councils. Paz 1989, 1–2.

20. See, for instance, the interview with Saliba Khamis in *Al Sinara*, March 22, 1991, and in *Kul al Arab*, April 4, 1991.

21. *Yediot Aharonot*, May 20, 1995.

22. As a result of the contest that developed in the expression of solidarity with the deported Palestinians in Gaza, the Front member of the Knesset, Mahamid, was censured by the Knesset after he encouraged a crowd in Gaza to continue the armed struggle against the Israeli army. *Ha'aretz*, Dec. 25, 30, 1992, May 3, 1994.

23. See an interview with Darwish, *Ha'aretz*, June 1, 1995.

24. CPI, 21st Congress, 1990, 75.

25. See *al Ittihad*, March 22, 1992.

26. In the vote by the new central committee, Vilner came in last with another member. The publication of these results is a novelty. See *Zo Haderech*, Feb. 12, 1993.

27. Muhamad Nafaa was elected to the post. Ibid.

28. See *Davar*, July 2, 1992. Ziad denied emphatically that his ultimate purpose was to replace the party with the Front. *Zo Haderech*, Oct. 21, 1992.

29. *al Ittihad*, June 6, 1995.

30. The efforts of the Front to identify itself as the most patriotic Palestinian political body among its Arab competitors intensified as the peace process got under way at the end of 1991. The CPI supported the PLO's decision to go to the Madrid conference and identified completely with its demands vis-à-vis the Likud government. By no coincidence, the Front's convention that year was held on November 15, the date of the Palestinian declaration of independence three years earlier. The guest of honor, who was also invited to speak, was the head of the Palestinian delegation to the Madrid conference, Dr. Abdel Shaf'i from Gaza. See *Zo Haderech*, Nov. 21, 1991.

31. *Ha'aretz*, May 23, 1995.

CONCLUSION

1. It is interesting to note that even the small political movement Abna al Balad, whose ideology followed that of the Democratic Front of George Habash, objected to the introduction of the Intifada into the Green Line, citing the "special role" of the Palestinians in Israel. The means at their disposal began with the leaflet and ended with the general strike (see Ozacky-Lazar and Ghanem 1993, 9–18).

2. See Ross 1992.

3. See interview with the party secretary, Meir Vilner, in *Davar*, May 12, 1989; also interview with Tamar Gozanski in *Hadashot*, May 5, 1989.

4. According to a poll conducted at the beginning of 1993 by the Jaffa Research Center, published in *Al Sinara*, Feb. 26, 1993, the Abna al Balad won a total of eight council seats in the 1993 local elections. Part of the Abna al Balad decided to take part in the 1996 national elections and joined the Front as part of the National Democratic Alliance.

5. Smooha (1989, 100–104) found that 71 percent of a sample of the Arab public supported an Arab university, 63 percent supported Arab labor unions, 63 percent wanted the Arab school system to be controlled by Arabs, but only 34 percent supported out-right political self-rule. In a 1993 survey by the Jaffa Research Center, 26 percent preferred that the Arab sector "integrate" into Israel, 22 percent preferred "autonomy," and 17 percent wanted the "existing situation" to continue. *Al Sinara*, Feb. 26, 1993.

6. According to Lewin-Epstein (1990, 27). However, a different study argues that Arab workers employed by Arab businesses attain jobs better matched to their education than in the Jewish private sector (Shavit 1992, 57).

GLOSSARY

Hadash: Hebrew acronym for the Democratic Front for Peace and Equality set up in 1977 by CPI-Rakah.

Histadrut: General Federation of Workers in Israel, established in 1920 in Palestine as an organization of Hebrew (Jewish) workers. By the 1940s it had become a "government in the making." In addition to acting as an all-encompassing trade union organization (with membership of 85 percent of salaried workers), it developed as a public sector conglomerate of health, welfare, cultural, economic, and financial organizations and up to 1948 commanded military units. Histadrut was the political stronghold of Mapai and its successor, the Labor Party, up to 1994. Arab workers were admitted in stages and as full members only in 1959.

Intifada: The uprising of the Palestinians in the West Bank and Gaza against Israeli occupation; it began in December 1987. At first a popular mass stone-throwing resistance to the presence of the Israeli army, it changed into acts of civil disobedience and acts of violence against Israeli military and civilians in the occupied territories and within Israel. These acts were organized by both PLO-affiliated groups and the Islamic Hamas, as well as by individuals. The inability of Israel to put down the Intifada by force led to the Oslo Declaration of Principles with the PLO in September 1993. The Hamas rejected the accords and intensified its acts of violence.

Knesset: The Israeli parliament and legislative body, made up of 120 members who are elected on party lists by a proportional electoral system.

Maki: The Community Party of Israel between 1948 and 1965, at which time it split into a Jewish faction and a predominantly Arab faction. The Jewish faction retained the name Maki until it disintegrated in 1973. The surviving faction—the New Communist List (Rakah)—has "repossessed" Maki as its official name since the mid-1980s.

Mapai: The leading labor party among Zionist political institutions and the Jewish community (the Yishuv) in Palestine since 1930. After 1948 it was the dominant party in all governments up to 1977. In 1968 Mapai formed an alignment with two other parties, thereafter referred to as the "Maarch" (the alignment). Its official name since 1969 has been the Labor Party of Israel (Mifleget Ha'avoda Ha'israelit).

Mapam: A Zionist-Socialist party based on the kibbutz movement, established in 1948 as a union between two Zionist socialist movements. It had Marxist and pro-Soviet orientations and was therefore strongly opposed to Mapai. In 1954 it was the first Zionist party to accept Arabs as members. In the mid-1950s it broke away from its pro-Soviet orientation and softened its Marxist leanings. In the 1960s and 1970s it participated in the government led by Mapai with which it formed an alliance from 1969 to 1984. In 1992 it joined an alliance with two other parties to form Meretz.

Rakah: The Hebrew acronym of the New Communist List, the Arab-Jewish Communist faction in the split in Maki in 1965. It consisted of the entire Arab membership and leadership of Maki and a section of the Jewish membership and leadership. Since the formation of the Democratic Front for Peace and Equality (Hadash) in 1977, the party's representation in the Knesset has included at least one noncommunist member of the Front in a safe seat. Since the mid-1980s, the party has readopted the name Maki—the acronym of the CPI—and has used it on its official publications.

BIBLIOGRAPHY

Abu-Gosh, Subhi. 1965. "The Politics of an Arab Village in Israel." Ph.D. diss., Princeton University.

———. 1972. "The Election Campaign in the Arab Sector." In Alan Arian, ed., *The Elections in Israel—1969*, 239–53. Jerusalem: Academic Press.

Al Haj, Majid I. 1983. "Family Life among Groups and Sects in an Arab Town in Israel." Ph.D. thesis, Hebrew University.

———. 1989. "Elections and the Arabs at the Shadow of the Intifada: Propaganda and Results" (in Hebrew). In Jacob Landau, ed., *The Arab Vote in Israel's Parliamentary Elections, 1988*, 35–49. Jerusalem: The Jerusalem Institute of Israel Studies.

Al Haj, Majid I., and Henri Rosenfeld. 1990. *Arab Local Government in Israel*. Boulder, Colo.: Westview Press.

Al Haj, Majid I., and Avner Yaniv. 1983. "Uniformity or Diversity: A Reappraisal of the Voting Behaviour of the Arab Minority in Israel." In Alan Arian, ed., *Elections in Israel 1981*, 139–64. Jerusalem: Academic Press.

Amitay, Yosef. 1988. *The United Workers' Party (Mapam) 1948–1954: Attitudes on Palestinian-Arab Issues* (in Hebrew). Tel Aviv: Tcherikover Publishers.

Anderson, Benedict. 1991. *Imagined Communities: Reflections on the Origin and Spread of Nationalism*. Rev. ed. London: Verso.

Ballas, Shimon. 1978. *Arab Literature under the Shadow of War* (in Hebrew). Tel Aviv: Am Oved.

Balti, Berl. 1981. *In the Struggle for the Jewish Existence* (in Hebrew). Jerusalem: Marcus.

Beinin, Joel. 1986. "Class and Politics in Middle Eastern Societies." *Comparative Study of Society and History* 28, no. 3 (July): 552–57.

———. 1991. "Knowing Your Enemy, Knowing Your Ally: The Arabists of Hashomer Hatza'ir (Mapam)." *Social Text* 28: 100–121.

Ben-Artzi, Yosef. 1986. "The Demographic and Spatial Development of Haifa from a Coastal Town to a Cosmopolitical Harbour City, 1832–1848." Paper read in a colloquium on "Palestine 1840–1948, Population and Immigration," University of Haifa, June 9–11.

Ben Avram, Baruch. 1978. *Parties and Political Trends during the National Home Period, 1918–1948* (in Hebrew). Jerusalem: Shazar Center, Israeli Historic Society.

Benziman, Uzi, and Attala Mansur. 1992. *The Goverment Policy toward the Arabs in*

Israel, 1948–1990: Processes of Decision Making and Implementation (in Hebrew). Jerusalem: Keter.

Berger-Barzily, Josef. 1968. *The Tragedy of the Soviet Revolution* (in Hebrew). Tel Aviv: Am Oved.

Brass, Paul. 1985. "Ethnic Groups and the State." In Paul Brass, ed., *Ethnic Groups and the State.* Totowa, N.J.: Barnes and Noble.

Breuilly, John. 1985. *Nationalism and the State.* New York: St. Martin's Press.

Budeiri, Musa. 1979. *The Palestine Communist Party 1919–1948: Arab and Jew in the Struggle for Internationalism.* London: Ithaca Press.

Carmi, Shulamit, and Henri Rosenfeld. 1974. "The Origins of the Process of Proletarization and Urbanization of Arab Peasants in Palestine." *City and Peasant: Annals of the New-York Academy of Science* 220, no. 6 (March): 470–85.

———. 1992. "Israel's Political Economy and the Widening Class Gap between Its Two National Groups." *Asian and African Studies* 26:15–61.

Czudnowski Moshe, and Jacob Landau. 1965. *The Israeli Communist Party and the Elections to the Fifth Knesset, 1961.* Stanford: The Hoover Institution.

Edelstein, Meir. 1973. "On the Split in Maki in 1965" (in Hebrew). *Measef* (March): 146–95.

Enloe, Cynthia. 1973. *Ethnic Conflict and Political Development.* Boston: Little, Brown.

Faris, Amin. 1993. *Beyond the Pitta-Bread: Poverty and Economic Gaps among the Arabs in Israel.* Bet Berl: The Institute for Israeli Arab Studies.

Flapan, Simha. 1963. "Planning for the Arab Village." *New Outlook* (October): 24–31.

Frankel, Jonathan, ed. n.d. *The Communist Movement and the Yishuv in Eretz Yisrael, 1920–1948.* Jerusalem: Hebrew University.

Freedman, Robert. 1975. *Soviet Policy toward the Middle East since 1970.* New York: Praeger.

Geertz, Clifford. 1963. "The Integrative Revolution: Primordial Sentiments and Civil Politics in the New States." In Clifford Geertz, ed., *Old Societies and New States.* New York: Free Press.

Geffner, Ellen. 1973. "Attitudes of Arab Editorials in Israel 1948–67." Ph.D. diss., University of Michigan.

Gellner, Ernest. 1964. *Thought and Change.* London: Weidenfeld and Nicholson.

———. 1983. *Nations and Nationalism.* Ithaca and London: Cornell University Press.

Ghanem, Asad, and Sarah Ozacky. 1989. *The Results of the Elections to the Histadrut in the Arab Sector* (in Hebrew). Givaat Haviva: Institute for Arab Studies.

Ghanem, Asad, and Sarah Ozacky-Lazar. 1994. *The Municipal Elections in the Arab Sector in Israel, November 1993: Results and Analysis* (in Hebrew). Givaat Haviva: Institute for Arab Studies.

Ginat, Yosef. 1980. *Employment as a Cause of Social Change in the Arab Village.* Working Paper no. 6-80, The Sapir Center for Development, Tel Aviv University.

Ginnor, Fanni. 1980. *Socio-Economic Disparities in Israel* (in Hebrew). Tel Aviv: Am Oved.

Golan, Galia. 1976. *The Soviet Union and the PLO.* Adelphi Papers, no. 13 (Winter).

Goldberg, Giora. 1981. "Adaptation to Competitive Politics: The Case of Israeli Communism." *Studies in Comparative Communism* 14, no. 1 (Spring): 331–51.

Gurr, Ted. 1993. *Minorities at Risk.* Washington: UN Institute of Peace.

Habash, Awni. 1973. "Society in Transition." Ph.D. diss., Cornell University.

———. 1977. *Processes of Change and Modernization in the Arab Family* (in Hebrew). Jerusalem: Hebrew University.

Haidar, Aziz. 1991. *Social Welfare Services for Israel's Arab Population.* Boulder, Colo.: Westview Press.

Haim, Sylvia., ed. 1976. *Arab Nationalism.* Berkeley: University of California Press.

Harel, Isser. 1987. *Soviet Espionage: Communism in Israel* (in Hebrew). Jerusalem: Yediot Aharonot.

Hechter, Michael. 1975. *Internal Colonialism: The Celtic Fringe in British National Development, 1536–1966.* London: Routledge.

Hen Tov, Jacob. 1974. *Communism and Zionism in Palestine: The Comintern and the Political Unrest in the 1920s.* Cambridge, Mass.: Schenkman.

Hobsbawm, Eric J. 1992. *Nations and Nationalism Since 1780.* 2d ed. Cambridge: Cambridge University Press.

Hofman, John, and Nadim Rouhana. 1976. "Young Arabs in Israel: Some Aspects of a Conflicted Identity." *Journal of Social Psychology* 99, 1st half (June): 75–86.

Horowitz, Donald L. 1985. *Ethnic Groups in Conflict.* Berkeley: University of California Press.

Hroch, Miroslav. 1985. *Social Preconditions of National Revival in Europe: A Comparative Analysis of the Social Composition of Patriotic Groups among Smaller European Nations.* Cambridge: Cambridge University Press.

Israeli, G.Z. [pseud. of Walter Laqueur]. 1953. *MPS–PCP–Maki* (in Hebrew). Tel Aviv: Am Oved.

Jiryis, Sabri. 1976. *The Arabs in Israel.* New York and London: Monthly Review Press.

Kana'naa, Sharif. 1976. *Socio-Cultural and Psychological Adjustment of the Arab Minority in Israel.* San Fransisco: R&E Research Associates.

Keating, Michael. 1992. "Do the Workers Really Have No Country? Peripherial Nationalism and Socialism in the United Kingdom, France, Italy and Spain." In John Coakly, ed., *The Social Origins of Nationalist Movements.* London: Sage.

Khalidi, Raja. 1988. *The Arab Economy in Israel.* London: Croom Helm.

Kimmerling, Baruch, and Joel Migdal. 1992. *Palestinians: The Making of a People.* New York: The Free Press.

Kipnis, Baruch. 1978. "Geopolitical Ideologies and Regional Strategies in Israel." *Tijdchrift voor Economische en Sociale Geografie* 78: 125–38.

Kriegel, Ann. 1972. *The French Communists.* Chicago: University of Chicago Press.

Landau, Jacob. 1969. *The Arabs in Israel: A Political Study.* London: Oxford University Press.

———. 1993. *The Arab Minority in Israel, 1967–1991: Political Aspects* (in Hebrew). Tel Aviv: Am Oved.

———, ed. 1989. *The Arab Vote in Israel's Parliamentary Elections, 1988* (in Hebrew). Jerusalem: The Jerusalem Institute for Israel Studies.

Levinson, Hana, Elihu Katz, and Majid Al Haj. 1995. *Jews and Arabs in Israel: Joint Values and Mutual Images* (in Hebrew). Jerusalem: Guttman Institute of Applied Social Research.

Lewin-Epstein, Noah. 1990. "The Arab Economy in Israel: Growing Population-Jobs Mismatch." Discussion Paper no. 14-90, Pinhas Sapir Center for Development, Tel Aviv University, October.

Lewin-Epstein, Noah, and Moshe Semyonov. 1993. *The Arab Minority in Israel's Economy.* Boulder, Colo.: Westview Press.

List, Nahman. 1964. "The Comintern Was Right" (in Hebrew). *Keshet* 22 (Winter): 157–68.

———. 1965. "The Comintern Was Right. . . ." *Keshet* 27 (Spring): 86–97.

Lustick, Ian. 1980. *Arabs in the Jewish State: Israel's Control of a National Minority.* Austin: University of Texas Press.

———. 1990. "The Changing Political Role of Israeli Arabs." In Alan Arian and Michal Shamir, eds., *The Elections in Israel 1988,* 115–31. Boulder, Colo.: Westview Press.

Mair, Peter, and Ian McAlister. 1982. "A Territorial vs. a Class Appeal?" *European Journal of Political Research* 10:17–34.

Malik, Ibrahim. 1990. *The Islamic Movement in Israel* (in Hebrew). Givaat Haviva: Institute for Arab Studies, August.

Mansur, Atalla. 1964. "Arab Intellectuals Not Integrated." *New Outlook* (June): 26–31.

———. 1975. *Waiting for the Dawn.* London: Secker and Warburg.

Mayer, Tomas. 1988. *The Awakening of the Moslems in Israel* (in Hebrew). Givaat Haviva: Institute for Arab Studies.

Meyer-Brodnitz, Michael, and Daniel Czamanski. 1986. "Industrialization of the Arab Village in Israel" (in Hebrew). *Riv'on Le'kalkala* 36, no. 128: 533–46.

Miller-Rubinstein, Sandra. 1985. *The Communist Movement in Palestine and Israel, 1919–1984.* Boulder and London: Westview.

Morris, Benny. 1987. *The Birth of the Palestinian Refugee Problem, 1947–1949.* Cambridge: Cambridge University Press.

———. 1993. *Israel's Border Wars, 1949–1956.* Oxford: Clarendon Press.

Nahas, Dunia. 1976. *The Israeli Communist Party.* London: Croom Helm.

Nakhleh, Khalil. 1973. "Shifting Patterns of Conflict in Selected Arab Villages in Israel." Ph.D. diss., Indiana University.

———. 1973. *Palestinian Dilemma: Nationalist Consciousness and University Education in Israel.* Detroit: Association of Arab American University Graduates, monograph series no. 18.

Narkiewicz, Olga A. 1981. *Marxism and the Reality of Power.* New York: St. Martin's Press.

Nevo, Yosef. 1977. "The Political Development of the Palestinian National Movement, 1939–1945" (in Hebrew). Ph.D. diss. Tel Aviv University.

Ozacky, Sarah. 1990. *The Positions of the Arabs of Israel toward the State, 1949–1967* (in Hebrew). M.A. thesis, University of Haifa.

Ozacky-Lazar, Sarah. 1992. *The Elections to the 13th Knesset among the Arabs in Israel* (in Hebrew). Givaat Haviva (July).

Ozacky, Sarah, and Asad Ghanem. 1990. *Autonomy for the Arabs in Israel—The Beginning of a Debate* (in Hebrew). Givaat Haviva (December).

Ozacky, Sarah, and Riad Kabha. 1991. *The Madrid Conference in the Eyes of the Arab Press in Israel* (in Hebrew). Givaat Haviva (December).

Ozacky-Lazar, Sarah, and Asad Ghanem.. 1993. *The Perception of Peace among the Arabs in Israel* (in Hebrew). Givaat Haviva (September).

———. 1996. *The Arab Vote for the 14th Knesset, May 29, 1996* (in Hebrew). Givaat Haviva.

Paz, Reuven. 1989. *The Islamic Movement in Israel following the Elections to the Local Authorities* (in Hebrew). Tel Aviv: Dayan Center, Tel Aviv University.

Peled, Yoav. 1989. *Class and Ethnicity in the Pale.* New York: St. Martin's Press.

———. 1992. "Ethnic Democracy and the Legal Construction of Citizenship: Arab Citizens of the Jewish State." *American Political Science Review* 86, no. 2 (June): 432–43.

Porat, Yehoshua. 1964. "The League for National Liberation" (in Hebrew). *Hamizrach Hachadash* 14, no. 4: 354–66.

———. 1968. "Revolutionism and Terorrism in the Policy of the PCP 1929–39" (in Hebrew). *Hamizrach Hachadash* 18, no. 34–4: 255–67.

Reiss, Nira. 1988. *Health Services to the Arab Population in Israel.* Tel Aviv: International Center for Peace in the Middle East.

Reiter, Yitzak. 1989. "The Arab Democratic Party and Its Position in the Orientation of Israel's Arabs" (in Hebrew). In Jacob Landau, ed., *The Arab Vote in Israel's Parliamentary Elections, 1988,* 63–84. Jerusalem: The Jerusalem Institute for Israel Studies.

Rekhess, Eli. 1976. *Arabs in Israel after 1967—The Intensification of the Orientation Problem* (in Hebrew). Shiloah Institute.

———. 1977. *The Arabs of the Galilee and the Land Expropriations* (in Hebrew). Shiloah Institute.

———. 1981. "The Intelligentsia" (in Hebrew). In Aharon Layish, ed., *The Arabs in Israel, Continuity and Change,* 180–96. Jerusalem: Magnes.

———. 1989. "Israeli Arabs and the Arabs of the West Bank and Gaza: Political Affinity and National Solidarity." *Asian and African Studies* 23, nos. 2–3 (November): 119–54.

———. 1992. "Arabs, Israel and the Intifada" (in Hebrew). In Gad Gilbar and Asher Susser, eds., *At the Core of the Conflict: The Intifada,* 99–112. Tel Aviv: Kibutz Hameuhad.

———. 1993. *The Arab Minority in Israel: Between Communism and Arab Nationalism* (in Hebrew). Tel Aviv: Hakibbutz Hameuchad.

Rosenfeld, Henry. 1978. "The Class Situation of the Arab National Minority in Israel." *Comparative Studies in Society and History* 20, no. 3 (July): 374–407.

———. 1980. "Men and Women in Arab Peasant to Proletariat Transformation." In Stanley Diamond, ed., *Theory and Practice*, 195–219. The Hague: Mouton.

Ross, George. 1992. "Party Decline and Changing Party Systems: France and the French Communist Party." *Comparative Politics* 25, no. 1 (October):43–61.

Rouhana, Nadim. 1986. "Collective Identity and Arab Voting Patterns." In Alan Arian and Michal Shamir, eds., *Elections in Israel—1984*, 121–50. New Brunswick: Transaction Books.

———. 1993. "Accentuated Identities in Protracted Conflict: The Collective Identity of the Palestinian Citizens in Israel." *Asian and African Studies* 27, no. 1–2: 97–127.

Samara, Samir. 1980. *The Actions of the Communists in Palestine: The Class and People against Colonialism* (in Arabic). 2d ed. Acre: al Aswar.

Schnell, Yitzhak. 1994. *Identity Draws a Territory: The Israeli Arab Space Perception* (in Hebrew). Beit Berl: The Institute for Israeli Arab Studies.

Schwartz, Walter. 1959. *The Arabs in Israel.* London: Faber and Faber.

Semyonov, Moshe, and Noah Lewin-Epstein. 1987. *Hewers of Wood and Drawers of Water: Non-Citizen Arabs in the Israeli Labor Market.* Ithaca, N.Y.: I.L.R. Press.

Shafir, Gershon. 1989. *Land, Labor, and the Origins of the Israeli-Palestinian Conflict 1882–1914.* Cambridge: Cambridge University Press.

Shafran, Nasia. 1983. *Farewell Communism* (in Hebrew). Tel Aviv: Hakibbutz Hameuchad.

Shaibi, Issa. 1976. "Following the Elections in Nazareth" (in Arabic). *Shu'un Falastinyye* 53–54 (January–February): 218–20.

Shalev, M. 1992. *Labour and the Political Economy in Israel.* Oxford: Oxford University Press.

Shavit, Yossi. 1992. "Arabs in the Israeli Economy: A Study of the Enclave Hypothesis." *Israel Social Science Research* 7, nos. 1–2: 45–66.

Sheingold, Carl. 1973. "Social Networks and the Voting: The Resurrection of a Research Agenda." *American Sociological Review* 38: 712–20.

Shilo, Gideon. 1982. *Israeli Arabs in the Eyes of the Arab States and the PLO* (in Hebrew). Jerusalem: Magnes Press, Hebrew University.

Shim'oni, Yaakov. 1977. *The Arabs of Palestine* (in Hebrew). Tel Aviv: Am Oved.

Shmaltz, Uziel. 1978. "The Labor Force" (in Hebrew). In Aharon Layish, ed., *The Arabs in Israel—Continuity and Change*, 45–76. Jerusalem: Magnes.

Smith, Anthony D. 1986. *The Ethnic Origins of Nations.* Oxford: Basil Blackwell.

Smith, M.G. 1969. "Some Developments in the Analytic Framework of Pluralism." In Leo Kuper and M.G. Smith, eds., *Pluralism in Africa*, 432–50. Berkeley: University of California Press.

Smooha, Sammy. 1980. *The Orientation and Politicization of the Arab Minority in Israel.* Monographs in Middle East 2 (n.s.). Haifa: Jewish-Arab Center, University of Haifa.

———. 1984. *The Orientation and Politicization of the Arab Minority in Israel.* Haifa: The Jewish-Arab Center, University of Haifa.

———. 1989. *Arabs and Jews in Israel.* Vol. 1, *Conflicting and Shared Attitudes in a Divided Society.* Boulder, Colo.: Westview Press.

———. 1992. *Arabs and Jews in Israel.* Vol. 2, *Change and Continuity in Mutual Intolerance.* Boulder, Colo.: Westview Press.

———. 1994. "Arab-Jewish Relations in Israel in the Peace Era." *Israel Affairs* 1, no. 2 (Winter): 227–44.

Soffer, Arnon. 1988. *The Demographic and Geographic Situation in Eretz Israel* (in Hebrew). Haifa: Gastlist.

Teitelbaum, Joshua. 1985. "Ideology and Conflict in a Middle Eastern Minority: The Case of the Druze Initiative Committee in Israel." *Orient* 26, no. 3 (September): 341–59.

Tessler, Mark. 1977. "Israel's Arabs and the Palestinian Problem." *Middle East Journal* 31, no. 3 (Summer): 313–29.

Tilly, Charles. 1990. *Coercion, Capital and European States A.D. 990–1990.* Oxford: Blackwell.

Touma, Emil. 1982. *The Path of Struggle of the Arab People in Israel* (in Arabic). Acre: Dar Abu Salma.

———. 1990. *The Palestinian National Movement and the Arab World* (in Hebrew). Tel Aviv: Mifras.

Tsimhoni, Dafna. 1986. "Demographic Trends of the Christian Population of Palestine during the Mandate Period." Paper read in a Colloquium on Palestine 1840–1948, Population and Immigration, University of Haifa, June 9–11.

Wolkinson, Benjamin W. 1989. "Equal Employment for Israel's Arab Citizens." Discussion Paper no. 48, Golda Meir Institute for Social and Labor Research, Tel Aviv University.

Yatziv, Gadi. 1979. *The Class Basis of Party Affiliation—The Israeli Case* (in Hebrew). Papers in Sociology, Hebrew University of Jerusalem.

Yiftachel, Oren. 1990. "Public Policy and Political Stability in a Biethnic Democracy: The Influence of Israel's Land Use Planning on Arab-Jewish Relations in the Galilee." Ph.D. diss., University of Western Australia, Perth; The Technion, Haifa.

Yinon, Avraham. 1981. "Toufiq Ziad: We Are the Majority Here" (in Hebrew). In Aharon Layish, ed., *The Arabs in Israel,* 213–40. Jerusalem: Magnes Press.

Zureik, Elia. 1979. *The Palestinians in Israel.* London: Routledge & Kegan Paul.

SOURCES FOR STATISTICAL DATA ON THE ARABS IN ISRAEL

Central Bureau of Statistics, *Statistical Abstract of Israel.*

———. *Moslems, Christians and Druze in Israel.* Data from the Population and Housing Census 1961, no. 17, Jerusalem, 1964.

———. *Labor Force Survey.* Special Series no. 68, 243, 715.

———. *Results of the Elections to the Knesset and Local Authorities.* Special Series no. 51, 111, 166, 216, 309, 461, 553, 680, 775.

———. *The 1983 Census of Population and Housing.* Publication nos. 3, 4, 5. Jerusalem, 1985.

———. *Population in Localities. Demographic Characteristics, 1994.* Pub. no. 1026, April 1996.

Cohen, Avraham. *Economic Aspects of the Arabs of Israel* (in Hebrew). Givaat Haviva, Institute for Arabic Studies, April 19, 1984.

Ghanem, Asad. 1993. *The Arabs in Israel: The 21st Century, A Survey of Basic Infrastructure*. Givaat Haviva.

Harari, Yehiel. *Facts & Figures on the Arabs in Israel* (in Hebrew). Givaat Haviva, 1968, 1973, 1974, 1976, 1981.

———. *The Elections in the Arab Sector in 1973* (in Hebrew). Givaat Haviva, 1975.

———. *The Elections in the Arab Sector in 1977* (in Hebrew). Givaat Haviva, 1978.

———. *The Municipal Elections in the Arab Sector 1978* (in Hebrew). Givaat Haviva, 1979.

Jaffa Research Center, 1990. *Arab Cities and Villages in Israel.*

Publications by the CPI

Central Committee, CPI, Vilner, Meir. 1970. *Fifty Years of Struggle of Our Communist Party* (in Hebrew). Tel Aviv: The CPI.

CPI, 1980. *Sixty Years of Struggle of the Communist Party of Israel.* Tel Aviv: The CPI.

Central Committee, CPI-Maki. *The 13th Congress* (in Hebrew). Tel Aviv–Jaffa, May 29, 1957.

———. *The 14th Congress* (in Hebrew). Tel Aviv–Jaffa, May 31–June 3, 1961.

Central Committee, CPI-Rakah. *The 15th Congress* (in Hebrew). Tel Aviv–Jaffa, August 6–8, 1965.

———. *The 16th Congress* (in Hebrew). Tel Aviv–Jaffa, January 30–February 1, 1969.

———. *The 17th Congress* (in Hebrew). Tel Aviv–Jaffa, June 21–24, 1972.

———. *The 18th Congress* (in Hebrew). Haifa, December 15–18, 1976.

———. *The 19th Congress* (in Hebrew). Haifa and Nazareth, February 11–14, 1981.

———. *The 20th Congress* (in Hebrew). Haifa, December 4–7, 1985.

———. *The 21st Congress* (in Hebrew). Haifa and Shfaim, May 21–25, 1990.

———. *The 22nd Congress* (in Hebrew). Givaat Haviva, January 28–30th, 1993.

CPI-Rakah. "A Plan for an Israeli-Palestinian Peace—A Joint Statement of the Communist Palestinian Party and the Israeli Communist Party" (in Hebrew). Tel Aviv, January 1983.

Party Papers

Kol Ha'am
Zo Haderech
Arachim
al Ittihad

Other Papers

Al Sinara
Bamerhav
Davar
Ha'aretz
Ma'ariv
Yediot Aharonot

Index